Bobby's
Life
Journey

Bobby's Life Journey

The Harsh World of Reality

Bobby Dutton

Library of Congress Control Number:		2010900877
ISBN:	Hardcover	978-1-4500-3158-5
	Softcover	978-1-4500-3157-8
	Ebook	978-1-4500-3159-2

This book was printed in the United States of America.

To order additional copies of this book, contact:
Xlibris Corporation
1-888-795-4274
www.Xlibris.com
Orders@Xlibris.com
71617

Dedication

Putting to writing many of the important events in my life has been a different experience for me. During the many hours of writing and reviewing what I had written, I took the time to reflect upon the road I had traveled. I have always been focused on tomorrow and rarely looked to yesterday with respect to "smelling the roses" of my ventures and adventures, merely using each as a stepping stone to the next. The major influencing factor that allowed me the time and strength to follow this road was my wife, Judy.

Married for over fifty-three years, she has—without exception—supported my efforts in every way. During the many long hours that I worked, she maintained the household, raised the kids, and kept our family going in the right direction and many times would fill in at the office for a day or so at a time when I was starting a new business or had an overload of work.

She has tirelessly dedicated her life to the family and has unfailingly supported whatever decision I made during the course of my many business ventures. I am pleased to dedicate this book to the love of my life.

Foreword

Have you ever had to make a real hard decision? The man who is known by his many friends as Bobby had to make many, starting at the very young age of eleven. Taking on the reason ability of an adult was something he felt he had to do while earning what he could to provide for his family and getting an education in rural Alabama. These early hard lessons would serve him well.

As a teenager, he decided he could do better moving north where job opportunities were better. This is not a "*rags to riches*" story, but a journey of a highly motivated man. He soon found work and a place to live using all of the money he had. And soon thereafter, he found the woman that he would share the rest of his life with. Now with his own family and responsibilities growing, he leaped into the harsh world of self-employment, starting and developing several different businesses over the years.

Bobby is a hands-on type of worker. I found that he would roll up his sleeves and solve a problem on the production line in the morning and attend a board of directors meeting of a Fortune 500 company in the afternoon. He was always well prepared at whatever he did. Over the years, he established and ran several manufacturing plants, established a bank, and built a golf course and golf community; and regardless of what he was doing or the degree of success he had attained, he never forgot his friends or the church, being a private but deeply religious man.

Now after the urging of many of his friends, he is taking the time from his very busy schedule to tell some of the details of his journey in life. It may inspire some and entertain others and may surprise his few detractors. I have greatly benefitted from my fifty-five-year association with him and have enjoyed the times we spent together. I'm very proud to call him my friend and am honored to write this foreword to an inspiring story.

David Kidder, 2009

Preface

Autobiographies and biographies are normally written about celebrities, very important or famous people, or someone who has contributed in a major breakthrough in their field of endeavor. So why am I writing this? I know who I am and where I've been, and I don't fit into any of the categories listed above; however, I think it to be important that as a part of my legacy, I leave to my family and friends the contents of this book. If it helps to inspire just one individual to work toward overcoming adversity, the time and effort will have been certainly worthwhile. Maybe, just maybe, someone who has given up to better themselves in life will read this story and conclude that through diligence and hard work, they too can take themselves out of poverty and make a better life for themselves and their family.

In this great land of ours, opportunity is always just around the corner; and for those who truly seek to better themselves and provide a better way of life for their family and loved ones, it is theirs for the taking. All that is required is a true desire and willingness to pursue it.

Success rarely comes without sacrifice and some failures, but if you trust in God and always face the light, the shadows of failure will fall behind you.

Chapter One

I was born February 4, 1938, and was the fourth child of James Archie and Esther Mae Dutton. I was born in a rural area near the old Indian town of Nauvoo, Alabama; and at the time I was born, we lived in a one-room farm outbuilding constructed of pine slabs and a dirt floor. There were no windows and only one door, which was a typical slab door with a Z-bar nailed to the face to hold it together. My recollection of this first home stems from a photograph that I viewed when I was about fifteen years old. From the photograph, the size of the building appeared to be about twelve by twelve feet, similar to two animal stalls in a typical old barn. During their short marriage, my mother and father had four children—Ella Mae, James O'Neal, Shirley Ruth, and myself.

Soon after I was born, we moved into another old farmhouse a couple of miles down the road; and by the time I was three years old, we had moved again. I vividly remember living in this place, although it was for a very short time. This was during the winter of 1941, and several things happened that are as clear in my memory as if they happened yesterday. I didn't know what money was, and someone gave me a penny. Like any three-year-old, I'm sure it went into my mouth immediately; nevertheless, I swallowed it.

Needless to say, we had no such thing as running water or an indoor toilet but had an outdoor one. I remember my mom supervising my visits to the outdoor toilet, and after a day or two, she retrieved the penny when I passed it. My dad thought I should remember this event; so he drilled a hole in the penny, put it on a string, and I wore it around my neck for a period of time. The old farmhouse was heated by an open fireplace in the living area, and a box of matches was always on the mantel above the fireplace. Late one evening, my sister Ella Mae was messing around the fireplace, striking matches; then she caught her beautiful long red hair on fire. Fortunately, she put the fire out before any major burns occurred.

Up to age three, I had not seen a snowfall that stayed on the ground. During that winter, we awoke one morning to one of the most awesome sights I have ever witnessed. During the night, a blizzard had gone through and left all the trees and ground covered with snow that was about eight or nine inches deep. I'll never forget that morning. As soon as we finished breakfast, Dad took Ella Mae and Jim to the front porch and cleaned the snow off; and the three of them sat on the porch steps, playing a game. The snow in the yard had not been disturbed, and Dad was tossing his knife into the yard, and Ella Mae and Jim were racing through the snow to retrieve it. Looking back at this activity, I'll bet that after a few tosses and a lot of footprints, the knife got harder to find. While this was going on, I was standing on the porch behind my dad. My sister Shirley, who was five at this time, came out on the porch wearing a big, long black coat that belonged to my mother; and the bottom of the coat was dragging some distance behind her. She instantly headed to the sack of hog food that was sitting on the porch, dug her hand into the sack, and began eating the hog food.

By the time I was four years old, we had moved again. This time, we moved into a little farmhouse a couple of miles down the road. The community elders had added a large room onto the side of the house, and it served as the local church. The denomination was Southern Baptist, and people came to worship several times a week. The church was very poor and could not afford a resident preacher, so the elders of the community took turns holding the church services. The entrance to the church was through our front door, with a small hallway leading by the bedroom where my brother and I slept. When the young couples who had small babies came to the church, they would put their babies on my bed to sleep during the services. Needless to say, those were the days before leak proof diapers were available, so it was a normal occurrence to have a wet bed after the services. Mom would take the bedding and hang them over the back of an old straight chair to dry next to the wood-fired heater before my brother and I could go to bed. I could hardly stand it and stayed angry most of the time because Dad would always tell the people to put the babies on my bed.

My dad worked in the coal mines and sometimes drove a truck hauling coal. He also filled in as a substitute preacher. Our church had a roving minister who would preach in different churches in the area and could only get to our church about once a month. All the other services were held by the community elders and my dad. At almost every service, Dad would bring us four kids to the front of the church, and we would sing old Gospel hymns such as "Amazing Grace," "Standing on the Promises," "The Old Rugged

Cross," and such while he and other members of the congregation played the music, using mostly stringed instruments. Since the church room had a flat floor, the people in the back of the room could not fully see us kids as we sang, so Dad proceeded to correct the problem. The miners Dad worked with used a material called carbide, which they burned in the lamp attached to their hard hats. Dad brought home three different-sized cans that the carbide came in and placed them in the front of the room. When we kids sang, my oldest sister, Ella Mae, would stand on the floor; my brother, Jim, stood on the shortest can; my sister Shirley was on the next tallest can. They would hoist me up to stand on the taller can. We then were all about the same height, and the full congregation could see us.

Once every year, the area churches would get together and hold a revival meeting. No area church had enough room to accommodate the crowd, so the directors of the area churches would collectively select a place in the area among a sprawling pine thicket and proceed to construct a temporary shelter called a brush arbor, in which to hold the services.

The second house I lived in.
(from left to right) At the back, Dad and Mom
In front, sister Shirley, brother Jim, Bobby, and sister Ella Mae

Every able-bodied man, woman, and child would help in its construction. Some of the men would fell the young pine trees, leaving the stumps at the right height to provide the base for benches, and the tree would be trimmed and used for the roof. Others would cut the tops from the trees that were located on the outer perimeter of the arbor, which were used for the upright posts to support the roof. They would then connect the structure together while the children and women trimmed and collected the pine branches and covered the entire roof, which would keep the sun out and slow down the water in the event of rain during the revival. A few of the trees were taken to the sawmill and ripped into slabs. These slabs were nailed to the remaining stumps and provided seating. A temporary pulpit was constructed, and now the structure is ready for the revival. It was at this time that I had my first experience of witnessing people talking in "tongues." Oh, by the way, it always seemed like if you needed rain, build a brush arbor. It rained hard at least once during every revival.

When I was five, my maternal grandmother, Sarah Jane Duncan, owned forty acres of land, which she and Grandpa received from my great-grandparents who had homesteaded the land years before. My grandmother was a Cherokee Indian whose lineage was through the Cherokee rebels who refused to march on the Trail of Tears. Her ancestors escaped into Georgia and Alabama when President Andrew Jackson sent the military to root them out from the Carolinas. She married an Englishman by the name of Henry Duncan. I had never seen Grandpa Duncan because he was in Bryce Hospital in Tuscaloosa with a terminal illness. Grandma was clearly the head of the family and proceeded in decision making without haste. She gave us one acre of land adjacent to her log house.

So Dad, with help from an uncle, constructed a little three-room house, which was about sixteen by forty feet. It had a front door and a back door straight in line with each other. Brother Jim and I could stand on either end of the house and toss a ball back and forth through the house. There were about six window openings, but none had glass. Each window was the same as the door, except they were a couple of feet above the floor. Instead of glass, they had hinged shutters that could be opened during the day and closed at night. The house had a tin roof and no ceiling with all the rafters exposed, and when you looked at the walls, you would see the exposed structure and the back side of the exterior siding. To me, this was a castle compared with the previous houses that we lived in even though during the day, pigs and chickens had as much access to the house as the kids did.

We moved into this house about the time I turned five. Within a very short period of time, we moved up the road about a mile into a rented house owned by the Ingles. Dad still worked at the mines and was helping Mr. Ingle farm. My brother and sisters were now attending school, which was about a mile from the house, leaving Mom and I alone until the kids came home from school. We were very poor and to this point had never had a purchased toy.

Grandmother

If we needed something to play with, we made it. One day, we four kids were playing in the road; and the two older ones were tossing a golf ball-sized rock back and forth, playing keep-away from Shirley and me. One of them tossed the rock high into the air, and Shirley reached out to catch it. She missed it, and the rock hit her in the center of the forehead. She began bleeding really bad; and my grandmother, who was visiting, came running. She grabbed Shirley, rushed her into the house, opened up the damper on the cookstove smoke pipe, scraped a handful of soot, and vigorously rubbed the soot into the wound. The bleeding stopped, but over the years, the scar remained. After over sixty-five years, Shirley still has a faint scar, which has a blue color, left from the soot. From that time on, we didn't play ball with rocks but began making balls by wrapping a small rock with cloth; and when it was the right size, Mom would sew it in a sock. My favorite toy was the click and wheel, which was easy to make. All that was required was a metal ring and a long piece of stiff wire. You would form a U at one end of the wire, then bend it at a ninety-degree angle and use the wire to roll the ring to see who could keep it rolling the longest time.

Until I was five, I always wore hand-me-down clothes. In the fall of 1943, during harvest time, Mom made me two pair of short pants using cloth she obtained from fertilizer sacks. I immediately put on a pair and went with my dad to the crusher mill to grind sugarcane. The mill had circular grinding wheels and a stone with a tongue extended to where a horse or mule would walk in circles around the mill as someone fed the cane into the grinder. My dad gave me the task of riding the tongue and holding the guide reins from the mule. Needless to say, crushing sugarcane is a sticky, messy job; and by noon, Dad and Mr. Ingle had straw, dirt, and everything else stuck to their clothing. It was about time to go home for lunch, and I thought Mom wouldn't believe that I had been working because Dad was so dirty and my clothes were still clean. I had to remedy this problem, so I proceeded to wipe a lot of cane juice on my clothing, followed by applying some dirt and debris. Mom was not impressed but let me change into the second pair of shorts, and after lunch, I went back to work with Dad.

Christmas came; and it must have been a good year because as I arose on Christmas morning and ran to the Christmas tree, I expected to see the normal popcorn balls, fudge, and peanut brittle candy. To my surprise, there was a toy under the tree for each of us kids. Mine was a beautiful multicolored spinning top. I was so happy. I played with it all day.

Soon after Christmas, things began to change. Dad would come home from work real late on Friday night, and most of the time, he had been drinking; and he and Mom argued violently about his drinking and not having enough money to sustain the family. This led to Dad becoming very abusive to Mom, and on more than one occasion during their arguments, he would order one of the kids to the yard to get what we called a hickory switch, a small branch from a tree. Then he proceeded to whip my mom with this small branch, leaving welts and stripes on her back and legs. This went on until around springtime.

One day, Dad was either at work or away somewhere, and Mom and we four kids had walked down the road to visit my grandmother. When we arrived back home in the midafternoon, all our belongings were stacked up on the front porch, and the house was boarded up. We inquired with Mr. Ingle, the landlord, and he simply told my mom that he was evicting us. I have no knowledge as to the reason, but we got Uncle Charlie to bring the wagon, and he hauled our goods back to our house next to my grandmother's house. Soon thereafter, Dad joined the army and went away to boot camp. We were just getting settled in our house next to Grandma's and began helping Grandma and her three unmarried children, who still lived with her, do the farming.

When boot camp was finished, Dad came home for a weekend. Even though he had mistreated Mom, I was glad to see him. He looked so nice and perky in his uniform because I had never seen him wear anything except overalls and farm clothes. On the last day Dad was home, he was lying in bed with his uniform neatly hanging over the foot of the bed. Brother Jim had seen that Dad had some ready rolled cigarettes lying on the floor under the edge of the bed. Now Jim had an experience with tobacco the year before when we lived at the Ingles' place. Dad chewed Brown's Mule tobacco, which came in a small rectangular shape about three-eighths of an inch thick. When he used it, he would use his pocketknife and shave off a few little slices. Brother Jim knew that Dad kept a new cake of chewing tobacco in the house, so he found it and proceeded to cut off a small piece and chewed it. When Dad found out what he had done, he called Jim and me into the house, and he was pretty unhappy. He sat Jim down in a chair right in front of the glowing fire in the fireplace and then shaved small pieces of tobacco, making Jim chew it. Jim would chew the amount Dad gave him and spit into the fire. As soon as he finished one mouthful, Dad would give him another. This continued until the last of the tobacco was gone. Jim got very sick, but to my knowledge, he has not touched chewing tobacco since then.

On this day, Jim, cousin Larry, and I were playing in the road in front of the house. Jim told us that Dad had these cigarettes lying on the floor and that he was sleeping. The three of us decided we would cast lots to determine who would sneak into the house and steal one of Dad's cigarettes. Jim picks up a flat rock, spits on one side, and tosses it into the air while each of us took our turn of calling whether the rock landed with the wet or dry side up. Needless to say, I lost. I sneak into the front door and, being very quiet, crawled about a dozen feet to the door opening by Dad's bed. I reached around the door casing and felt the cigarette pack, which made a slight noise as the package crinkled. The next thing I knew, Dad had his hand on my wrist, asking what I was doing. Of course, I blamed Jim, so I told Dad that Jim and Larry sent me in to steal a cigarette. Dad told me to go get my brother, which I did right then.

When we entered the bedroom, Dad sat us on the floor and said, "Now, boys, you know you're not supposed to smoke." Having said that, he opened up the cigarette pack, which contained only two cigarettes. He broke one in half, handing each of us a piece, put the other one in his mouth, and proceeded to light all three. He made us puff on the cigarette until we could no longer hold it in our fingers. When we finished, Dad reached for his pants, put his hands in the pocket, and removed six cents. He handed the six cents to brother Jim and said, "If you're gonna smoke, you're gonna have to roll your own." He then instructed us to go to the store, which was owned by my mother's uncle John, and get our own tobacco.

It was Sunday afternoon, and when we reached Uncle John's store, he was working in his garden area behind the store. We told him that Dad was home on furlough and needed some tobacco. Uncle John sold us a little bag of Bull Durham tobacco and a pack of OCB cigarette paper for the six cents. The next hour was very frustrating. As we were walking the mile or so home, we would stop along the side of the road several times and try to roll a cigarette, each time without success. It really didn't matter because we weren't smart enough to take matches with us. As we approached the edge of our property, there was a huge tree with a hole in it. We knew that if Mom or Grandma caught us with tobacco, we would be in serious trouble, so we put the tobacco and cigarette papers in the hole in the tree.

Before that day, we had never attempted to smoke a cigarette using tobacco but had followed in the footsteps of the older boys in the community and had smoked "rabbit tobacco, corn silks, and cross vine." We never went back to retrieve the tobacco we put in the tree.

Dad left the next day, going back to camp, and was later shipped overseas. Just before he shipped out overseas, he came home for a weekend, and he brought a bicycle to be shared among the four kids. He then shipped out, and I don't remember ever receiving any mail from him except on one occasion when he sent us a small record containing a song or two that he had recorded somewhere in the South Pacific. The next time I saw him, he was out of the army, and he and Mom were considering getting a divorce.

We kids helped work the farm, and Mom went to work in uptown Jasper, which was about ten miles away. The four of us kids took turns sleeping at our house and at my grandmother's house. Mom would take the bus to her job in town, taking care of her sister who had tuberculosis, and would return home late Friday evening. One of the main events of every week was walking a little over a mile to meet the bus and walking home with Mom. This lifestyle continued where we raised almost everything we ate and used. On Grandma's farm, we raised cotton, corn, hay for the animals, and peanuts. We also had a huge garden, a lot of peach and apple trees, grapes, and a very large wild plum orchard. On the property, we also had one female beech (nut) tree, which bore wonderful-tasting beechnuts. Across the road on the neighbors' land, there were several huge oak trees that had wild muscadine, and we had wild blackberries growing in several places. Several hickory trees, scattered throughout the farm, produced an abundance of hickory nuts. As kids, we spent many hours gathering the fruit and nuts, which we either canned or dried. Of course, in those days, we had no electricity to freeze anything nor even an icebox to keep things cold. There was a hand-dug well next to the house that had plenty of water, but it contained so much sulfur and other impurities that it was only good to do laundry or other tasks where the water would be boiled.

During the time Dad was away in the army and Mom was working uptown during the week, we had gotten accustomed to living part-time with my grandmother and part-time in our own house. I had started to school at a two-room schoolhouse about two miles from home, and all four of us kids would walk to and from school together. The school, Macedonia, was grades 1 through 3 in one room and 4 through 6 in the other. The rooms were separated by a huge folding door, and each room was heated by its own large coal- or wood-burning heater. We had no electricity nor running water and had two outdoor toilets, one for the girls and one for the boys. During my first year, the entire school had about twenty or twenty-one students. I was fortunate to find a picture of all the boys in all six grades for my first year. There were only nine. (Please see the picture below.) The year I started school, a new first-through-third-grade teacher was hired. Her name was Mrs. Garrison, and she was a beautiful lady who treated all us kids like we were her own. I immediately fell totally in love with her. Mrs. Garrison learned that my brother, sisters, and I always walked to school, unlike some of the students who lived much closer to the school or were transported by their parents in wagons or buggies; and she insisted on picking us up in the morning since she drove past our house on her way to school.

Our neighbors the O'Rears had a girl about my age. Every morning, as the weather permitted, the parents would put her on a horse; and the horse would take her to school, walking up close to a small porch at the school so the little girl could get off. As soon as she was safely off, the horse would return home. Just before school let out, her parents would send the horse back to school to pick her up, always getting close enough to the porch that she could get on its back. Once Mrs. Garrison got to know me, my brother, and sisters, she became aware that we were very poor and that our father was in the army. She began bringing us little things like a cookie or a small piece of candy and would give it to us during the ride to school. She learned that none of us had ever been to a circus or fair; so when the Walker County Fair came to town in September 1944, she drove the ten miles from her house to ours, picked all four of us up, and treated us to a full day at the fair. She paid for every ride and bought us something to eat; and when the day at the fair was over, she took us to her home and treated us to more food, then drove the ten miles back to take us home.

I have never forgotten this beautiful, kind, and generous lady and the impact she had on my life. For a number of years (about fifteen), I lost track of this fine lady; and even though I couldn't find her, I continued looking. When I was a little older, I moved away from that area but continued searching for her. Finally, a couple of years after I was married, I found Mrs. Garrison. She was a clerk at the county courthouse in Jasper, Alabama. I drove from Indiana to see her; and upon greetings in her office, I gave her my profound thanks for the positive influence, help, and inspiration she had given me. She was the same bubbly, wonderful lady she was when I was a child, even though she had recently been permanently confined to a wheelchair.

All the boys grades 1 through 6 at Macedonia 1944-45 Bobby

I haven't said anything about the health of the family, but living in the conditions we were forced into, it is a wonder that we were not sick all the time. When we lived in our second home after I was born, all four of us kids came down with whooping cough at the same time. I remember having this disease but don't remember much of the conditions and circumstances of that time. All of us either had been inoculated or would be by the time we were first or second graders, and being a pretty hardy group, we had little sickness. When I was six, my oldest sister came down with the mumps, which lasted maybe a week. As soon as she was out of bed, my brother was put to bed with them; and just before he recovered, my youngest sister got them, and all three of them received a lot of special attention. Obviously, they did not have to go to the fields to work and were given some things we were not used to having.

One of these extra things was Coca-Cola. I had never had a Coke but tasted one of theirs. I asked for one for myself but was denied because I didn't have the mumps. It became obvious that the only way I would get one would be if I contracted the mumps. I began getting as much contact with each of them as I could. At the height of their sickness, I would crawl in bed with them; and of course, they couldn't eat a lot, so I would finish eating something they left on their plate. I expected to have the mumps any day and finally came down with them but only on one side. By the time I had them, harvest time was upon us, which made available the old standby Indian remedy. Instead of getting the Coke I had tried hard to get, my grandmother ripped off some dried corn leaves, boiled them, and put something else into the mix. She called it fodder tea and made me drink it daily.

Of course, Grandma had an old Indian cure for everything; and usually, her formulas worked, but they were nasty tasting and sometimes worse than the ailment. Her cure for colds, chest congestion, allergies caused from breathing pollen, and such was chopped onions, a tablespoon of sugar or molasses, and one teaspoon of kerosene, which she boiled for a while and made us drink it. Believe it or not, it usually worked. By the time I reached seven years old, all four of us had gone through German measles, red measles, chicken pox, and a whole lot of rashes from stinging nettle, poison oak, and poison ivy, which we came in contact with while working the farm.

My brother, sisters, and I had acclimated to our circumstances of Dad not being around; and all of us kept very busy working on the farm. When we spent the night in our house, Ella Mae would cook and feed us, clean the house, do the laundry, and then do her part working on the farm. When we stayed with our grandmother, Ella Mae would help with the household chores, as well as farmwork.

We grew almost everything we needed. We had plenty of trees that we used for firewood to heat Grandma's log house and our little house. We had a cow that we milked every day and made our own butter. To keep the milk from spoiling in the heat, we placed it inside a bucket and submerged the bucket in the well. The well and the water were used for special purposes, but all our drinking water was carried up to the house from an artesian spring down the hill. We had a mule that was used to pull the farm implements, and we raised our own hogs. Every fall, when the weather cooled, we would kill and dress a hog or two. Part of the meat would be smoked and/or salt-cured at the smokehouse while some parts, like the hocks, were canned. We made our own lard, which ended yielding pork cracklings that were used for food in several dishes. When all the processing of the meat and lard were done, we made soap, which we used to do laundry, bathe with, wash the dishes with, etc.

Cotton was our staple crop, but if you've never pick cotton, I can't explain well enough to you as to how hard the work is. Everyone in our community grew cotton, and it would be ready to pick on some farms before others were ripe. All the neighbors would swap out labor during cotton-picking time, and the swap was based on the number of pounds that you pick. Any difference in the number of pounds that a neighbor picked on our farm and that which we picked on their farm had a dollar value of three dollars per hundred pound. When the cotton was taken to the gin, it usually resulted in our getting about one bale of ginned cotton; and the balance, including the seed, went to the gin in payment of seed and fertilizer. When the ginned cotton came back to the farm, Grandma would get a group of the ladies together; and with looms, spinning wheels, quilting racks, and such, they made thread, cloth, quilts, and whatever needed to be replenished. Our underclothes were made from flour sacks, and other garments were made using the cloth fertilizer bags.

We raised enough corn to store up for winter feed for the animals and hand selected enough to make our own cornmeal. At harvest time, Grandma would select the corn she wanted ground into cornmeal; and for several nights after supper, she would spread a sheet on the floor in front of the fireplace, and we kids would hand shell every kernel of corn that was to be ground into meal. While we were shelling corn, Grandma would make us a treat such as popcorn, peanut brittle, or parched peanuts.

We would then take the shelled corn to the gristmill and stone grind it into cornmeal. We then bagged it, stored enough to get us through to the next season, and used the balance to barter for the goods we couldn't produce ourselves. Every other Thursday, the rolling store (huckster) would come to the farm. Grandma would usually get some coffee beans, which she would grind herself. We made our own syrup from sugarcane and used the settlings of sugar in most uses; but on occasion, she would get a bag of sugar, a salt block for the animals, and a gallon of coal oil (kerosene), which was used to fuel the lamps at nighttime.

The man who owned the rolling store was Mr. Rutherford. When Grandma finished selecting all the items she needed, then came the time all the kids were waiting for. Mr. Rutherford and Grandma would count the number of kids present and then line us up. Each kid was allowed to enter the rolling store to select one of two or three items that Mr. Rutherford had placed on the counter. Sometimes it would be a Snickers bar, a PayDay candy bar, or maybe some Bazooka bubble gum. Each child was allowed only one minute to make their selection and leave the vehicle. When all were finished, Grandma would give Mr. Rutherford the value of what she purchased in the form of cornmeal, live chickens, or eggs.

Working together on the farm and caring for one another in my mom's absence brought the four of us kids close together, but a major change was about to happen. Mom and Dad's divorce became final; and Dad, whom I hadn't seen in a long time, came to the house and took the girls. It was very difficult for me to understand, and I missed them so much and longed for them to be back home with brother Jim and me. During the time Dad was in the army and Mom was away during the week, the girls and my brother had become my family, and I missed them so. I have never understood how the split of the children came about except to say that the court ordered the girls to go with Dad and ordered my brother and me to live with Mom. This was a very, very traumatic experience that caused me to find something that I enjoyed doing and immersed myself in it. I loved to go to church and had been attending services with part of my family at a Baptist church called Antioch, which was real close to my school. That helped me to adjust, but just wasn't enough. I buried myself in my schoolwork (first and second grade) and virtually memorized all the textbooks used in my class.

Chapter Two

A few months after I turned seven, things began to get better. Mom was marrying again, and a man by the name of Coleman James would now become my dad.

Coleman was a fine man, and we immediately bonded. He was a lumber grader at a lumber company in Jasper called Brakefield Lumber, about ten miles from our house. We began to have a steady flow of income. Before he and Mom were married, he lived closer to his workplace and hitched a ride to work with people going to town. When he moved into our house, he had to buy an automobile for transportation to work. We had never owned an automobile; as a matter of fact, only one family in our community had a car. My mother's uncle Charlie Alexander owned a Model T, which he used to transport vegetables to the market; the mailman had a car, and then there was Mr. Rutherford's rolling store, and Mrs. Garrison, my teacher, also owned one. Other than these, all you would ever see on the roads in our community were horses, wagons, and horse-drawn buggies. This little country road was pure red clay and had three ruts on which to drive. Even when two wagons would meet, each would have to hug the outside of the road to pass by each other.

Coleman was really good to the family. Knowing that I had never seen my grandpa, he drove me and the family to Bryce Hospital in Tuscaloosa. I'll never forget what I saw. When we approached Grandpa's room, there was a closed door, which had a very small pane of glass that was interlaced with wire. After the adults looked through the glass, Coleman held me up so I could see. What I saw has stayed with me without diminishing. As I peered through the small window, I saw a man—very frail and flailing about the room, the same as one would expect a wild animal to do. This was my grandpa. There was padding on the floor and on every wall to about five feet tall. There were no solid objects of any kind such a table, chair, lamp, or such.

Here was this man bent over, flailing his arms constantly and moving around the room in extreme jerky motions, unable to communicate with us.

It was a super hot day, and on the way home, we stopped at a park to replenish our jug of drinking water. Coleman and I went to the well, which had a hand pump. While he pumped, I held the jug. As the water began flowing, the smell was so bad that I had to turn my head. We capped the jug, and without drinking any of the water, we headed for home. Upon arriving home, I set the jug aside; and about a week later, I needed it to carry some water to the field. When I opened the jug, the sulfur smell about knocked me out as there was about one-fourth of the contents that had settled to almost a solid state.

After the shock of seeing my grandpa subsided, I asked my grandma about Grandpa. She replied with the same message that she had told us many times before. She told the story of how an accident happened while one of her sons, Uncle George, and Grandpa were in a storm. She said the two of them were in the wagon on their way back to the house from the bottomland. On their way, a bad storm rolled through, taking out many trees; then a tree limb broke off and hit Grandpa in the head.

Within a few months of my first seeing Grandpa, he died. During the funeral, when I viewed him, he sure looked so peaceful compared with the way he was when I visited the hospital. In later years, I would learn the full truth. As time went by, someone would mention the name of Bryce Hospital, and I learned that it was commonly called an insane asylum. In later years, it became known that Grandpa had a disease that, in those days, no one was willing to talk about. Little did I know at that time that this same then-unknown disease would prove to be the largest adversary in the lives of my family who descended from Grandpa Duncan.

My relationship with Coleman began to blossom. He had become my real dad, and I was loving it. Soon after he married Mom, he sat me on his knee and called me son. I asked him what I should call him. "Should I call you Dad?" I asked.

His reply really set the stage for our forever-great relationship. He said, "Son, you have a real dad. I'm your stepdad, and I'll always be here for you, and you can just call me Coleman." He gave me a big hug and kissed me on the forehead and went about his business. Coleman only had a third-grade education, but I thought he was the smartest person I knew. He taught me so much through his actions. Although he believed in God, he didn't go to church; but over time, as opportunity presented itself, he would teach me certain values by quoting from the Bible. He had a thousand sayings of his own, such as "Don't do as I do, do as I say do," "The early bird gets the worm," "Truth hurts less than a lie," "It's better to be early than late," and a thousand more. He would say those kind of phrases and then explain exactly what he meant regarding the effect of doing or not doing what he said. He bought me the first new pair of shoes that I remember having. Before that, I either went barefoot or wore hand-me-downs that someone had outgrown. I was seven years old and couldn't properly tie my shoes. Mine always ended with a hard knot, and he was the one who usually had to untie them.

Mom and Coleman, 1945

When he gave me the new shoes, he sat me on his lap and said, "When you get the knot right, you can go play." I learned quick because for the first time in my life, someone took the time to teach me things that theretofore I had been muddling through on my own.

Mom and Coleman had been married for a few months, and one day, he had not come home from work. As usual, I had all my chores done and was looking forward to spending time with him. It grew later and later, and I really began to worry as I remembered back to when Dad had left us, and I began to think that Coleman was never coming back. We had no telephone or any way to communicate with anyone who might know where he was. Finally, his old car pulls into the yard. The car was a mess. Coleman had been involved in wreck that pretty much destroyed the car. He wasn't hurt, but the car would never be put back on the road again. I didn't care about the car. I was super happy that Coleman was home.

Our first Christmas with Coleman was growing near, so he brought home this beautiful Christmas tree. We set it up in the corner of the living area and decorated it. The room was very small and had a bed where Mom and Coleman slept, along with a small wood-fired heater. We had not had a Christmas tree in this house before, and the only place to put it was in the corner next to the heater. I was really looking forward to Christmas. I had only ever had one toy in my life, and that came from my dad. Its importance diminished when Dad left us alone, and I knew that Coleman would provide us with the best Christmas we'd ever had. The tree had been up for a few days, and obviously, it was getting dried out sitting next to the heater. I really don't know how it happened; but Jim and I were messing around the tree, and all of a sudden, it burst into flames. Jim grabbed the tree, I opened the door, and he dragged it outside. I don't remember what happened after that because I was so upset over the tree burning that everything else was just a blur.

After the wreck, Coleman had a difficult time getting to and from work, hitching rides with whomever he could, some of which only went partway; and he would walk the remaining distance. His job was very important, so he and Mom made a decision to move our family closer to his work where he could walk to work. The farmhouse next to his mother and father's house became available, which was close enough that he could walk to work; therefore, the decision was made to move.

Soon after my eighth birthday, Coleman hired a Mr. Pruitt to move us. We didn't have much, so we knew we could get all our belongings on Mr. Pruitt's truck and only have to make one trip to the new place. It had rained all week before the move was to take place, and the little Blackwater Creek between our house and the main road was swollen beyond its banks, and the road was underwater. There was no way any vehicle could get through. There was a back way to our house from another main road, but it was several miles of rutted, slick clay country roads. The move was to happen on Saturday morning. On Friday night, we had a huge ice storm, which left hundreds of trees laden with ice and their branches drooping to the ground. The country road that we would have to take was lined for several miles with long-leafed pine trees, and these ice-laden branches would prove to be a problem to get a large loaded truck through without getting stuck or hung up among the trees.

Mr. Pruitt arrived early and said that he thought we could make it through. The truck was loaded; and as we headed out, brother Jim rode on one running board, and Coleman rode on the other while Mr. Pruitt drove with me and Mom inside the truck. As we approached ice-laden trees, Jim or Coleman would push the branches aside or lift them high enough that the truck could pass under them as the limbs scraped the canvas covering on top of the truck. After a few hours, we made it to the main road and continued a few miles to our new location.

Before moving, I had been making straight As in school; and when Mrs. Garrison learned we were moving away, she told me if I would stay with my grandmother and finish the year at Macedonia, she would double promote me to the fourth grade, skipping the third grade. Even though Mom and Coleman would allow me to do it, I absolutely refused. I was not about to give up my newly found security of having a dad and all the pleasure that gave me. I looked forward to going to a new modern school that had automatic heat and electric lights and to a place where there would be other kids my own age.

The old farmhouse we were moving into had really high ceilings. It had four rooms, and there was a fireplace in the living room and one in the kitchen. It also had something that was new to me. It had electricity! In the center of each of the four rooms, hanging from the ceiling, was an electric wire that had a lightbulb fixture attached. They all had a pull-string switch, and Coleman had already tied the strings to a height that both Jim and I could not reach other than standing in a chair. The first thing he explained was that electric lights cost a lot of money and that all of them had to be turned off no later than 8:00 p.m. Any light needed after this hour would have to be from a kerosene lamp. This was no big deal because kerosene lamps or the light from the fireplace was all we'd ever had. There were no electrical receptacles, but we didn't need them because we did not have any tools that required electricity.

After a few days in our new home, we got a big surprise. Coleman had bought us a stuffed sofa and two stuffed chairs. The only chairs that we ever had were homemade straight-back ones with a wood seat; and when that seat broke or wore out, it would be repaired by interlacing one-inch strips of rubber, woven in both directions of the seat frame. The stuffed chairs were so heavy that I couldn't even slide them across the floor. They were placed a long way from the fireplace since the fireplace was not screened, and sometimes burning logs would pop and spit fire outside the fireplace.

I looked forward to going to the new school, which was about two miles from home if you walked the railroad tracks, but by roadway was several miles. The school bus came by my house, so I began riding it to school. I was amazed when I reached the school. It was a sprawling one-story brick building with a quarter-mile drive coming off the main highway and a beautifully landscaped yard that actually had green grass lawns. All the previous houses, churches, and school that I had been associated with had clay yards; and when a weed or a sprig of grass began to grow, someone would take a hoe and remove it. This new Farmstead Junior High School was certainly different from what I'd previously seen. There were ten grades, kindergarten through the ninth grade, and several of the grades required more than one room. There were just under four hundred students in the entire school. It had a large auditorium with a great basketball court, an outside tennis court, a baseball diamond, and a large kitchen and lunchroom where they could feed half of the students at one time. Going to school here was going to be fun.

Things went along really well. I grew accustomed to my new environment, was doing well in school, and was making a lot of new friends. It was fairly easy since there were a lot of kids my own age at Farmstead. The rural area we lived in was different. Most of the kids from that general area were closer to my brother's age, and very few were my age. When you're eight and all the others are twelve to thirteen years old, a wide gap of interest exists, so I was left out of most of the activity that the boys in my area were involved in.

I hadn't seen my sisters in a long time even though they lived only about fifteen miles away. Dad had gotten married to a woman named Evelyn, who had a son a year or so younger than me. I was used to them not being at home but still missed them every day. I began talking to Mom about the girls, the divorce, and such because I still did not understand what had happened with respect to splitting up the kids. Mom would never give me the details but simply stated that the court made the decision and that when each of us children attained the age of sixteen, we would be free to choose which parent we wanted to live with. This was great news to me because I knew that both girls would come back home as soon as they could.

During the summer of 1946, I spent a lot of time with my mother and helped her around the house, along with doing my other chores of cutting firewood, keeping the water buckets filled, cleaning out the fireplaces, and so forth. Sometimes after Mom and I would finish the daily chores, we would sit and talk, but she would never discuss Dad and didn't talk much about the girls. Mom always had a fetish for her toenails. She always kept them in perfect shape and polished. During this summer, I began to notice that Mom would have trouble trimming and polishing her nails. Further, on occasion, she would drop something; or her coffee cup might rattle in the saucer she would be holding. I volunteered to do her nails, which I did about once a week for a couple of summers. Soon, it got to the point that I began to notice some unusual jerky movement in her eyes and a twitch in her cheek. She was in her early thirties at this time, and then she began experiencing problems with indigestion and stomach-related issues. No one else seemed to notice, but Mom finally decided see a doctor. The result was that the doctor prescribed some type of bromide to relieve the stomach disorder. Over the years, Mom's health continued to worsen, and the only treatment for it was she continued taking the bromides.

Bob and Jim, 1945

It was near Christmastime, and I still had not seen my sisters. A few days before Christmas, my dad drives to our house and gives me and my brother one pig as a Christmas present. I didn't really care much for the pig because it came from Dad. Good ole Coleman—the smart, very perceptive new dad of mine—took the bull by the horns and resolved the issue. He called Jim and me together and told us that this pig was very important and required someone to care for it and raise it until it was grown and that the two of us would not be able to share that responsibility. Only one of us could claim ownership of the pig. Brother Jim, in keeping with his normal ways, instantly said that it was his pig. Coleman agreed with Jim, and ten minutes later, he walked me down the road to a small farmer named Mr. Sparks. Coleman knew that Mr. Sparks's old sow had just had a litter of pigs, and he took me there to pick one out. I chose one. Coleman paid Mr. Sparks, and we took the pig home. For the next year, I cared for my pig and helped my brother care for his.

Coleman was a lumber grader at Brakefield, and his workstation was right at the end of the shed-type building where he would put a blue chalk mark on each piece of lumber that came off the planer and stack it on a skid to be hauled to the storage area. There was no heat at his station, and it was very cold in the wintertime. We kept a five-gallon can of lard in the kitchen; and every morning before he went to work, he would take a big spoon, dip it into the lard can, and gulp it down. After he had done this a few times, I asked him why he kept doing that because it was obvious that it was very unpleasant to do. He told me that he basically worked outside and that the lard helped him to stay warm. About the second year we lived there, he changed jobs and went to work at Walco Lumber Company, which was up toward a community called Manchester.

Coleman loved to rabbit hunt and always hunted with a .22 rifle. He was a great marksman and rarely missed his target. He taught me how to rabbit hunt, but I never handled the gun because Mom was violently opposed to it. While hunting without the help of a dog, we would kick up a rabbit or spot one sitting. Coleman would always make the rabbit run before he shot it. He did it because rabbits with certain diseases that are harmful to humans just won't run. Once the rabbit started running, Coleman, knowing that it was safe game, would whistle very loudly. The rabbit would momentarily stop and perk up his ears to detect where the sound was coming from, and at that time, Coleman would shoot the rabbit . . . always in the head. We spent a lot of time together, and I became his target man. After making the targets he was used to and blowing them away as accurately as Annie Oakley ever did, I began to devise new targets for him to test his shooting skills. Some were very simple, such as hammering a nail partway into a tree and seeing how many shots it took him to drive the nail completely into the tree without bending it first. He became almost perfect on this target. I would take six fireplace matches and stick them in the ground about two inches apart. He would put six bullets in the rifle and proceed to strike and light one match per shot until all six matches were burning. He did this dozens of times.

Sometimes around dusk, brother Jim and I would throw rocks as high in the air as we could, and Coleman would shoot down what we called nightingales. Actually, they were large bats. Jim and I would wear one of Coleman's split leather lumberman's gloves and retrieve the downed bat. I can't remember him killing one, but he would hit them with the shot, and they would fall to the ground. For the longest time, he wouldn't tell us how he did it. He would just say that it was a secret. After many times of doing this, he finally explained how he did it. He said, "You see, son, bats use radar to guide them through the air. When the bat senses the presence of the rock, his radar always directs him to the exact apex of the rock's flight. I just sight the rock in, follow it to its apex, and stop. When the bat crosses that spot, I pull the trigger." I understood what he said, but I could never do it, and I don't know anyone else that can.

I would stick a double-bladed axe in a tree and put a piece of paper behind the blade to make it easy to find where the bullet goes. He would walk twenty paces away, turn, fire, and split the bullet every time; and I always confirmed it with the two holes in the paper behind the axe. I developed a lot of different targets; but my most favorite and, I think, the most difficult was driving a nail into a tree with one shot, having to fire through a three-eighths-to-one-half-inch washer that was swinging to and fro in front of the nail. The washer had a piece of cellophane taped over the hole to confirm that the bullet went through the washer. He got very good at this one too.

I had never fired a gun, and shortly after my ninth birthday, I persuaded Mom to let Coleman show me how. Coleman's father was a night watchman and owned a .38 Special pistol. We found an old can and set it on a fence post. Coleman put one bullet in the cylinder and rotated it to the proper place at the barrel. Standing behind me, he slipped the gun over my head into my hands, helped me to aim, then cocked the hammer. He took his hands off, and I pulled the trigger. I don't know where the bullet went because I had the gun too close to my face; and when I pulled the trigger, the recoil of the gun and my reaction caused the hammer of the gun to hit me in the mouth, cracking my lip and bringing a fair amount of blood. That episode didn't help with my mom's attitude about me shooting a gun.

We raised our hogs that Jim and I had gotten for Christmas, raised most of our vegetables in our garden, and owned quite a number of chickens. When the vegetables began to ripen, I would take my saltshaker to the garden and eat tomatoes, cantaloupe, watermelon, and several other vegetables. In the spring, we'd go along the railroad track and pick gallons of blackberries and dewberries; and on occasion, we'd find a wild huckleberry patch. We always took the blackberries and dewberries home to make jam and jelly, and

Mom would always can some for the winter. We always had an abundance of eggs and would trade eggs for milk as we no longer owned a cow.

One Saturday, Mom and Coleman went to town and left Jim and me alone. Usually, they would take us with them. Sometimes while they shopped, they would allow us to go to a movie; but this particular day, we were left alone. In midday, we both got hungry and shared the bright idea that we would go to the chicken house, which was in an old barn, get some eggs, and boil them. We rummaged through the hay in an unused old part of the barn and found two nests that were full of eggs. We gathered about a dozen and a half, knowing that Mom and Coleman would be happy that we had found a couple of new nests with eggs in them. We took four eggs and boiled them on the open fireplace and put the rest of them in the egg storage bin. As soon as the eggs were boiled, with saltshaker in hand, I cracked my first egg open. It appeared to be undercooked. I then cracked the second one and quickly took a bite. Oops! Believe it or not, the eggs were rotten. Obviously, an old hen had been setting on them, trying to get them to hatch. When they didn't hatch, she abandoned the nest. Needless to say, we went without lunch.

All year long, I had cared for my pig, and now it had grown into a full-size hog. We had become buddies, and many times, I would jump the fence into the hog pen and play around with my hog. A couple of times, I even tried to ride it like you would a small horse. I wasn't very successful with the riding thing, but my hog and I liked each other. When cool weather came, it was slaughter time. Coleman borrowed his father's .38 Special, and he and I walked down to the hog pen. My hog immediately came to the fence as I approached. Coleman put the end of the barrel on my hog's head and pulled the trigger. He then jumped the fence, and using a long sharp knife that we called a pig sticker, he proceeded to cut a slot in the hog's throat to bleed it. I had helped slaughter and dress hogs many times when I was at Grandma's house, but I hadn't realized that the reason we were growing this hog was to slaughter it for meat. I cried for a long time; but finally, Coleman, in his great fatherly fashion, explained to me the merits of what we were doing.

After slaughter time was over, our next chore was to store up firewood for the winter. Coleman bought both Jim and me a trimming axe, and off to the woods we went. We would fell medium-size trees with a crosscut saw and then cut them to lengths that we could handle to get them back to the woodpile near the house. Jim and I would trim the trees and cut the smaller limbs into short lengths that could be used in the cookstove. We always cut at least one big oak tree and keep it from drying out as long as we could. The large oak logs would be used for a backlog, which helped to radiate the heat out into the room where the fireplace was located. Jim and I were responsible for splitting the wood and stocking the wood bin in the house, and we took turns building a fire in the fireplace and cookstove every morning.

Winter came, and the weather turned foul with rain and sleet. Coleman's father had been ill, and during this stretch of bad weather, he passed away. They brought his body in the casket to lie in state at their house, which was about three hundred yards from our house. The weather was very brisk; and after supper, we put a big backlog on the fire, then walked to the father's house, where all the family was gathered. Everyone inside the house was preoccupied with the death of the father, and no one had looked outside. At about two o'clock in the morning, we opened the door to leave, heading home. To our amazement, there on the ground was the second largest snowfall that I had ever seen. By this time, the storm had moved through, and it was a beautiful moonlit night.

When we arrived home, brother Jim decided he was not going to bed because he wanted to get an early start playing in this beautiful fluffy snow. He wrestled one of the big overstuffed chairs close to the fireplace so he could keep warm. I tried to move the other big chair but could not, and Jim wouldn't help me, so I went to the kitchen and got a straight-back chair. I was pretty cold, so I placed the chair real close to the fireplace. The heat from the open fire felt so good, and the warmer I got, the sleepier I got. Coleman was ready for bed; and as he passed behind our chairs, he looked at us and said, "Boys, you ought to go to bed." I pleaded with him to let us stay up so we could get an early start playing in the snow. As I pleaded, he told me he was concerned that I might nod off to sleep and fall in the fire. I continued pleading for him to allow us to stay up, and he relented.

Shortly after he went to bed, I caught myself nodding back and forth in the chair and once reached out and touched the top of the fireplace to steady myself. I should have gone to bed right then, but the anticipation of tomorrow's activity kept me there. Within minutes, I fell forward from the chair and tried to grab the top of the fireplace, which I missed; and my right arm got buried up to just below the elbow under the backlog in the glowing coals. I began screaming; and Coleman, hearing my scream, instantly came, grabbed me, and headed for the wooden water bucket on the back porch. The water was frozen; so he took his fist, broke the ice, and put my arm down in the bucket in the ice-cold water.

After a minute or two, we went to the kitchen where he gently dried the arm. He then reached into the lard can and spread about a half cup of lard on the burns. Mom heard the activity and came in to help with bandaging the burns. I managed to get through the night, and about midday, Mom and Coleman wrapped my arm with thick clean bandages. Coleman put one of his split leather gloves on my burned hand and carried me outside and played alongside me for a few minutes. Due to Coleman's fast thinking and actions, my arm healed. The scars were visible for a long time, but eventually, they became unnoticeable.

Coleman was never a big drinker of alcohol, but on occasion, he would make five gallons of home brew (beer) with ingredients he purchased at the A&P Supermarket. Brother Jim and I would collect old soda pop bottles and caps, and when the home brew was ready, we would bottle and cap it. By the time it was ready, Coleman had sampled it a few times, and the remaining home brew would fill fifty-four or fifty-five bottles. We stored the bottles in an old blue-colored chest that was between our beds.

We had done this a few times without incident; but on one occasion, a couple of days after bottling the brew, we were in bed. Sometime during the night, we were awakened by some fairly loud popping and spewing noise. We got up, lit the lamp, and were very surprised to see home brew running out of the chest onto the floor. Upon opening the chest, we discovered several broken bottles, and more bottles exploded. We woke up Coleman, and he explained that the problem was that we had bottled the brew before the yeast had finished working.

The first neighbor to the south was the Bradbury family, whom we had purchased our milk from since we lived here. Other neighbors suspected that Mr. Bradbury was a moonshiner, but no proof existed. No one had seen a moonshine still on his land, but the word was out that you could buy whiskey from him. The county we lived in was a "dry" county, so it was illegal to have whiskey.

One day, Coleman sent me and Jim down to the Bradburys' and gave us two dollars to give to him. Mr. Bradbury came out on the porch; and Jim, handing him the two dollars, said that Coleman had sent us. Mr. Bradbury told us to wait there while he walked across the road near the railroad tracks and then returned with a very small paper bag, which contained a half-pint bottle of moonshine. We had done this three or four times during our first year there, so we knew that Mr. Bradbury sold whiskey, but no still had been found.

One Saturday morning, Jim and I were outside near our barn, and we heard several gunshots. We were used to hearing guns fired, but this was different from the sounds that came from guns used for hunting. A short period of time passed, and then it seemed like every police car in the county had converged at Mr. Bradbury's house. The police arrested Mr. Bradbury and took him to jail. By late afternoon, everyone in the area knew exactly what had happened.

Earlier that morning, Mr. Bradbury and his small son had walked to the store about a mile away, leaving his wife and young daughter at the house. While he was gone, the city police, who had no jurisdiction, (we were in the county) had sent two officers to his house, apparently trying to find illegal moonshine; and without a search warrant, the officers proceeded to rip the house apart, including tearing off the wallpaper in several places. They did not find anything and left before Mr. Bradbury and his son returned home.

When he saw what they had done, he walked back to the store to use their phone and called the police chief, whose name was Harbison. Mr. Bradbury told the chief that the city police had no jurisdiction because the city had just passed an ordinance and posted appropriate signs on the road advising everyone where their jurisdiction ended, and this line of jurisdiction ended about one mile before getting to the Bradbury house. They argued on the phone, and Mr. Bradbury told the chief that if any city police came to his house again, they would not leave.

Chief Harbison immediately dispatched two officers in one car to go back to the Bradbury house. They arrived within minutes of Mr. Bradbury's return to his house from making the phone call. The police car pulled into the dirt driveway, slamming on the brakes; and by the time the car had come to a complete stop, both officers, with guns drawn, rushed to the house. One officer reached the front door first as the second one was going around the house to the back door. The officer in front kicked the door in, and Mr. Bradbury shot him twice. The downed officer managed to stagger the few feet to the road, and a motorist picked him up. Immediately following the gunshots, the officer at the rear kicked the door in, and Bradbury shot and killed him. The first officer, being transported to the hospital by the motorist, died en route. Very soon thereafter, the Bradburys' yard and the road were filled with both police and sheriff cars. They arrested him, but it was a long time before the trial was held; however, the jury found him guilty, and he was sentenced to life. He died in prison about ten years later.

Things were going pretty well for our family except I kept noticing that Mom had some kind of ailment. Coleman's job was good, and he worked a lot of overtime. The company was growing, and he had a good job position. He came home one day and told us we would be moving soon, and it was great news. His company was constructing four houses along the road at the entrance to the lumber mill, and they wanted Coleman to move into one of them. The other three were to house the superintendent, the production manager, and the machinist. Our move into the new house was uneventful, and the house was great for our family. It had three bedrooms, a living room, a kitchen with an enclosed back porch, and an open front porch. It was constructed from planed lumber inside and out, and the owner would not allow anyone to paint the houses. They remained this way for many years.

Our house was built on the corner of the entrance to the mill where they used to keep all their mules and horses that they had previously used to pull the wagons and sleds. Now they had purchased tractors, so this lot was no longer needed. One of the houses where the superintendent lived had indoor plumbing, with a sink in the kitchen and a bathroom. The other three only had water that was piped from the well on the superintendent's lot to the back porch of the other three houses, and each of the three had outdoor toilets.

Our yard was overgrown with kudzu vine, which is tougher than nails, and you almost have to sterilize the soil to get rid of it. If you've ever driven through the south and saw vines that had completely encased fences and trees, you've probably seen kudzu. Under President Roosevelt, kudzu was imported from Australia to the United States and planted in areas to protect the land from soil erosion; but through the years, it spread wildly and got out of hand. Using a scythe, sling blade, hoe, and axe, I worked daily to remove this stuff. I poured kerosene on it and burned it, only to see it sprout new stems and leaves very quickly. Coleman taught me how to use the tools I was using and always seemed to be pleased with my efforts in removing the kudzu.

When we moved into the house, we installed linoleum on the living room floor and set a heater plate under the coal-burning heater. When the ashes were removed, some of them would almost always get outside the pad and on the linoleum. Mom would walk into the room, and when she sat down, I began to notice very slight involuntary movements of her feet. I knew this was happening with her hands, but the slight scraping of the soles of her shoes on the ash and small cinder residue made a very noticeable sound, which was more irritating than fingernails being scratched on a blackboard. She was still taking some medication, and about every week or two, I would ride my bicycle the five miles to town and get her medicine at the drugstore. Coleman had quit driving and had not driven a car since his accident that happened soon after he and Mom were married. Coleman's work was steady, so he decided to buy another car, which was a '47 Chevrolet. He still would never drive; so even before Jim had his driver's license, he would drive out in the country, and we would visit some of our relatives.

Since we moved to this location, it was much closer to school than before, and I walked to school every day. Coleman bought us boys a bicycle. Several times during 1948, Jim and I would ride the bicycle ten or twelve miles to visit my sisters; and sometimes we would stay with Dad and help him on the farm, particularly when the corn needed thinning, which we did by hand with a scraping hoe. During one of these visits, I learned that sister Ella Mae would soon be sixteen years old, and she told me she was coming to live with us on her birthday. I have never been happier in my life. Nothing more was spoken about her coming; and in August, on her birthday, she showed up at the house. A neighbor or friends of hers brought her. Sister Shirley came with her; but within a few hours, Dad drove to our house and made Shirley go home with him because she had not reached the court-appointed age of sixteen, and the choice of where she lived was not yet hers.

Dad and my stepmother, Evelyn, had two children, in addition to Evelyn's son that she had before she and Dad were married. Before Ella Mae came home, Dad had five children under sixteen years old and his wife living in a four-room house on a very small farm, and he relied upon the work efforts of all of them to make the farm go and to feed his family.

After Ella Mae came, things became much easier for me. Until that time, with Mom becoming less able to get all the house chores done, I had helped her with the meal preparations. I'd peel and cut up potatoes, set the table, clear the table after the meal, and wash the dishes. On laundry day, I'd prepare the washer and hang the clothes on the line to dry. Brother Jim was rarely home, except at mealtime. After school, he was always gone somewhere and spent little time at home on the weekend. Now that Ella Mae was home, I had the time and freedom I looked for and found some odd jobs where I could earn some money of my own. I began mowing the lawn for a family who lived about a mile from us. They had an old push mower, which I cleaned up and sharpened the blade. When I first started, it would take me a half day to complete the job because I definitely wanted to please them, so I would go over the area nearest the house more than one time. They found out why it was taking me so long and made me stop. They were pleased when I went over the yard only once. They paid me $1.25, and I mowed once every week.

I never asked Coleman or Mom for money, but when I needed something for school, they always got it for me. Now I could buy pencils and paper and an occasional soft drink and candy bar with my own money. Although our family was doing very well compared with the way it was before Coleman came on the scene, we were still very poor. My school principal, Mr. Burt Richardson, knew our financial condition and knew that on many days, I would not bring a lunch. I could not afford the twenty cents per day that the lunchroom charged, so Mr. Burt (our school had two Richardsons, so we called them Mr. and their first name) called me into the office and gave me the job of operating one of the two concession stands that were open only during the morning and afternoon recesses. I was making excellent grades, so he let me out of study hall to work in the lunchroom.

Occasionally after school, I would help our janitor, Mr. Land, polish the hallways and clean up the classrooms. I was very happy to do this. I got my lunches free and a soft drink or an ice cream bar during the two recesses; and if I needed pencils, paper, or other school items, Mr. Burt made sure I had them without charge. On the weekends, I would ride my bicycle to his home and mow his yard. He had a gas-operated mower, and even though I had to push it, the job was much easier than the other yard I was doing. Mr. Burt always fed me lunch or dinner on the day I mowed and then paid me two dollars. He had a small farm where he raised a few acres of corn, and when the corn was ready to harvest, he would pay me to help. I began paying for all my own things, including shoes and clothing. If I didn't need anything at the end of a particular week, I would keep enough money to buy a Coke or a candy bar per day and give the balance to Mom.

Ella Mae was with us for about two years; and all the time she was home, I did the yard work, and she did most of the work inside the house. When I finished my work at home, I would be mowing one of the two yards that I was doing or working for Mr. Burt. I still had time left, so when I was eleven, I started caddying at a small country club near our house. The golfers had to take the road we lived on to get to the club, and I would hitch a ride with one of them and caddy every chance I could. I got paid sixty-five cents for nine holes and $1.30 for eighteen, plus a small tip. Since I was a new caddy, I was classified as a C caddy, which indicated to the golfer that I had very little experience.

Every Monday during the summer months, the course was closed for maintenance. This was also caddies' day. The club provided all the caddies with clubs, and of course, all of us had balls that we had found. There would usually be two sets of clubs for each foursome but the C caddies got what was left over. When I first began, the leftovers were left-handed clubs, which I started playing with. As soon as we finished playing golf, our job was to finish cleaning the huge swimming pool at the club. Before we started golfing, we would open all the drains on the pool; and by the time we finished, most of the water had drained into the creek just below the pool. There sometimes was three or four feet of water left, and we all would swim and mess around until the water was all gone. We'd finish up the cleaning job, turn the fill pump back on, and our job was done.

I loved golf and was real pleased when Mrs. Mary McCutchon wanted me to become her regular caddy. Her old caddy was about eighteen years old and ready to move on to something else. Ms. Mary, as I called her, always played from the men's tees. She was the best golfer in the club and many times would compete within a foursome of three of the best men players in the club—and beat them most of the time. The way the course was laid out required the caddies to be forecaddies on most of the holes. Some of the tees were located way back in the woods, and many blind shots would be encountered. Ms. Mary would select the teeing club she would use and proceed to the tee. I would continue to the fairway area near where her tee shot should end up. I would go to her ball, and when she arrived, she would hit the next shot; then she would drop another ball and have me hit it with her right-handed clubs. Before the year was over, I would occasionally break forty for nine holes using right-handed clubs.

Bob, 1948. Jim had just cut my hair for the first time.

Chapter Three

Things were going very well for me, but Mom's disease was quickly progressing to a point she could not sit still. Her limbs began to have constant involuntary jerky movements, her speech was becoming slurred, and she couldn't walk without wavering.

Ella Mae had been dating a guy since she moved home, and it was obvious that she would marry and leave us very soon; but while she was home, I was going to make the best of it. When I was in the sixth grade, Mr. Burt called me to his office. He gave me some additional responsibilities, which included distributing payroll to all the teachers and employees, and gave me charge over the school cash box. I prepared the orders to replenish the concession stands and maintained inventory on all the soft drinks and kept the drink vending machines filled. He made arrangements with all my teachers and approved my being out of classes where I continued getting As.

Two or three times each week, I would count all of the income from lunches, the two concession stands, soft drink machines, and any other function we'd had. I'd make an accounting sheet, verify the totals were correct, and then sort and wrap all the bills, then roll all the coins. Mr. Burt would verify my work and then deposit the funds in the bank. Mr. Burt knew I spent most of my time working, so he insisted I try out for the elementary basketball team. He bought me a new pair of basketball shoes, and after several days of tryouts and practice, I was selected as one of the eight players to make the team. I worked real hard and practiced on my own basketball court that Coleman had helped me build by bolting the hoop to a pine tree in our yard.

We had a really good basketball player from our neighborhood who had finished school. His name was M. A. Woodley, and he was left-handed. M. A. was taller than most other area players; he loved the sport and liked to help young players learn the ropes. He had been teaching us how to shoot

41

a hook shot, which would be more difficult for the opponent to block. I was short, so this sounded good to me. I practiced for hours and got pretty good, making baskets as long as no one was guarding me.

Now the day came when we played our opening season game. It was to be played at a school named Thatch just a few miles away. The coach told me he only had room to take seven players and that I was either the seventh or eighth one, tied with a kid named Bobby Ashley. The coach determined which one of us would go with the team by a flip of the coin. I won the toss.

I sat on the bench and watched the game intently, knowing that the coach would not put me in. It was a very close game. Shortly after the second half started, he slapped his hand on my knee and told me to go in at the forward position. I checked in with the officials and headed for the floor. The coach called me and motioned me to him. With both hands on my shoulders, he said, "Dutton, I don't want to see any hook shots."

I replied, "Yes, sir." And in the game I go.

On the first offensive play, our guards brought the ball down court and attempted a bounce pass to our center. The defense got a hand on the ball and deflected my way as I was breaking across the top of the key. I grabbed the ball, and two defenders immediately cut off my progress to the right. I swiftly turned to the left, looking for an outlet receiver, and all there was to my left was the defense. I was scared to death and didn't want to make a mistake, but practice and instinct took over. I pivoted to my left, and with full extension, I shot the most perfect hook shot I'd ever seen. It made a noise as it ripped through the net. The instant that the coach could, he called for a time-out, pointed to me, and motioned me to the bench. As I got to the bench, he restated that he did not want to see any hook shots. I learned a great lesson that day. Regardless of circumstances, do what the coach says to do and don't do that which he said not to . . . (We won the game.)

The world seemed to be turning in my favor, and I began to have time to do a few things other than work. I really loved to play basketball and improved a little every day. Ella Mae would be finishing high school soon. She attended school at Curry, which was a twenty-minute bus ride from Farmstead, where I attended. She and I would walk to Farmstead, and she caught her bus to Curry from there. I knew she would get married as soon as she graduated. Her boyfriend, Jack, and I got along real well. One day, Ella Mae had gotten mad at Jack, and he was supposed to come to the house that afternoon to pick her up. Jack had a '36 Ford and had taken me for a ride a few times, so we were getting to know each other pretty well.

Ella Mae told me that when Jack arrived at our house that she wasn't going with him because she was mad at him and that I should tell him she wasn't home. I was in the yard working and see his car coming down the road. I walked to the side of the road and met him at the car. When he asked where Ella Mae was, I told him she wasn't home. He started the car up, drove down the road, turned around, and came back. He reached out the window and said, "Here's a quarter. Now tell me where she is." At that point in time, Ella Mae came out of the house, so I told Jack she was mad at him. He told me to keep the quarter, and he'd make everything right with Ella Mae. Within a few minutes, they were off doing their thing together.

By this time, I had inherited the sole responsibility of making Coleman's home-brewed beer; and as a normal routine, I would make five gallons about five or six times from spring through fall. He never drank anything from Sunday night through Friday night; but on Fridays—payday—he would come home from work, give Mom his paycheck, and then drink one or two bottles of the brew. Saturday afternoon was the drinking day. I would go to the golf club on Saturday morning and caddy, then stop on my way home and mow the yard I had been taking care of. By the time I got home, Coleman usually had a brother or one of his nephews at the house. They loved to participate in competitive target shooting, and of course, I was still the target man.

Now I also became the brew man and would make sure that there was enough brew so that each of them could have a couple or three. Occasionally, there would be an extra person involved in the target shooting; and of course, I provided them with a brew or two. After a couple or three weeks of this, the stock would begin to run low because of the extra person and also because every time there was an extra, all of them would drink an extra bottle. When the supply got to a certain low point, I would make another five gallons, which might not be ready for their next gathering. I always tried to keep enough for Coleman and his friends, but once, I ran out. Coleman had invited a couple of extra guys, and there wasn't enough bottles for each of them could have two. One of them made a statement after he learned the brew was gone. He said, "Boy! I'd give a quarter for a brew." That day, the new batch wasn't ready, and all the bottled brew was gone. But I'd fix this situation in the future.

From that day forward, every time I bottled the brew, I would hide three or four in a safe place; and I was the only one that knew about it. After a couple of months, I had built the reserve up to a dozen or so bottles. I continued making the brew based upon the amount of drinking that went on, but one Saturday, I put my plan to work. There were four people competing in the target shooting, and I had exactly eight brews left. They all knew there were only two brews for each of them before they started. When the last one was gone and they confirmed it by looking in the storage box, one of them said, "Man, it's a hot day, and I'd give a quarter for a cool bottle of brew." Then another one chimed in and said the same thing. I told them I had a special stock set aside for Coleman because it was my job to have brew ready when he wanted it. Coleman kinda laughed and asked me if I really had some hidden away. I told him that I did, and each of them paid me a quarter. What they didn't know was that just before they came to the house, I had gone to the drugstore and spent all the money I had for Mom's medicine.

My Sunday schoolteacher, who had a car, was going to take me and three friends to the drive-in movie that night; and I was broke, so I planned this scheme so I would have enough to pay for the movie and have a Coke and popcorn. I would never ask Mom or Coleman for money, and after just spending all I had for medicine, the seventy-five cents these three guys gave me was more than enough for Saturday night. Later, they all found out why I did it; and from that time on, they would usually give me a small tip of ten to twenty-five cents when their target shooting was over.

Chesley Lockard was my Sunday schoolteacher's name. Chesley was a very young man just out of college, had his own car, and became a friend of my close group. That Saturday night, Chesley and his friend Kenneth Cornelison picked us up. The two of them picked up my best friends, Walter and Ronald Harris, then picked me up; and we then picked up Charlie Harris, who was not related to Ronald and Walter. We drove to the Manchester Drive-In Theater, and all six of us paid for a ticket. The reason I emphasize that we all paid for our ticket is that the first time Chesley had taken us to the drive-in was the year before on a Sunday evening where, for some reason, the study service was cut short and our group decided to go to the movie. Among all of us, we could not muster enough money to pay for tickets, a Coke, and popcorn for the five of us. We decided to do what we knew a lot of young country boys did. We would sneak some of us into the drive-in.

The five of us loaded into the car; and when we were at a short distance from the drive-in, Chesley stopped the car, and three of us got in the trunk. Chesley (my Sunday schoolteacher) drove up to the ticket booth, paid for two, and proceeded to a dark corner of the area where he let the three of us out of the trunk. We walked to the concession stand while Chesley parked the car, took the Cokes and popcorn back to the car, and made it just in time as the movie was just starting. Needless to say, we all felt pretty bad about what we had done, but didn't have the guts nor the money to confess and then pay for what we had done. We all agreed that a good solid prayer for forgiveness would do the trick, and we never did it again.

When we moved away from next to Grandma's house, I stopped going to church because when we lived on the airport road next to Coleman's parents, the church was too far away for me to walk. Once we moved into the new house at the lumber mill, they began holding church services in the auditorium at the Farmstead school. This was a Methodist church, which didn't make any difference. I went by myself because Mom was getting to the point that she could not attend because of her medical condition, and brother Jim and Coleman wouldn't go for reasons that I never knew. All my family strongly believed in God but did not frequently go to church. I loved it and attended the Sunday school classes that were held before the main service. Every week, I remember it to have been on Wednesdays, there was MYF (Methodist Youth Fellowship), which I attended most of the time; and then on Sunday evenings, there was a special service for the young people that was held in a huge room that had once been the workshop at school.

I got to know and became good friends with a number of kids my own age, and over the next few years, some in this group were involved in everything I was involved in. Four of five of the boys became Boy Scouts at the same time I did. Six or seven were included on our junior high basketball team. Two or three of them caddied at the country club where I caddied; and two of the girls, one boy, and I developed a great friendship and bonded very well.

Ann Mauldin, JoAnn Geeslin, Paul Osborne, and I had been in the same grade from third through the ninth grade and over that time had developed a fierce competitiveness in academics. Every year, starting at the final year-end grading, the four of us had the best grade average of the class. This continued from the third grade through the ninth, where we broke up and went to different high schools. Our school system was a 6-3-3, meaning six years of elementary, three years of junior high, and three years of high school; and a graduation exercise was held for the ninth-grade finishers. There would be a valedictorian and a salutatorian based upon the highest finishing grade. Each one of the four of us had been vigorously vying for this honor for six years.

Adjacent to Paul's house was a small building that was heated, had running water, and an indoor toilet. Paul's parents agreed to allow the four of us to use the building for studying. They provided us with a large table and four very comfortable chairs. We would meet once a week until two weeks before our final exam; then we studied every night. All four were so intent on getting the best grade that not once was there any horseplay nor even a conversation other than the school subject matter. Our study times were as disciplined as any had ever been at school and maybe more so.

On Thursday evening, the day before the finals, we wrapped up our studies, and Mrs. Osborne brought us a glass of lemonade and some cookies. We wished one another well and left. After the finals on Friday, the four of us discussed the test, and each one talked about how they thought they would score. It obviously was going to be a toss-up since our grades were virtually identical to this point. The following week, the test results were in; and as our homeroom teacher began handing out the graded papers to the thirty-three students, the four of us were on pins and needles. The end result was that Paul finished one-tenth of a point above me. I finished one-tenth of a point above Ann, and Ann finished one-tenth of a point above JoAnn. Paul gave a brilliant speech at graduation; and I spoke on the merits of knowledge, diligence, and effort relating to future success and used the study habits of the four of us to drive the point home.

Ella Mae got married and moved into her own place near town. This placed a burden on me because Mom's health continued to worsen; and I had to go back to helping her cook, clean, and do laundry, in addition to keeping the kudzu and weeds chopped down in the yard. I still was working at school, doing two lawns, caddying when I could, and trying to play basketball while keeping my grades as high as I possibly could.

One day, the superintendent of Coleman's company moved out of the only house of the four that had a bathroom. The company offered the house to Coleman, so we moved. It was only about five hundred feet away. Soon after we moved, Jim quit school, got his driver's license, and went to work at a used-car lot. Now all the chores fell to me because he was homeless now than he had been before. Mom's illness continued to progress, and she had to be very selective with what she ate. Bananas were her favorite because she liked them, and since it was becoming difficult for her to swallow, their softness made it easier to swallow.

Basically, now it was just the three of us. Jim would come home from work to eat and sleep, but to my knowledge, he never contributed even one penny toward our expenses. He began dating and frequently borrowed Coleman's car. Coleman had some strict rules regarding the car, which included restricting the mileage traveled to a total of thirty miles, and he never wanted the car to be driven over fifty miles per hour. He would always inspect the car the day after Jim borrowed it. He began to suspect that Jim was not adhering to his rules about the speed and the mileage, so he set out to correct it.

One Saturday night, Jim took the car and got home well after midnight. On Sunday morning, Coleman questioned him as to where he had gone the night before; and when Jim answered, the mileage on the odometer didn't equal nearly what Jim had told. He told Jim he suspected him of lying and gave Jim an opportunity to tell the truth. Jim stuck to his story. Coleman then took Jim to the car, reached under the dash with a flashlight, and showed Jim the evidence that proved he was lying. The seal of red fingernail polish on the threads of the speedometer cable was broken. Jim broke the seal when he disconnected the speedometer. Coleman never let him drive the car again. The following week, Jim purchased a car from his boss at the car lot. It was a green '41 or '47 Chevy Coupe. I really don't know much about his car because I was never in it. He wouldn't let me ride in it.

The yard at the new house was a lot easier to take care of, and when Mom was feeling OK, I had some free time. I worked hard practicing basketball. Mr. Burt would give Walter, Ronald, and me permission to practice at the gym and provided us with a key so we could access it as our time permitted. I spent a lot of time in this gym. Church on Sunday morning, basketball practice several times a week, plus the ball games themselves. While I was in the ninth grade, I went to church on a particular Sunday; and Walter, Ronald, and I made plans to practice basketball in the late afternoon before the evening studies began. We had about two hours before time to come back to the gym, so we all went home for Sunday dinner.

When Mom felt OK, we would usually have fried chicken on Sunday. When I got home, Mom asked Coleman to kill her a chicken, which he normally would kill with the rifle by shooting it in the head, then wring its neck so it would bleed out. When I killed them, I had to sneak up on the one selected and would throw some type of food on the ground to get them to congregate. I'd catch the chicken and wring its neck or sometimes cut its head off with a hatchet. As Coleman readied his single-shot .22 rifle, I pleaded with him to let me shoot the chicken. He reluctantly agreed. He put one bullet in the gun, made sure the safety was on, and told me which chicken I should shoot.

I grabbed a chunk of leftover corn bread and headed for the yard. I crumbled up the corn bread and called the chickens. As they got in sight, I threw the corn bread on the ground, moved back away from the spot, and positioned myself for a good shot. Lying on my belly with my elbows on the ground was a perfect position to sight my target. As the chickens fought over the corn bread, they were jumping all around, and the one I wanted to kill was right in the middle of the flock of about thirty chickens. When chickens eat, they pick up their food with their beaks and then toss their heads back, making it easier for the food to pass to their craws. My target had raised her head a couple of times, so I leveled my sight to where she had last popped her head up. Up came her head, and I pulled the trigger. The chickens scattered everywhere, most of which went into the high weeds next to the yard. When they cleared out of where the food was, there was no chicken left, so I began looking for the one I had shot at. First, I found one of our prized laying hens. The bullet had hit her in the leg. Next I found another good layer that had a broken wing. My targeted chicken was nowhere to be found, but she showed up later, healthy and certainly not having any bullet wounds.

After hearing the shot, Coleman came out and hollered, "Did ya git her?"

"No, sir," I replied with my head down, and then I told him I had found two hens that the bullet hit. He began helping me look for others that the bullet may have struck; and after accounting for all the chickens, I had hit a total of three, injuring two of them beyond repair. That day, we dressed two chickens, one for Sunday and another for Monday's dinner.

By late 1951, things were going pretty smoothly as a whole. Ella Mae was married, Jim had his driver's license, and sister Shirley was about the age at which she could come and live with us. I had given up cutting the two lawns but continued to caddy when I could and also did odd jobs for Mr. Burt. I was still running the concession stands and working in the lunchroom at school. I had turned thirteen, and after my studies and work were finished, I concentrated on basketball.

The planer mill at the lumber company was just a short distance from our backyard, and there stood a pretty large, tall metal building that had been used in the past for temporary storage of shavings and sawdust coming from the planer. The company no longer used it since now, they were free blowing all the sawdust in huge piles on the open ground; and through spontaneous combustion, they would ignite and burn. They burned very slowly, but fast enough to be able to reuse the same spot for sawdust storage. This building was completely enclosed and had huge ventilation ports about fifteen feet above the concrete floor. It would make a perfect indoor basketball court.

Coleman got me permission to use the building, and with help from Coleman and a few others, we installed the backboard and basket. I bought a new net and marked the floor for the playing court, designating the out-of-bounds and free throw lines. My friends and I played there frequently; and even though the weather was usually very warm and the building was metal, it was comfortable to play in there because even on a still day, there would be air movement through the huge ventilation ports, where the heat would exit and fresh air came through the door.

I was doing real good in school and was earning enough to make ends meet. Coleman's work was still good, but Mom continued a downward slope with her health. I had turned thirteen a few months back, and Shirley was about to turn fifteen, so I knew she would be coming home in about another year.

Disaster struck! The company Walco Lumber Company, where Coleman worked, had to close its doors. A yard foreman and another employee got into a fight, and the foreman hit the employee in the head and killed him. The dead man's family sued the company, resulting in closing it down. The owner, Mr. Roland Short, asked Coleman to keep living in our house; and we could have it rent free if he would occasionally walk around the premises and keep a lookout over the property. Coleman could not find another job, so I found one at a Frenchy's Drive-In, which specialized in smoked pork barbecue and catfish. My best friends and one of their brothers worked at Frenchy's.

Since I knew how to fell trees and use a bucksaw and axe, my first duty was to provide green hickory wood to fire the barbecue pit and smoker. On Friday after school, I would help clean the catfish that would be prepared that night. These fish were transported live from the Tennessee River from northern Alabama, so Frenchy's advertising was dead-on when he said "Fresh Catfish." When these jobs were finished, I cleaned the smoker and the pit, stocked the wood bins, removed the trash, and then curb hopped for short periods of time. Mr. French paid me pretty good, and he was aware that three of his employees were on the school basketball team, which he fully supported. He always set our work schedule around our practice and game schedules and would never let our work interfere with school studies or activity.

I took home all the money I earned, sometimes keeping fifty cents or maybe a dollar. I didn't go anywhere, except a couple of times that year, my friends and I walked to the drive-in theater for a movie. (Yes, we bought a ticket.) Mr. Burt had a project going at the back of his land and needed the land cleared to the point it could be plowed. Coleman's nephew, Joe, who had spent nine years at Farmstead but was now going to high school at Walker County High in Jasper, had worked for Mr. Burt while he was at Farmstead and did exactly the same jobs and routines that I was doing at school at that time. Joe was an ornery cuss, but he was a good-sized boy and a hard worker. Mr. Burt agreed to pay us based upon the number of cords of pulpwood we produced. That would be the extent of our job. We did not have to pile up the brush or remove any stumps. Mr. Burt had someone with big machinery lined up to do that. We knew if we worked really hard, we could make a lot of money in a short period of time. We gathered all our saws and equipment and had someone take them to the job site.

From that time on, we would ride our bicycles to the job site and work as hard and fast as we could in ninety-degree weather. I didn't do any caddying during this job but did work four or five hours at Frenchy's every day that I was scheduled. Once all the trees were cleared and the pulpwood cut to length, all the measurements were verified. Now all we needed was a log truck to make a few loads to the rail yard, and we could collect our pay.

Joe had a friend whose father owned a log truck. We hired him to make the loads for us. We'd load the truck as full as we could and still chain down the load; then Joe and his buddy headed for the rail yard, which was about three miles away. While they were gone, I would snake up as many logs as I could and place them so the truck could drive between the piles. This way, we could load from both sides. They'd return; we'd load the truck and repeated that for two days. When the last load was loaded, we loaded up our tools and bicycles on the truck, and all three of us headed for the rail yard. Joe's buddy was going to transport us home after we unloaded and collected our money. We finished our delivery and were driving up a cinder drive that intersected with the U.S. 78 Highway, which was only a couple hundred feet away. There was a small service station on the corner of the intersection, and just before the station was a huge drain culvert about five or six feet in diameter.

As we topped the little ridge where we could see the road and the station, we got a huge awakening. The sun was shining very bright, and it was over ninety degrees. There were cars stopped everywhere, and people were running to hide in the culvert. The rock wall on the opposite side of U.S. 78 was about sixty or seventy feet high; and as we gazed to the top, there was a huge tornado blowing forty- and fifty-feet balls of trees through the air, and it began to sound like a lot of freight trains were coming. The cloud cover came, but only lasted less than an hour. We called Mr. Burt from the station and told him we would bring his money later because we were going straight home and didn't know where the path of this tornado was heading, but it appeared to be headed toward the area where my grandma lived.

We gave Mr. Burt his money a couple of days later, and Joe and I each made over a hundred dollars. I took the money home to Mom. I didn't need any of it because Frenchy had paid me on Friday night.

When I got home after seeing the storm, Mom and Coleman had heard the news on the radio, and the storm had gone directly toward Grandma's place. Coleman still didn't drive, but I had learned to drive, so I told them I could safely drive to Grandma's if we stayed off the main highway. I drove us up there; and thank God, Grandma's place was not hit, but the area from the Ingles' home place (where we had once lived) to about a mile north had been totally wiped out. That included the old two-room Macedonia school and the Antioch church that I used to go to.

I stated earlier that Colman's nephew was an ornery cuss. As I got to know Joe, I realized that he was ornery and sometimes, I guess you could call it, a downright mean streak. Soon after I met him, brother Jim, Joe, and I were down in the pastureland at our house, shooting our slingshots at targets and sometimes birds. We walked over to the asphalt road next to the pasture to replenish our supply of small chunks of iron and steel. The roadway had been top dressed with tar and slag that came from the steel mills in Birmingham, and among the loose gravel was an ample supply of these small chunks. They were perfect for slingshots and far more accurate and penetrating than small rocks. As we finish collecting our ammunition, Joe saw a huge Missala transport bus coming down the road, and he told us he was going to shoot the windshield out. We told him not to, but all three of us hid down in the ditch. As the bus approached, we were out of sight. Joe pulled the pocket back from the stock as far as the rubber would stretch and let one of those small chunks of iron go flying. It hit the windshield and made a loud noise as the glass only cracked. By the time the bus stopped, we were long gone. Joe went to his house, and Jim and I went home.

The previous week, when the school nurse came to our school to give shots, they ran out of serum. Neither Jim and I got the shot and were instructed that the nurse would be at a place straight through the woods from our house on the next road over. We were to be there in about another hour to get our shots. While we were gone, a sheriff or some investigator came to our house trying to locate the person that shot the windshield on the bus. They were gone by the time we arrived at home, and when Coleman questioned us, we simply denied that we had any part in shooting at the bus, which was the truth.

I was following the same work path at school that Joe had taken, and this particular year would be his last at Farmstead. Some of our duties overlapped regarding our lunchroom work, so we both carried a key to the entry door.

We were having a Halloween party in the auditorium, and it was a grand event. The old workshop, where we held our Sunday evening studies, had been made into a really great and fun spook house. There were booths throughout the auditorium where for a nickel, you could win a dollar prize. There were a couple of water tubs filled with apples for bobbing, and the decorations were great. There were a couple of booths where you could purchase orange juice, which was something no one in our area could normally afford.

I hadn't seen Joe this evening, but I knew he would find me. He was the biggest moocher you ever saw, and a few days before, I told him I had bought my first pack of ready rolled cigarettes for twenty cents. He wanted me to bring them to the Halloween party, which I had done, but I wouldn't bring them in the school; so I hid them in a special place about a hundred yards away on the railroad tracks. I took a walk outside and spotted Joe a long distance away; so I snuck around behind the bushes, made my way to the tracks, and got my cigarettes. I had a plan to stop Joe's constant mooching. I didn't really smoke at that time. I bought the cigarettes to impress the older boys, and my mistake was in telling Joe in the first place. I'd had the cigarettes for a couple of days and hadn't gotten up the courage to light one; but I opened the pack, pulled out one cigarette, took a ladyfinger firecracker, and embedded it in the end of the cigarette. I pulled the fuse out and exposed a small hole to the powder. I put it back in the pack and marked its location so I would be sure to get the right one when Joe came a-begging. I got within a hundred feet of the school building, and Joe saw me. He came running, hollering, "Hey, Rusty (he always called me Rusty), ya got them cigarettes?"

I didn't want to overplay my hand, so I quietly muttered, "Yes."

"Well, gimme one so I can see if they're any good."

I slowly found the marked one and handed it to him, making sure that when he put it in his mouth, the charged end would be on the outside end of the cigarette. He grabbed a match and quickly lit the cigarette. Nothing happened. He proceeded to take a second big draw, and *BOOM*, the whole end of the cigarette blew off and about scared him to death. He wasn't too happy, but after a few seconds, he patted me on the back and said, "That's a good one."

We walked back into the auditorium, and it had begun to close down. We helped for a few minutes, and when everyone was gone, Joe asked to borrow my key to the lunchroom. He knew the rule that the key never leaves the holder's hand, so I told him no. I asked him where his key was, and he said that he left it at home. I asked him what it was he wanted in the lunchroom, and he said, "Man, didn't you see all that orange juice in the booths tonight?"

"Well, why didn't you buy some?"

"I don't have any money."

I began to feel sorry for him and told him I would open the door but would not enter the lunchroom. I stuck the key in the door and instantly heard footsteps a few feet away. It had to be Mr. Land, the janitor, who was coming up the winding metal stairs from the furnace room. We knew if you could hear him, he was at the top and, at any second, would be opening a door about eight feet away, directly across from where we were standing.

Joe, myself, and one of his buddies jumped into the kitchen; and while I quietly closed and locked the door, Joe and his buddy raced by the serving counter, grabbed a gallon can, and the three of us hightailed it at top speed down through the tennis courts and deep into the pine thicket. When we felt we were safe from getting caught, the three of us squatted, sitting on our feet. Joe placed the can between his knees and with his pocketknife cut two holes in the top. Now Joe was a guzzler. Every time he drank something, he would guzzle and gulp it down. He put the can to his mouth and quickly guzzled a couple of mouthfuls. Suddenly, he threw the can down and began coughing, spitting, and sputtering. He was getting paid back for some of the stuff he had done. This happened to be a can of hot Tabasco sauce.

Mrs. Bunch, the manager of the lunchroom, was very organized. She had put the orange juice away and had set out the cans of Tabasco sauce in preparation of cooking the next day's meals.

Things started getting really tough. It was becoming obvious to me that Mom would never get well. The doctors had no idea what was wrong, so they kept prescribing medicine for digestive- and nerve-related symptoms. Some names of neurological diseases were beginning to surface, but no doctor actually knew what her disease was. Coleman would occasionally find an odd job, but both our incomes were not enough to buy Mom's medicine and enough food for the three of us.

I had joined the Boy Scouts the year before and was struggling to find the time to attend the meetings. We had a great camp back in the woods about two miles from home. I rode my bicycle to the meetings. One night before our meeting started, about a dozen of us were playing a pretty rough game called tackle breakup. It was a version of "no man stands," and the object was to tackle and put down as many as you could before someone put you down. We were all wearing our uniforms and real hard soled shoes. Someone hit me hard, and I went down, and then I received a hard kick directly in the mouth.

The following day, Mom and Coleman took me to the dentist to clean up the mess. I lost six of my upper teeth over this incident and three dollars paid to the dentist to remove the broken ones that did not fall out of my mouth upon impact. I quit the Boy Scouts, which gave me a little more time to do odd jobs because enough money to live on was getting harder and harder to earn, coupled with the cost of putting a partial plate in my mouth where the six teeth were missing. I got to the point I would eat very little at home. It was difficult to eat, and the less I ate, the more there would be for Mom and Coleman. Occasionally, I would pour some oatmeal in a dish and put some water and sugar on it, but not very often. When lunchtime came at school, I would chose the soft foods, and I started eating an ice cream bar at recesses since that was a part of payment for my work.

Chapter Four

We managed to keep our lives going until early 1953. Jim got married and moved to a place of his own; but he, Ella Mae, and other relatives either wouldn't or couldn't help us. I had turned fifteen, and it was obvious that Mom needed someone with her most of the time. It was going to be either Coleman or myself. Coleman could only work a little time each week, and conditions were not getting any better. I learned that my dad had quit farming and had gotten a job in the auto industry in Ypsilanti, Michigan. That was a foreign place to me because the farthest I had been away from home was about ten miles inside the Mississippi line.

I contacted Dad and explained our circumstances and asked him if he could help find a fifteen-year-old a decent-paying job. He said he could and would, so he contacted a person he knew and got me a good-paying job roofing new houses. He then told me that he would be coming home to move his family to Ypsilanti the following week, and he had a rented house in a government project that was big enough for him, Evelyn, the four kids at his home, and myself and that I would be welcome to ride back with them.

I made arrangements with Mr. French and Mr. Burt to be gone for the summer, and they promised to give me my job back when I returned. I packed up a change of clothing and a pair of work shoes in a brown paper bag and went to Dad's house on Friday evening, the night he was leaving for home from Ypsilanti. I was real apprehensive about living with them. I thought I might be able to find a room on my own. I didn't really know my stepbrother, half brother, and half sister that well; but I would get to be with my beloved sister Shirley.

That night, everything that they were taking was packed. They were leaving almost everything, except clothing because the house in Ypsilanti was completely furnished, and they intended to move back home in about a year and start the farm up again. I slept with the boys; and at about five o'clock in the morning, Johnny, my little half brother, got out of bed and ran across the road to the barn. Five minutes later, he came screaming into the house. "Mama, Mama, the cow's stall is full of water!"

My stepmother, Evelyn, knew that the cow was about to give birth; so she asked me if I could drive, and I told her I could. She sent Allen, my stepbrother, and I over a wagon road in Dad's old truck to Dad's uncle Willie's house. Obviously, that had been the plan all the time if the cow came in before Dad got home. Uncle Willie was up, and when he saw us, he said, "She must be ready." So he jumped in his truck and followed us to Dad's house. The boys and I went to the barn to help Uncle Willie, and he sure needed it. By the time we got there, the birth was breaching, and Uncle Willie required extra hands to help turn the calf.

By the time this was done, Evelyn had prepared breakfast, and we washed up and sat down to eat. Johnny left the table, ran back to the barn, and once again came back to the house screaming. We weren't sure what was happening, so we hurried back to the barn, and the old cow was giving birth to a second heifer. This one came out fairly well on its own. In just a few minutes, both newborns were scampering around the barn lot. Dad had made arrangements for someone to care for his farm while he was gone. Dad got home in the early afternoon, immediately packed the car, then slept for a few hours.

Near nightfall, we headed out on this long trip in what was called a six-passenger automobile, but we had two adults and five kids. Barbara, my half sister, was pretty small; so she sat on my lap the entire way. We arrived in Ypsilanti early Sunday evening and began working Monday morning. I began work at seven the following morning, and after carrying two bundles of shingles up the ladder at a time, I was tired and sore by night. We worked ten hours a day and a half day on Saturday. When my paychecks began rolling in, I told Dad to set a price for room and board for me because I wanted to pay my own way. He said instead of doing that to just give him all the paychecks, except for a little spending money, and he would hold it for me. I told him I couldn't because I had to send money to Mom and Coleman. I finally decided to send half of my pay home, kept a couple of dollars for myself, and gave Dad the rest to hold.

I worked fifteen hours of overtime every week and grossed $78.20 per week. That was *big* money to me. I don't remember what the take-home pay netted out, but I sent exactly half home every week and gave Dad a little over thirty dollars per week to hold for me. I worked for three months and grossed over nine hundred dollars and netted somewhat over 750 dollars. I sent just under four hundred dollars home and thought that Dad would be holding about 350 to give me when I left.

I purchased a bus ticket home; and when I was ready to leave, Dad's math wasn't anywhere close, or he decided to charge the full house rental to me. I arrived home with very little cash. This was a great learning experience in many respects. It confirmed that decent wages could be had if one was willing to work. It gave me an opportunity to get to know Dad's family, but the greatest lesson was that I had made a big mistake that would never be repeated by me, and that was to have a clear understanding of all agreements and that if it's important, put it in writing—even if it's family. At that time, I had enough street smarts; but my ways, respect for elders, and trust in others got in the way.

The bus ride back to Alabama took about forty hours. We stopped several times, changed buses a few times, and covered somewhat over eight hundred miles on little narrow two-lane roads with traffic lights about every time you came to a place that had four or five buildings clustered together. We got into Birmingham early morning before daylight. I had to wait until noon for a bus to Jasper, which was about forty-five miles, and then I walked about five miles home.

I'll never forget how tired and disgusted I was—tired from the trip and disgusted about the little amount of money I was able to bring with me based upon what I had earned. I had started smoking, but I had never smoked a cigarette in my mother's presence. I lit a cigarette while sitting on the overstuffed sofa Coleman had bought us a few years earlier. I dozed off and dropped the cigarette in the crack between the cushions and burned a two-inch-deep hole in the base of the sofa. Mom wasn't too happy about the burn but was sure happy that I was home. She was really happy when I told her some other news. "As soon as Dad returns to the farm, Shirley is coming to live with us." Less than a month later, about the time school started, Shirley finally came home.

Chapter Five

Mom and Coleman still had a few dollars that I had sent them. I returned to school, began working again at Frenchy's, and had all my old jobs back with Mr. Burt and the school. Even though I was only gone three months, I could detect a change in Mom's condition. When we accumulated enough money, we took her to a doctor. This doctor thought she might have St. Vitus's Dance disease but didn't know for sure. By this time, several of her brothers and one sister were developing similar symptoms.

Many times, I would concentrate in deep thought about what I had seen regarding these symptoms. Then I remembered that when I was four and five years old, when it came time to repay some of the other farmers by helping them pick their cotton, we would go to my grandfather's brother's farm. He had a son whose name was Clinton. Clinton was about thirty years old but had the mind and physical abilities of a child who had not learned to walk or talk. The elders would tie a rope around Clinton's leg and tie the other end to a good shade tree near the field they were working in. Dad would leave me with Clinton and tell me to watch after him.

My mother's brother Elmer, one of twins, had returned home from service while we still lived by Grandma's house. Elmer had the same symptoms that Mom had, but he had been seriously wounded in the arm and chest, rendering his left hand to a partial claw. When I was a child, I attributed his actions and demeanor to his war injury. This proved to be wrong. The other twin, Delmer, began with the same symptoms. Then the older living son, Uncle Charlie, came down with the same thing; and then Mom's youngest sister, Susie; and next, the baby brother, Leon, who was my favorite, began showing physical signs the same as Mom's. Leon was ten years older than me, and when I started dating at age seventeen, Leon and I would double-date. He had just gotten home from service and had a car, so it was convenient for me to go on double dates.

When Uncle Elmer came home from service, he had been injured by an exploding mortar and had spent quite some time in the veterans' hospital in rehab. When he first arrived home, he had a hole completely through his left arm just below the shoulder; and it had healed well enough that the doctors were ready to do reconstructive surgery, which would include skin grafting. He also had injuries to his chest. Having been subjected to a tremendous amount of drugs, Elmer became addicted to alcohol. Periodically, he would spend a month or two in the veterans' hospital. While he was there, the hospital would save his veteran's paycheck and give him his money upon his release.

By the time he got home to Grandma's house, the only thing he had left was a partial jug of moonshine. He became delirious when he was drinking and would grab the chopping axe and march around the log house, slamming the axe into the logs. He said there were demons present in the gap where the clay was between each log. Finally, one day, the demons became too great for him; and he set fire to the house, burning it completely to the ground.

Grandma bought a small Jim Walter house and constructed it on the site, and after a short period of time, she moved Elmer into our little house next to hers. Elmer had just about completed his hospital visits, and his arm had been reconstructed, but he showed a lot of the same symptoms that Mom had. One day, Elmer was in the house alone. I don't know if he was drinking, but he piled all the clothing and bedding in a large pile on the bed and set it on fire and walked out of the house. Witnesses said that as the house was in full flames, Elmer ran back into the house and, within seconds, came back out, holding his rifle with outstretched arms in front of him. The rifle had a plastic stock, which had begun to melt.

I wondered if he had the same disease as Mom, but Mom and the others who had similar symptoms never did crazy things like Elmer had. I remembered a time when he first came home. My uncle Charlie had married and built a little house behind Grandma's place. Uncle Charlie had a dug well in his backyard that was about twenty feet deep. The well had a curbing that stood about four feet high with a removable lid on top. One day, Elmer was sitting near the back door, drinking a cup of coffee. My aunt Aroni said that all of a sudden, Elmer threw the cup one way and the saucer the other, ran out the back door, and, with a single move, slapped the lid off the well and dove in headfirst. She went screaming for Uncle Charlie and others who came immediately. They tied a rope around Uncle Charlie, and the others lowered him in the well, and he pulled Uncle Elmer to safety. Elmer was not hurt.

Soon after my teeth were knocked out, Coleman put together enough money (about fifteen dollars) to pay for my partial plate. Since I was only thirteen when the accident happened and my teeth were growing very fast, the dentist replaced the six teeth with only five, and the plate had one tooth dead center. He said my other teeth needed room to grow. I wore the partial plate until I was fifteen.

Dad and his family moved back to the farm from Ypsilanti, and immediately, Shirley came to live with us. Things were much better because Shirley helped Mom a lot, which gave Coleman the time to work at odd jobs and gave me the opportunity to really concentrate on basketball. This was my last year at Farmstead, and I was hoping that one of the two area high schools would want me to play for them, which meant they would provide me with some form of work around the school so I could afford to attend.

Shirley and I had a lot of catching up to do. We had not seen each other very often during the last eight years, except for the three months when we were together in Ypsilanti. We talked a lot and did goofy things together. We were very much alike and had a much closer bond than I had ever had with brother Jim. Jim had always been very independent and wanted everything to go his way, whereas Shirley was giving and considerate of me and was willing to be a good friend.

One day, we were reminiscing and talked about some of the things we had done during the few times we had visited over the past eight years. We talked about what we had learned and how things were really different that day from what they were just a few years ago. I reminded Shirley of one of those great differences—money. I recalled that on one of her visits, she and I were playing jacks on the floor. Shirley had several pennies, which she counted, and gave me half of them. We had pretended to be gambling, and the winner of each game would be paid a penny. She was much better than I and, of course, ended up with all the pennies. During this activity, I told her that one day, I was going to do something where I could earn a penny a minute. We were probably about nine or ten years old when this occurred. I then reminded her that during the three months that I was with them in Ypsilanti, I had earned almost three cents a minute. I deemed this as a sign of progress and was pleased.

I was in the ninth grade, still working every odd job I could find and loving every minute of playing basketball. I was a starter on the team, along with my two best friends, Walter and Ronald. I began having problems with my teeth. They were beginning to decay—in particular, the upper ones where the prongs of the partial plate touched the teeth—and all my teeth were becoming very brittle. Little chips started breaking off different teeth. Obviously, my diet had not been the best, but I always brushed my teeth. I had never had a toothbrush but used a sassafras twig dipped in a mixture of salt and soda. The dentist advised me that all of my teeth would have to be removed.

I saved every penny that I could, and soon after school began, I had all my teeth pulled. I still wore the partial plate, which contained five teeth. At first, it was embarrassing. When I talked or smiled, the plate would begin to fall because there was nothing to hold it in place. I learned to keep pressure on the plate with my tongue, but it was difficult to talk. When I smiled, you could see the gaping hole where the dentist had omitted the sixth tooth when he made the partial. I learned to cock my head so that my five teeth would be facing whomever I was talking with, but I still made funny noises when I talked.

The most difficult times were during a ball game. It was hard to shout loudly without opening my mouth pretty wide, and when I did, the teeth would almost fall out. As our basketball season was coming to an end, I had been going to the dentist where he was preparing my gums for impressions for a full set of dentures, but they wouldn't be done by tournament time.

The tournament came, and most of the sixteen teams had larger players than we had. We were a play making team and worked together very well. Although I had become real accurate in my shooting ability, I was not a high scorer. I was the smallest starter and close to the smallest player on the floor. I was a play maker and worked to set up one of our taller players. I did have one advantage in that I was the quickest and fastest player on the floor. I could run the 100 in ten seconds. The competition was tough, but we won both our games the first weekend and barely scraped out a win from a much bigger team on the following Friday night.

Now came the test. It was Saturday, and the game that night would determine the champions. All our players were confident that we could win, but this team's players were considerably bigger than our players, so we all knew we had to play smart. The best scorer was our point guard, Buddy, and the second best was my friend Walter. I had the lowest average of the five starters, but was number one in assists and was considered by most to be the third best overall player behind Buddy and Walter. The coach and Mr. Burt had the team arrive about three hours before the game. We went through some very important practice drills in slow motion and spent some time reviewing the plays the other team had been using, and then we were ordered to the dressing room where all of us rested for about two hours. We were given a cup of chicken soup and half of a Hershey's chocolate bar.

Coach Upton had graduated from Alabama, and this was his first year of coaching at Farmstead. He was a good coach, but strict and tough, but all the players loved him. About thirty minutes before the game, Coach Upton and Mr. Burt came to the dressing room. The team was dressed and ready to hit the floor. They talked for a while about team spirit and the importance of the game since it would be the last one at Farmstead for half of the team. They concluded the pep session with a prayer, and we hit the court.

The three-minute prestart horn sounded, and we cleared the court and headed to the bench. The starters huddled around the coach, and he told us the game plan he had devised for this game. It was entirely different from any game plan we'd ever played. Buddy was known throughout the basketball system as a great scorer, so the coach knew that he would be double-teamed; and Walter, equally well known, was our center and would get a lot of secondary defenders sagging to his position. Since I rarely scored more than three or four points, the defense would not be focusing on me. Coach Upton described the exact play he wanted us to do in every detail and told us to make that play every time we brought the ball down the court. His objective was to get a quick start and outscore the opponents early, and he felt that it would take a number of repeated plays before the defense could adjust to a play we had never used before.

Buddy was the point guard, and his brother Jackie played the other guard position. Walter was center, and Ronald was in the forward position on the right side of the offensive court, and I was a forward on the left side of the offensive court. The play was simple and relied upon the other team defending our two top players, Buddy and Walter. The coach laid out the plan. Buddy was to inbound the ball to Jackie, who would bring the ball to center court to the extreme right. Buddy would move to center court as Walter came out to the center of the key. The defense was playing zone and would shift to the right and center. Ronald was to stay deep in his corner to keep from clogging up the middle and helping to hold the defense to the right side.

My most favorite shot was about fifteen feet at about forty-five degrees from the basket, and the coach began to give me my instructions. He told me to go deep in the corner on the left as we came down court, and the instant that Buddy received the ball back from Jackie at center court, I was to go to Buddy and set a pick; then the zone defense would move out. As Buddy moved toward the basket and to his left, my defender would go around me and double-team Buddy, leaving an open, unguarded area on the floor. As soon as my zone defender doubled Buddy, I was to turn to the basket; and Buddy was to lob the ball to me, which I would receive. And without putting the ball on the floor, I was to shoot. Since the floor was fairly cleared, Walter or Ronald would have the best chance of a rebound if I missed.

The game started, and on our first possession, we executed the play perfectly; and with a wide-open shot, I hit a bucket for two points. We repeated this exact play for the entire first quarter, and the defense still hadn't corrected itself. When my defender didn't double up on Buddy, Buddy could maneuver around his single defender and get a good shot off. Basically, what happened is that four of their defenders were occupied guarding Buddy and Walter as our play was developing.

We continued this play, and with about a minute before halftime, a time-out was called. I had been playing zone on both offense and defense, plus all the movement back out to Buddy's position; and I was drenched with sweat, but happy as I had ever been. Both the high school coaches were there watching, and I was making a good showing. As we hovered around the coach during time-out, I was dripping sweat all over the floor; and the coach had a towel in his hand, wiping up the sweat. He looked up at me and said, "Dutton, you're really hot." I thought he was referring to the sweat and was about to bench me for this last minute of the half, so I pleaded that he not take me out of the game. He replied, "No no, I mean you're really playing well." I stayed in the game; and at halftime, all the players were telling me how good a job I was doing, and then I realized I had scored nineteen points.

During halftime, the coach changed the strategy since the opponents were now leaving Buddy and Walter a little more open. During the last half, I made several assists, stole the ball once, and picked off a couple of rebounds. I shot the ball one time during this half and missed. The other four players did a great job, and we succeeded to become the champions.

Immediately after the game, the awards presentation was held, and the entire crowd stayed in the gym. After we received our trophy, the announcement was made as to those who made the all-star team. I never had any expectations that my name would be included, but I was really looking forward to my two friends Walter and Ronald making the team. The announcements began, and the first name called was Buddy Roberts. The crowd expected that and gave a big applause. Then the second player selected was a big center from a school named Townley. Another big applause. The announcer then said, "And the third choice by unanimous vote, Bobby

Dutton!" The crowd roared and applauded, and it was the happiest moment of my life. I was stunned and somewhat embarrassed because both Walter and Ronald were better players than I. Walter made the fourth spot, and Ronald was in the ten that were selected. So here we had four of Farmstead's players voted to the all-star team out of the ten selected from sixteen teams. This was worth a celebration, so the coach and Mr. Burt took the team down to Frenchy's and treated us to a great celebration party with great food and ice cream dishes.

As I grew older, I went through numerous periods of times that I was frustrated, experiencing difficulty, starting a business, or whatever that got me nervous, unsettled, or upset. I would mentally go back to that night; and I can still feel the elation, pride, and happiness that swept over me as they never had before. I have and will forever thank God for inserting this garden of peace and happiness in the soul of a boy who really never had a childhood.

My basketball team

Chapter Six

I finished at Farmstead in May 1954 and immediately followed up with the dentist and got my new full set of dentures. They were hard to get used to, but now I could talk and laugh without them falling out of my mouth. Now that school was out for the summer, I had to get a job to make enough money to go back to school. I continued going to church at Farmstead, and our little group of six spent a lot of time together, especially on Saturday nights and Sundays. Chesley, Kenneth, Walter, Ronald, Charlie, and I were a sixsome.

None of us drank beer or any alcoholic beverage, and even though I had previously smoked a few cigarettes, I never smoked one for all the time the six of us ran together. We all went to church and would sometimes go to a drive-in movie together. Many Sundays after church, we would pack something for lunch and head up to one of the many abandoned old lakes and ponds left over from strip mining. The largest one was called the Rock Crusher but had become a public swimming and park area. We preferred to go to the ones very few or nobody frequented. Most of these pits were infested with cottonmouth snakes, along with copperheads, so we had to always be on the lookout for them. A couple of times, we took cane fishing poles with the intention of catching some bream and hoped to clean and cook them on sight. We would take along some food just in case this did not work out, and it never did. We never even got the poles out of the car. We'd swim, sit, talk, and just enjoy being together.

Some Sunday afternoons, we would go to a community named Manchester, which had Black Water Creek flowing through it. There was a great swimming hole in the creek, which had a swing on a big tree that we used to compete with one another, doing dives or other tricks swinging out over the water, using this rope swing. This was the same creek that flowed just below my grandma's house, which had a great swimming hole as well.

This was the place where I was baptized at when I was a youngster. I also swam in the creek many times at the country club where I caddied. While we waited for a golfer to show up, we would dive in the creek and hunt for golf balls.

My basketball season was over, and I knew I had to find work where I could make enough money to attend school. I found a job at Copeland's Dry Goods downtown. This would be my only source of income since it's the only job I had time for. I signed up for summer school. I rode my bicycle to town and attended Walker County High. As soon as class was over, I went to work at Copeland's. This was a retail clothing and shoe store. My primary job was keeping the shelves stocked and organizing the stockroom, which was across the alley from the back of the store.

When I first worked in the stock warehouse, I found a huge oak barrel that was filled with dentistry equipment. Upon inquiring with the owner, I learned why it was in the warehouse. The man who owned the store was Mr. Weinstein. It was actually Dr. Weinstein. He told me the whole story. Dr. Weinstein was a Jew and had come to Jasper from New York. He had been a practicing dentist for several years, but for some reason, the Jewish council had blackballed him.

I didn't understand what he meant by "blackballed," so he proceeded to explain it like this. He said that the Jews maintain a high profile in the business world because they have internal rules and regulations that prohibit Jews from doing certain things. Their procedure is simple. If a Jew goes outside the rules once, he is forgiven and helped by the Jewish community to grow and prosper in his field of endeavor. They then allow a similar situation at the second offense; but upon a third offense, the council votes upon what the decision will be as to whether that person remains and retains his then-current status with continued support from the Jewish community, or whether he is ousted and is then on his own. The council vote is done in secret, and each member passes privately into a voting area that has a container of white balls and a container of black balls. They select and deposit their choice of balls into the voting receptacle. The balls are then counted, and the course of action to be taken depends upon the color of the balls having the largest quantity.

Dr. Weinstein said he had been blackballed and could never work as a dentist in New York again. Copeland's was a national chain of stores, and Dr. Weinstein had married one of the daughters of the Copelands. He gave me a big discount on clothes so I could afford to buy some new clothes for summer school. Coleman was still working odd jobs, Shirley was helping

Mom, school was going well, and we were getting by. We still did not have to pay any rent because Coleman was still watching over the defunct lumber mill property. That all was about to change.

We were notified that they were going to move all the houses away from the mill, and we would have to find a new place to live. That was all right with me because we found a house right at the edge of town where I could walk to work and to school. My old bike was on its last leg and would have to be junked, and I could not afford a new one. I worked at Copeland's for a short period of time and then found a full-time job at Vine's Motors, which was a Lincoln Mercury dealership. They were going to pay me $22.50 per week, and I would be working about forty hours a week. My job was to quick wash the cars on the used lot every morning, which I did starting at about six. I would spray water on four or five cars at a time and wipe down the glass and front end with a chamois cloth. Usually, there were about fifteen or twenty used cars on the lot. I would be done by seven thirty and would walk to school, which was only about a half mile away.

I went to school until noon, then walked back to work. In the afternoons, I would wash new cars being prepared for delivery and install the floor mats, which were shipped loose when we received the cars. I also washed many customers' cars when they were in for service. When I wasn't busy on the wash rack, I greased and changed oil in cars that were being serviced.

Things were still tough at home. Mom's health was continuing to fail, and we didn't have quite enough money to get by now that we had to pay rent. We had a government food warehouse and commodity outlet that had been established in town for the people that were in need. Reluctantly, Coleman signed up for the commodities. Once a week, he would go and stand in line for quite a while. He left with a big cake of cheese, potted meat, powdered milk, and powdered eggs. Sometimes he would get a cake of margarine that was pure white; but it came with a sealed packet of orange coloring that you had to put the two together, and after kneading them for a few minutes, you ended with something that looked like butter.

One day, I had the opportunity to go to the commodity line with him. I wanted to see what it was like. I have never been more embarrassed nor humiliated as I was that day receiving handouts. I vowed to myself that barring major disaster that will never happen to me again.

Shirley was liking living there in town. Our next-door neighbors were the Burgetts. They had three or four boys, and one of them had just returned home from service. I think his name was Terrell. He asked Shirley for a date, and when I found out about it, I really objected and talked to Mom and

Coleman to try to get them to prohibit her from going out with Terrell. They were reluctant to take any action, so on the day she was supposed to go on the date, I took her into her bedroom and tied her up. When Terrell came for her, I told him she had to go somewhere and to tell him she was sorry.

Sister Ella Mae was a member of the Church of God, and Shirley joined her in going to that church. Ella Mae and her husband, Jack, were renting a farm owned by the Blackwells. The lady, Perni Blackwell, was the reason Ella Mae began attending this church. Perni's brother who lived in New Orleans was a minister, and he came to visit Perni. Shirley met him at the church, and after a period of time, they decided to get married. I began to tell Shirley how right I was about not dating that Terrell guy, and it became a joke between us.

Their wedding day was coming soon, so they rented an apartment at the government projects at the edge of town. On a Saturday, they drove over to Mississippi, about forty miles away, and were married. They returned to town in the late afternoon; and her husband, Jack, told her he had to run uptown for a little while. I had a friend that worked at the corner drugstore as a soda jerk; and sometimes on Saturday, when my work was over, I would go to see Charles at the drugstore and maybe have a Coke until he was off work at six. Charles finished checking out, so he and I walked out of the drugstore and sat down on a set of concrete steps leading to the Cave Billiards, which was a pool hall known for heavy gambling. No one under twenty-one was allowed to enter. We both peered through a small window, and I was shocked. There was my brand-new minister professing, "just married three hours ago" brother-in-law shooting pool with a large group watching. This was a big game. The money box was very visible, and there was a stack of bills that would choke a horse.

I'd seen all I needed to see. Charles and I jumped in his car and drove to Shirley's apartment. Coleman's sister lived in the projects, and she and Shirley were standing in the yard, visiting. I told Shirley what I had seen, and she too was shocked. At first, she thought I was kidding; then I convinced her to go see for herself. She went down and watched through the same window Charles and I had watched through, and she began crying. It was OK to pretend to gamble as she and I had done, but this kind of gambling was against God and everything she believed in. She went home and refused to see Jack when he got there. On Monday morning, she went to the courts and had the marriage annulled. I believe she spent the night with Coleman's sister or alone in her apartment. She was back home the next day.

She started dating one of the Burgett boys next door. His name was James, and I liked him, so I didn't tie her up anymore. They dated for a period of time and then married. They have been married for about fifty-five years.

I finished up my summer session at school and could not afford to go to the regular session of school that was ready to begin. I chose to work during the day and go to the night classes that were offered. I continued working at the dealership, and it was difficult making ends meet. I never had any spending money, and I was tired from working and going to school. We just couldn't make it. I was tired of having to walk everywhere. Coleman still had the old '47 Chevy, but it was important to him even though he didn't drive it. When he and Mom wanted to go somewhere, which was rare, I would drive them in the Chevy. I had never been on a date, but had always had several friends that were girls.

One Saturday night, I was going straight home from work and decided to stop by the roller rink. I had never been inside it and never been on roller skates. Once inside, I saw this very attractive girl that I had seen during summer school. I didn't know her name but wanted to meet her. She had another little girl with her that was about seven or eight years old. This little kid was a picture of beauty. I walked over and introduced myself. She said her name was Vida Yvonne Black, and she also told me her little sister's name, which I don't remember. She told me to get a pair of skates, and she would teach me how it was done. I had some change in my pocket but wanted to decline to spend the quarter to rent skates. This was too important, so I hurried to the counter and rented the skates.

Out on the floor, both she and her sister were very graceful. They would go around the rink as easy as if they were walking. I thought to myself, *I can do that.* I stepped on the floor and could hardly stand without holding on to the railing. Vida came to me, took one hand in hers, and put her arm around my waist. "Now let's go," she said. We went around the rink a few times, and I was beginning to get the hang of it and told her to turn me loose. We skated side by side for a round or two, and then ego set in, and I had a little cocky streak, but it didn't last very long. I broke away from Vida, hit the straightaway, and was flying down the rink. When I got to the first corner, I attempted to walk through the turn. That was a big mistake. Both feet came out from under me, and I skidded across the floor. I'd probably still be going except that the kick rail and my tailbone came together, resulting in momentary excruciating pain.

That, coupled with my embarrassment, was about all I could handle. Vida was very kind and understanding, and when I asked her for a date, she immediately accepted. We set the date time for the next Saturday night. I had never asked to borrow Coleman's car, but I thought it would be OK; but if it wasn't, my friend Charles could get his father's car. I really wanted Vida and me to go on the date alone since it was my first, so I was hoping Coleman would loan me the car. When I asked him if I could borrow the car, he was pleased and kidded me about my first date. He said there were no longer any restrictions on how far I could drive the car, but the maximum speed was still fifty miles per hour.

I went to Vida's house and met her parents. Mr. Black was a state representative, and I remembered seeing his picture in the newspaper. Her parents were very nice and kind people and simply asked what time we would be home. We told them that we were going to a movie uptown that would be over about ten and then we might stop and get a Coke or something but that she would be home by eleven. We took the movie in, stopped and got a Coke to go, and drove back to her house. We sat in the car, talking for a few minutes. We held hands a couple of times, but that was the extent of our contact. I never attempted to kiss her and did not want to ruin my chances of seeing her again. I saw her at a distance once after that, but something happened that kept me from asking her on another date.

Since we had moved uptown and I went to summer school and was now going to night classes, I didn't get to see much of Walter, Ronald, and my other friends that I had made over the eight years at Farmstead. I missed them, and I envied them. They would be going to the regular daily session of school, trying out for the basketball team, and enjoying all that would be going on. I thought that I would sure like to do that, but it was out of the question. There wasn't enough time to work, go to school, and have any time for myself. Mom was getting sicker and now needed some much attention that she couldn't be left alone for more than an hour or so.

I had been at the automobile dealership for a year and worked between forty-two and fifty-five hours a week. My pay was $22.50 a week when I started and still was $22.50. The family needed much more than that, and something had to be done. Mom was on medication, which helped ease her discomfort. Everybody else was gone from home, except Mom, Coleman, and me; and so far, no one ever offered one dime or one hour of help. I was too proud to ask anyone and dedicated myself to do whatever had to be done and vowed that I would never ask anyone to help us unless I could pay for their help. When Mom was well, she once told me that decisions in life are easy if you don't have a choice.

There were no other jobs available for a sixteen-year-old, so something else had to happen. I didn't know what I was going to do, but I knew that I had to do it very soon. My seventeenth birthday came and went. The man who owned the dealership, Mr. Vines, had died; and his family sold half of the company to Mr. Price, who had been my boss since I started work. Mr. Vines's daughter Mary Ellen and I became friends. Mary Ellen worked in the office when she was home from school. She had graduated and was going to college.

One day, one of the young boys from a rich family in town bought a new Mercury, which was decked out with everything you could get on the car. He immediately wrecked it, and Mr. Price ordered him a new one. While he was waiting for the new Mercury to come in, he bought a beautiful old '39 Chevy that had been modified. It was really fast. When his new car arrived, I asked him what he was going to do with the Chevy. He said that he was going to turn it in to Mr. Price, but if I wanted it, I could have it for fifty dollars. Coleman's old car needed some repairs, and I thought it might be less money to buy this car. I agreed to take it, and Mr. Price agreed to let me buy it from the company and deduct two dollars per week from my pay.

I knew Coleman would not drive this car even in an emergency because it simply was too "hot." I made a deal with one of our mechanics. He needed his car painted, and I had become a good painter by helping out in the body shop in my spare time. He told me that if I would buy the parts for Coleman's car, he would repair it; and he would buy the paint and supplies for his car, and I would paint it. We both completed the jobs we had agreed to. Coleman's car ran fine, and the mechanic's car looked like a new one. We were both happy. I was paying for the parts the same as I was paying for the '39 Chevy, so four dollars a week was being deducted from my pay. This would continue until school was finished in May. I would sign up for the summer school session. I would only need one or possibly two credits to get my diploma. The parts for Coleman's car would be paid off, and I would only owe a few dollars on my car. I had only driven the car one time because I couldn't afford the gas.

In desperation, I went to a man who had once taught our Sunday school class for a short period of time. He was the recruiting officer for the air force. I explained to him our current circumstances, my age, and educational background. The air force had a special training program and would in fact allow a seventeen-year-old in the service, with certain restrictions. I discussed this with Mom and Coleman, and they agreed to sign the approval papers for me to get in. After all the work was done by the recruiting officer, I was accepted, but my mother changed her mind and would not sign. Her reason was that she did not want me going off to war.

Registration for summer school came, and I registered for my classes. I decided that I would take a full load in the event I was able to go to college. I told Mary Ellen that I was all set for summer school, but a need for a few dollars came up at home. I gave Mom the money I had saved for my books and school supplies, and on the first day of school, Mary Ellen walked through the garage and saw me. She came running over and asked me what I was doing and told me I was supposed to be in school. I told her what had happened, and she left.

About an hour later, here she came with all the books and supplies required for my summer session. She handed them to me and said, "This is what friends are for. Now GET YOUR ASS TO SCHOOL!" I refused to do it because I could not pay her back. She told me that she and her mother owned half of the dealership and had the money. She told me she really wanted me to do this and jokingly said, "One day, when you're rich, you can pay me back."

I went back to school the following day. Life went on for a couple or three weeks, and things simply got tougher. Now was the time I had to do something. My brother, Jim, had moved to Indiana and was making good wages; and he was in town. He had not stopped to see the family, but relatives told me. As much as I hated to, I devised a plan. I would ask Mr. Price for a small raise, and maybe I could mow lawns on Sunday so I could get through school. If I couldn't get a raise, I would locate my brother and negotiate a ride with him back to Indiana.

Mr. Price was gone for the day, so I would have to wait until Saturday morning to set my plan in motion. I knew that Jim would be leaving for Indiana late Saturday, so I had to act fast and make some quick decisions. At nine in the morning, when Mr. Price came to work, he walked through the garage. I approached him, said good morning, and then recited the words I had carefully planned and rehearsed for the past twenty-four hours. "Mr. Price, I've been with you for going on two years. I've never missed a day's work, and I work hard. My family and I are struggling to make ends meet, and I really can't afford to go to school. Could you see your way clear to give me an increase of two dollars per week?"

Without hesitation, Mr. Price responded in a tone of finality and said, "Well, Bobby, I don't think I'm gonna need you anymore."

I was shocked at his response. He was not known to joke around, and the tone of his voice was serious. I thought he might say he couldn't afford it, which would have been acceptable, but now here I stand greatly offended because of his lack of appreciation for my diligence and steady work. I told him, "Very well, let's go to the office and settle up. I still have a balance, owing you on the parts for my stepdad's car. And you can have the '39 Chevy back, which has only been driven one time. Take out what I owe you, and we'll part company." That is almost word for word what was said.

He kind of grunted and said, "Well, I was just kidding."

I told him, "You're not dealing with some wet-nosed kid, and I'd been around long enough to know the difference. Just pay me, and we'll part company." He reluctantly ordered the girl to figure out the account and cut me a check. I had two weeks' pay coming, and after everything was completed, the girl wrote me a check for somewhat over twenty dollars. I left the '39 Chevy where it had been parked, on the rear lot of the dealership, since I bought it; and I gave the keys to the girl in the office.

I found a telephone and located brother Jim at his in-laws' house and made a deal to ride back to Indiana with him. This was about ten in the morning, and he was planning to leave town around four in the afternoon.

My walk home was a hard one. I knew that Coleman would understand, but Mom would take the news very hard. When I got home, I went to my little hiding place where I kept a few dollars for emergencies. I had seven or eight dollars in my stash. I put all my money together and counted out nineteen dollars, which I calculated I would need to live on, assuming I could get a job quickly. I was positive I could get some kind of job because I was willing to do any kind of work. I put the nineteen dollars in my wallet and had about ten dollars left over. I got Mom and Coleman together and told them what had happened and that I would be leaving for Indiana in the late afternoon. I told them that as soon as I got a paycheck, I would send them some money, and I gave them the ten dollars. Mom began crying. I hugged and kissed her and told her that someday, I will earn enough money that we can get her a special doctor. In the meantime, I guaranteed her that I would provide enough for her and Coleman to get by on.

With that, I went to my room, selected the best shirt and pants I owned, grabbed my favorite harmonica, and packed away a full change of work clothes, a pair of work shoes, and my little white Bible. I put them in a paper grocery bag and folded the top of the bag, so now I'm about ready to travel. I sat down on my bed, and a few tears began creeping down my cheeks. I prayed to God to keep Mom and Coleman and to guide me in this strange land where I was going. My tears stopped flowing, and I began to be filled with anticipation.

I washed up and changed into my best clothes and spent the rest of the day around Mom and Coleman. I kept asking them if there was anything else I could do before I go, and they insisted there wasn't. At around four in the afternoon, brother Jim and his wife, JoNell, picked me up. They hurriedly said hello and goodbye to Mom and Coleman; then we hit the road.

At that time, gasoline was about twenty-nine cents per gallon, and it would take close to two tanks for the trip. Jim and I agreed on my contributing two dollars for gas, which I paid as we made our first stop in Nashville.

The trip would take about twenty-two hours, and I hardly slept at all. Jim and JoNell took turns driving, and I sat in the backseat, alone with my thoughts. I was already missing and worrying about Mom and Coleman. I was worried that they would need something, or Mom would get sicker, and then I began feeling sorry for Coleman. He was such a good man, and I knew he would look after Mom, but that was a very difficult job to do by yourself. I was already missing my friends, and I thought about Vida and the fact I probably would never see her again. I thought about Charles (whose last name was Gibson), who had been a real good friend for the past two years; and my thoughts kept going back to my best friends, Walter and Ronald.

Once again, I could feel tears on my cheeks, and I had a big lump in my throat. I was never afraid. I was never uncertain about being able to make it on my own. The biggest thing was that I had missed my childhood, but I always had Mom and Coleman to lean on; but beginning now, I really had to be a man. Occasionally, I would have to mentally go back to my happy place, which was the night I made the all-star team. That happening was and would be a mainstay in my life.

I still needed another credit to finish high school, and I had aspirations of going to college. All of this became uncertain earlier that day when Mr. Price told me he didn't think he was gonna need me anymore.

My first and foremost influence and the true mainstay in my life is God. God has always been a source of strength for me, and I have prayed almost every day of my life. Many times, I was so busy for fifteen or sixteen hours a day that my prayers were made on the run; nevertheless, God heard me and has been by my side, without fail, in every endeavor in which I've participated. I praise him to the absolute highest degree and profoundly thanked him for giving me the strength, fortitude, and will to continue trying to make wherever I go better than when I came.

Our trip to Elkhart, Indiana, was uneventful. There was not a lot of conversation as it was a long and tiring ride. Jim and JoNell told me I could stay with them for a while. They had a one-bedroom duplex on South Main Street, but I could sleep on the sofa. I appreciated their offer and thanked them, but I knew that real soon, I would have my own place.

As we were getting close to Elkhart, JoNell said that she could close her eyes and tell me when we entered the city limits. She closed her eyes, and as we passed the green sign welcoming motorists to Elkhart, I noticed two things. First, there was a change in pavement with a small bump; and second, the sign stated the population to be 43,557. The town of Jasper that I had just left was 8,559, and I thought as we passed it that it was now 8,558.

The date was June 19, 1955; and just after two in the afternoon, we were at brother Jim's house. It was real nice even though it was a small three-room downstairs duplex or apartment. The floors were carpeted, and it felt so good to my bare feet. We had never had any carpet at any of the many houses we had lived in. There was a bathroom with a shower, and while JoNell fixed us something to eat and made me a bed on the sofa, I took a shower. I scrubbed myself extra hard because I wanted to have clean nails and hair when I went looking for a job the following morning. Jim was working at the Old English Door Company and got off to work early on Monday morning.

After breakfast, I left the house and walked downtown to see the new town I would be living in. I got the address of the state employment office, and after getting directions from several people on the street, I found it. It was located within one block of Elkhart Central High School, and as I passed the school, I wondered if they might have night classes where I could complete the credit I needed to finish high school. The town was much larger than Jasper, and everyone I spoke to indicated that there were some jobs available and that work had been very good all year. When I entered the employment office, I knew I would have to lie about my age. It seemed that you had to be eighteen to get a job in the factories, and I was only seventeen. When I inquired at the desk about applying for a job, the lady took my information and, after some time, instructed me to be back at the office the following morning at nine. They had scheduled a testing session for those that were applying for a job, and I was lucky to get my name on the list at this late date.

That night, we were all still tired from the trip and went to bed early. I silently said my prayers, for I knew that I would need more than luck on Tuesday when I would take the test. I had to find a job quickly, and I was already uncomfortable being at brother Jim's house.

Chapter Seven

Tuesday morning seemed to come quickly, and I was filled with anticipation about taking the test for possible employment but had no idea as to what kind of test it might be. Until now, I had taken numerous tests in school and also a series of tests in preparation to join the air force. In every previous case, I had an opportunity to prepare for the test; but not knowing what to expect, I reconciled myself simply to do the best I could.

It was about a twenty-minute walk to the employment office. I showered and spruced myself up as best I could and left the house at eight o'clock. I had no knowledge as to how many applicants would be taking the test, so I was going to make sure that if there was a line, I would be near the front. I couldn't afford to take the chance of being left out. The office had not opened when I arrived, and no one was waiting in line. I sat down on the benches located in the hallway, and soon, I saw a lady unlock the entry door. I scampered right in and told the lady I was there for the tests. She directed me to a large room that looked like one of our classrooms back at school. There were desks for each individual that had a chair attached to it. I was the first one in the room, so I took a seat in the front of the room.

People began coming in, and pretty soon, I had counted about thirty-five. In walked a lady who introduced herself as the instructor and began to explain the test and the rules that would apply. She stated that this was an aptitude test, which would assist the agency in placing people to jobs they were suited for. We were given forty-five minutes to complete the test, which included some paperwork that was in much more detail than the paperwork the day before. Stacked upon a table in the front of the room were about fifty wooden cases that were about one and one half by two feet and about three inches thick. The instructor asked each of us to come to the front and get one of these cases and instructed us not to open them until she told us to.

When everyone had their cases and returned to their seats, she asked us to open the case and fill out the paperwork, which took about ten minutes. Then she gave us about five minutes to read the instructions. The case had numerous compartments that contained nuts, bolts, screws, washers, studs, and an array of irregular-shaped objects, all of which had several sizes. There was a mixture of colors, sizes, different threads on the nuts and bolts, different lengths, and various diameters. When the five minutes for reading the instructions had passed, she told us to follow the instructions; and we would be allowed thirty minutes to complete this part of the test, and then we would be finished for this session.

The test required finding the right color and the right size of studs, bolts, washers, and nuts and securing them together. If you followed the instructions, you would be able to finish during the thirty-minute time allowed. I had very nimble fingers, so it appeared that this test would be a breeze. It also helped that I knew the difference in some of the mechanical properties of the parts, such as the difference in a machine thread and a pipe thread. I could tell by looking at the nut or bolt. When each segment of the job was completed, there was a designated place in the case to put them. Now that I had seen everything and understood what I was supposed to do, the rest was a breeze. After about fifteen minutes, I leaned back in my chair. I had completed doing everything the written instructions asked for and had double-checked everything, and everything was correct.

The instructor saw me leaning back in my chair and walked over by me. I was the youngest one taking the test, and she assumed I was having a problem. She asked if I had any questions or required some help. I told her, "No, thank you, I'm finished." She looked at my case, then asked me to wait in the other room. I knew I was in trouble and thought I had done something wrong. I sat outside the room for the balance of the test period, and it seemed like it was forever. Things were not looking good, and I was thinking what I would do next. I decided that as soon as I left the employment office, I would stop at every garage, car wash, service station, and paint shop until I had a job. I knew how to do this type of work.

Finally, the people came filing out of the room; and as the last one passed, I got up with the intention of following these people back out to the street. As I started to leave, the instructor came to the door and asked me to come back in. We sat down at her desk, and she began to talk. She was an older lady and was very pleasant. She began by telling me that she had given this test numerous times, and many people don't quite complete it, and some who do don't score very well because they did not follow the instructions.

She then said that I had completed the test in less time than anyone she had ever had in her class and that everything was correct. She opened my case and said, "Son, I've got a job for you." She asked me if I had transportation, and I told her I had just gotten in to town but could get to a job regardless of where it was in the area. The place she was going to send me was about a forty-five-minute walk from where we were.

She made a phone call; and after she finished, she wrote down the company's name, address, and the name of the person I was to see and told me they needed someone right away. The name of the company was Leggett Manufacturing Company and was located on the south side of town. I knew where it was because we had passed it a few blocks inside the city limits as we entered Elkhart on Sunday. I was instructed to see a Mr. Lyle Syson, who was production superintendent.

I was the happiest that I had been in a long time and began walking toward where my new job was located. I had to walk right past my brother's house, and when I was there, I just kept on walking. I arrived at Leggett's sometime after eleven and went to the office. The girl called Mr. Syson in. He entered the office, took one look at me, and smiled. "So you're my new man," he said. He told me I was kind of small for the job, which was handling mobile home and travel trailer axles in the welding shop. I smiled back and assured him that I was like a Bantam rooster, a strong person in a small body. He told me that he would start me at the rate of $1.75 per hour and explained insurance and other benefits, including the union and such, and he asked me when I could go to work. By now, it was their lunchtime, so I told him I could start after lunch. He laughed and called me an eager beaver and told me to report to work the following morning at seven.

I had left home with nineteen dollars in my pocket and had given Jim two dollars for gas. JoNell had made sandwiches for the trip, so I had not spent any more money. Now I had seventeen dollars in my pocket. I headed down Main Street back toward town, and when I was about halfway to Jim's house, I saw a sign on the door of a two-story house that said Room for Rent. I rang the doorbell, and this real nice elderly lady came to the door. She opened the door, and I inquired about the room. She took me upstairs and showed me the room. There were three bedrooms upstairs and a bathroom with a tub and shower. The room was clean as a pin and smelled really good. It was perfect. She explained that she had two other men in the other rooms. The three of us would share the bathroom, and she took care of the cleaning, but we had to keep our room orderly. She told me the rent was seven dollars a week, and she required two weeks in advance. I asked her when it would be available, and she said, "The room and bedding are clean, and you can move right in."

I really wanted this room, but I had to think for a minute to determine if I could eat on three dollars for the next ten days because that would be how long it would be before I received my first paycheck. The math was pretty simple. Three dollars for ten days was thirty cents. Hamburgers and a Coke would be twenty-five cents. Heck, If I had one hamburger and one Coke each day, I could make it all right, and I'd still have enough maybe for a milk shake. I gave the lady fourteen dollars and went whistling down the sidewalk for the few blocks to brother Jim's house.

I got my bag and told JoNell where I was going and that I would come back that evening to talk to brother Jim.

I didn't have any way to let Mom and Coleman know that I had found a job and that I was going to be fine. I moved into my room and lay on the bed, thinking. I was real happy that I had a job, but longed for Mom and Coleman and my friends. I knew Mom was worrying about me, and I had to make sure she knew I was fine. Later toward evening, I walked to Jim's house and told him where I would be staying, thanked him for the ride to Elkhart, and started to my room.

I had spotted a little store a couple of blocks away and decided to see if they sold writing paper. I bought a tablet and a pencil for ten or fifteen cents and proceeded to my room. I kind of chuckled to myself, "Whoops, there goes my milk shake for next week." I returned to my room and met the two other men who were there. One was a much older fellow, and the other was probably in his thirties. As time passed, we would see one another coming and going, but we never sat down to conversation. It was rare if either of them were home during the evening.

I pulled out my pencil and paper and wrote Mom and Coleman a letter explaining what had happened to this point and that I had a job that would pay me well and was further living in a room in a real nice lady's home. I wrote that I would receive my first pay on the second Friday from then and would send them some money. I knew they would never write me. Mom couldn't because of her illness, and I don't remember Coleman ever writing a letter. That didn't matter as long as they got along OK. I finished the letter and folded it. *I'd have to get an envelope and stamp tomorrow.*

I went downstairs to the front porch, and my landlord was sitting on the porch swing. I sat on the steps, and we talked for a while, and I told her some of the reasons that I had come to Elkhart and told her I had just written my mom a letter but had to get an envelope and stamp to mail it.

She went into the house and brought back one of each and gave them to me. I cannot remember her name even though we spent a great deal of time together. I went to my room, said my prayers, and went to bed. Tomorrow would be a big day.

Work went very well. I was loading two welding tables with axles that weighed about eighty to ninety pounds each. The welders would install the brake flange; and I would move the axles to my table, chip off all the weld slack, and position them on a skid, which was forklifted to the assembly line. I handled each axle three times, and we were welding 170 per day. That meant I was lifting 510 axles per day, and I was tired by the end of the shift.

We had about one hundred employees, and most of them took their breaks and lunchtime on the assembly line where it was comfortable to sit. A lot of the guys played cards at lunch. I got to know most of them, and they all kidded me because I was from the south. I developed a daily routine. When the bell rang ending the shift I would clean up my area, clock out, and walk home. After resting a little while, I would shower and change into tomorrow's work clothes, which were rented through the company, and then walk to a place called Wray's Ice Cream, which was across the street from brother Jim's house. I ate my hamburger and drank my Coke and then walked home.

I was lonely and worried about Mom and Coleman. If we'd had a telephone on both ends, things would have been a whole lot easier. Many times, I thought about going home but knew that I couldn't. Back at my room, I would sit and doodle on my pad of paper, trying to estimate money matters and when I would have enough to get some transportation. I would get down in the dumps mentally, and I knew this was not good; so every time I began feeling sorry for myself, I would read my Bible or play my harmonica.

After playing the harmonica a few evenings, I was in my room, playing a fast song, which was a little louder than normal. A knock came at the door. I opened the door, and there stood my landlady. I thought she was going to chew me out for making noise. Instead, she told me she had been listening to me play for several nights and asked if I would sit with her on the front porch and play. I was very relieved and pleased and immediately headed for the porch. I played several songs, and then she excused herself and went into the house. Moments later, she returned and handed me a big piece of coconut pie and a glass of lemonade. This became a regular routine, and at least a couple of times each week, we would sit on the front porch, I would play, and she would always bring me pie and a drink or something to eat.

Work was very good, and I usually got off between four thirty and five thirty. I would work as much overtime that they would let me. A few days before, as I was walking home, I saw a real pretty young girl in the yard. She waved at me, and I kept going. This day, as I was walking by, she came out of the yard to the sidewalk and began to talk to me. She was really pretty and very nice, and I thought about asking her out, but she looked very young, so I didn't. This episode got me thinking about Vida and my friends back in Alabama, and I would start feeling lonely again. I'd read my Bible and play my harmonica and begin to feel better.

I didn't think it would ever get here, but payday finally came. My first check netted me seventy-two dollars and some change, and believe it or not, I still had a few cents in my pocket. I had worked late and had to work on Saturday. I was very tired, so I bought myself a Pepsi Cola with the change I had; and as soon as I finished the drink, I went to bed. When I finished work on Saturday, I found a place that would cash my check. I put half of the money in an envelope and sent it to Mom and Coleman. I paid my rent and then went to a café and ate my first full meal that I had in almost two weeks.

My checks got larger and larger because after thirty days, I got a small increase, and I volunteered for overtime in any department that needed me. I could do mechanic work, sweep floors, assemble goods, store goods in the stockroom, and paint; so there was extra work for me most every day. I had been there for about a month and still had not joined the union. All jobs that become available were posted on the board, but you had to be a union member to bid on the job. In addition to building axles, our company had a government contract to provide the entire running gear for ammunition carts that the air force used at every airfield they occupied. Their paint specifications were exacting and would reject the entire assembly for the slightest flaw in the paint.

One day, the painter left, and the job came up for bid. The company tried two or three union workers, and they could not do the job. It was beginning to hurt production as the fenders, springs, and axle parts were accumulating all over the plant; and production would have to be cut until they found a qualified painter. I went to Mr. Syson and told him I could definitely handle the job and would work day and night and clean the mess up within two weeks. He knew I was not in the union, but after he discussed it with the union steward, he gave me an opportunity but told me he didn't think I could possibly have enough experience to hold the tolerances and quality that was required by the air force. He then took me to the paint department, and I showed him what I could do. He was very satisfied and told me that if I could do in production the quality I had just shown him, my pay rate would go from the then rate of $1.85 per hour to $2.35 per hour.

The following morning, another employee took my job in the welding department, and I went to the paint department. I worked my butt off and rarely stopped for a break. At lunchtime, I would take about fifteen minutes, and back to work I'd go. They let me work up to about twelve hours a day, and I loved it. About the third day, Mr. Syson came to me, put his hand on my shoulder, and told me he was so pleased that he would make my new pay rate retroactive to the day I went into the paint department. The air force inspector came in two or three times during this catch-up process and measured the paint with a micrometer and fully inspected the parts. I only saw him once a month the balance of the time I worked there. It took a little over two weeks to clean the mess up, and we maintained normal production throughout the plant during the process.

When the old painter was there, he sometimes worked overtime, getting the regular production done. I could understand why as I got accustomed to the overall timetable, equipment, and routine. I changed several procedures, modified the paint booth, and cleaned the place up so that 100 percent of the space was usable every day. Soon thereafter, I only spent about six hours a day in the paint shop. I would go to the mill room, furnace room, or machine shop and offer to work in my spare time. You have to remember that these people are staunch union employees, and I wasn't a union member, so my getting my job done quicker by using better methods and organization didn't set real well with them.

The foreman in the machine shop liked me and showed me how to run the machine that threaded the U-bolts that were used to mount the axles. I began running the threading machine in my spare time. The plant manager, Mr. Markle, was aware of my work habits and was looking for someone to help one of the machinists on a big project that he was having done.

Mr. Markle loved to race quarter midget cars and was having the machinist mill all the parts and build the race car from scratch. He needed help, and by now, they knew that I had some experience and, of course, that I could paint. Mr. Markle asked if I would be willing to help on the project, which was all to be done after the machine shop closed for the day. I jumped at the opportunity, and for the next few weeks, the machinist and I worked almost every night and on Saturdays to complete the car just before the big local race was scheduled.

We formed all the parts to the body, and while the machinist worked milling spindles and suspension parts, I prepared the body. With body shop tools, I removed any slight imperfection in the body and sanded it until it was ready for paint. We assembled the car and put the body on it, and I spent two or three nights painting it. It was a beautiful brilliant blue that I had modified and put a combination of different-colored metallic dust in. Some was silver, and some was gold colored. When light reflected off the car it gave off a deep iridescent glow. *It was gorgeous.*

There was a quarter-mile racetrack at the old airport location where the big race was to be held. We loaded the car on a trailer we also had built; and Mr. Markle, the machinist, and I took it to the track. While we were building it, I had told Mr. Markle that I wanted to drive it someday, not in a competitive race, but just on the racetrack. We unloaded it and rolled it on the track.

Mr. Markle told me to take it around a few times. I buckled up and put the helmet on, started her up, and away I went. It would do almost 50 at top speed, but there was a maximum of 35 mph rule in quarter midget racing. We had installed a governor, but had not adjusted it yet. I tried to hold the maximum at 35, and that was plenty fast when your butt was only three inches off the track. The car handled very well, and I had a ball cornering and racing around the track. Both the other fellows tried it out, and we took it back to the plant and made some final adjustments, including setting the governor to conform with the rules of the race. We played around with the car on the cinder parking lot and deemed it ready.

On Friday night, we were all really anticipating that the trophy would be presented to Mr. Markle. We knew the car would be the best or equal to the best that was entered in the race. Mr. Markle had won a front-row starting position by winning a couple of heats, which confirmed that we should win. The race started, and Mr. Markle continued to lose ground. By the time the race finished, there were a couple of cars that didn't make it, but Mr. Markle came in dead last. He was a good and experienced driver, so we asked him what had happened. We thought something had not performed correctly on the car. He laughed and told us that the car was so pretty, he was afraid to scratch it, and it performed great.

There were times I became so lonely and missed everybody back home. I sent word to my good friend Charles Gibson, telling him jobs were plentiful, and I would help him find one if he would like to come to Elkhart. I figured we could get an apartment and share expenses, and then I would have someone to pal around with. Charles came and stayed with me in my room. He got to my room on Saturday, and by Monday, he could not stand being away from home and decided not to look for a job. He did not have enough money for a bus ticket home and told me he was going to pawn his ring for twenty dollars. I couldn't talk him into staying and gave him the twenty for his ring. The ring was worth a lot more than twenty dollars. Charles left on the bus, and I was right back where I started.

Time went by in a hurry. I was busy all the time and was making good money. Over the next several weeks, I had over $150 take-home pay because of the overtime. I continued sending money home and had begun to save some for myself. I bought some new clothes and a pair of shoes, and I wanted to go visit Mom and Coleman.

My mother's brother Leon had come to Elkhart, and I learned that he was driving to Alabama the next weekend. I contacted him and offered to pay half the expenses if I could go with him. On Friday, I took my things to work with me that I was taking to Alabama, and Leon picked me up at about four o'clock. I had been gone from home just under two months, and all I had done was work and miss my family and friends. I had devised a plan that I would present when I saw Mom and Coleman. I had promised them that I would take care of them, and my plan would make it a lot easier for all of us.

Leon and I drove all night and arrived home late Saturday morning. He had driven much faster than we had driven on the way to Elkhart, so we made it in two or three hours less time. He dropped me at Mom and Coleman's, then went about his business. We did everything in a hurry because we would have to leave, heading back to Elkhart around noon on Sunday in order to make it back to work on Monday morning.

We were all glad to see one another. Mom and Coleman were both doing OK and shared their appreciation for the money I had been sending them. I told them about my job and how well the management treated me, and I felt assured that my job would remain very good. I told them that I was going to rent a place in Elkhart and that when I had everything ready, I wanted to come home and take them there with me to live. They were apprehensive about it and wanted to think it over. I visited several people until near noon on Sunday when Leon and I headed back to Elkhart.

I had not slept more than two hours since Thursday night and could barely keep my eyes open. Leon seemed a lot fresher than I, so I suggested that if I was going to do part of the driving, it would have to be in the daylight. I had stopped at the drugstore and picked up some NoDoze, which was supposed to help you stay awake, and had taken two pills about two hours before we left. I was confident that it would work, at least during the daylight hours.

I got under the wheel, and we had not gone twenty miles when we approached a real long hill that was straight as a string. About a half mile in front of us was some type of farm implement, which I clearly saw, and I was gaining on it. I was going about 50 mph, and the vehicle was never out of my vision. I was fully aware that it was there but could not respond. I did not slow down nor attempt to pass it. Leon was very alert. He grabbed the steering wheel and jerked it really hard, and the car came up on two wheels. It was probably at least a hundred yards before the other two wheels came back in contact with the pavement.

It was as if I were in a trance. I saw everything but could not respond. When Leon grabbed the wheel, I slid as close to the driver's side door as I could, for I immediately realized the circumstances and gave him full control. He steered us to the side of the road. I got out the driver's side and walked around to the passenger side, and while doing that, I reached in my pocket and tossed the NoDoze alongside the road. They had kept the eyes open, but put the brain to sleep. Leon drove the rest of the way without incident.

Work was good, and I was earning a pretty good paycheck every week, but work was about all I had done. I had to develop a long-term plan for my future; and I now felt that I had enough information, experience, and knowledge to make such a plan. I set down the parameters under which the plan would be developed and listed all the important things I wished to accomplish in my life. The first thing I had to put to writing regarding a lifelong plan was a creed—one that would guide me through the ups and downs that I was sure to face; one that would say exactly who I am, who I wanted to be, and what I wanted to do; and one that would provide the rules under which I would conduct my life.

After many nights of working on my creed, I was able to commit to writing one that I felt was good and would become my guidepost. I had once read something similar and wrote in pencil the following. It would be another six years before I typed it and framed it for my wall.

Bobby R. Dutton Creed

I do not choose to be a common man.
It is my right to be uncommon, if I can.
I refuse to barter my incentive for a dole.

I refuse to be a kept citizen, humbled, and embarrassed
By having the welfare state look after me.

I do not seek the stale calm of utopia, but search for challenge.
For it is my right to try, to fail, to succeed
That I might taste the fulfillment of success
And the bitterness of failure.

I seek to establish myself with my fellow man
That he will look upon me as a brother.

I refuse to worship idols.
I accept my ever-loving God and will hold his covenants nearest and
     dearest
To my heart, that I may pass through this life with his blessings.

I will always face the light so the shadows of failure will fall behind me.

I will trust God to give me the wisdom and strength to travel
A righteous path that where I go will be better than when I came.

I will retain my dignity.
I will keep my morals high.
That in the end, I will proudly proclaim

THESE THINGS I HAVE DONE.

When I finished my creed, I set forth an objective and a plan to reach
that objective. I was going to further my education, someday get married,
and vowed that when I did nothing short of death would end it on my part.
I planned to have four children, to own my own home, and one day own
my own business. The question is, how can all this be done? I had no one
to guide me nor tutor me and no one to turn to in the event of trouble or
failure. I planned to retire at age forty-seven.

I knew by this time that there was a horrible disease that ran like wildfire through my family; and I further concluded that regardless of the stories that Grandma told about Grandpa, his death was due to a disease, and all of the people I knew who had it were from the same lineage. Because of my constant exposure, from the time I was about seven years old, to those who had the disease, I realized that the onset normally began as the person reached their very early thirties; and based solely upon my experience, I determined that the diseased would either be dead or could not care for themselves past the age of fifty. I assumed I would follow that same path. I would not find out that this was in fact a hereditary disease until I had put my total plan in operation.

Had I known then, I would have excluded or changed a couple of my objectives. My plan included my commitment to save or invest one half of the money I kept from my earnings. Any such investments would be a house, a business, insurance that provided a cash return, etc. Automobiles and personal possessions that depreciated in value with age and use would be considered as disposable goods and must be purchased using the retained 50 percent of earnings.

Work was going well, and I spent my evenings in my room or on the front porch with my landlady. We enjoyed each other's company. It was late August, and Mom and Coleman had agreed to let me move them to live with me in Elkhart. One evening, while sitting on the porch, I told my landlady that I would be finding an apartment soon because my parents were coming to live with me and that I was planning to go get them on Labor Day weekend. She told me she would be sad to see me go, but was happy for me.

She had never seen me drive because I had walked almost everywhere I had gone, so she assumed that I couldn't drive. When I told her I would drive my parents back to Elkhart, she was surprised and then asked me if I would do her a big favor. I replied that I would be happy to and asked of her what she needed. She asked if I would drive her car and take her and her lady friend to Warsaw, Indiana, to the big fair that was to be there the next week. She said she would pay all the expenses of food tickets and any rides I wanted to take. She said that she could not drive at night and that unless someone took them, they would not be able to go. The following week, I took them, and all three of us had a great time. She had become kind of a substitute grandma to me, and I was very comfortable around her.

I began looking for a place to live that I could afford. I found a two-bedroom apartment with everything we would need on Sycamore Street on the north edge of town. It was much farther away from my job, but I planned to own a car real soon.

Chapter Eight

On Friday after work, the beginning of Labor Day weekend, I hitched a ride to Alabama to get Mom and Coleman. When I got there, I was pleasantly surprised that Mom was doing pretty good. When I left three months before, she wasn't doing well. Her speech was faltering, and it was difficult for her to eat. Now I could understand her most of the time, and she was eating better and able to do a fair amount of cooking and housework.

Coleman was doing great and had almost everything we would be taking packed into the old '47 Chevy. We closed down the rented house and stored their meager belongings, and on Sunday, we were wrapping up getting ready to head to our new home in Elkhart. The trunk on the car wasn't very big, and it was filled to the brim. The backseat was loaded, leaving enough room for Mom to sit comfortably. Coleman had taken the spare tire out to load, and there was no room to carry it. We didn't dare start on this long trip with old tires and not have a spare, so we rearranged the trunk and put the tire in with about six inches of the tire extended rearward beyond the bumper. We secured the spare and tied the trunk down to the frame of the car. This left the bottom of the trunk lid resting on top of the spare tire. We put plastic around the goods in the trunk to keep water away in the event it should rain. Then we hit the road.

I was rested very well and would do all the driving. Coleman still would not drive, except sometimes on back roads where there was little or no traffic. We had packed away some sandwiches and something to drink, so the only stops would be for the potty or for gasoline. Things went really well until we were about fifty miles south of Louisville, Kentucky. It had started raining just enough to make driving difficult when it was dark. The pavement absorbed the light from the headlights; and in those days, all of the roadways were not marked with white-and-yellow stripes as they are today, so sometimes the edge of the road was hard to see.

There was very little traffic, but we came upon where an accident had happened earlier. A policeman had the northbound traffic stopped while the wrecker pulled this old Nash Rambler back onto the roadway. There were two cars stopped in front of me, and when the wrecker cleared, the officer motioned the traffic on. The two cars in front moved out; and as I let out on the clutch to begin moving, I realized we were still in high gear, so the car barely starts moving. To change the gear to low required that you come to a complete stop because the transmission was operated by vacuum. I touched the brakes, and we came to a complete stop a few feet short of the officer.

From out of nowhere, a pair of headlights was on our tail. I screamed to hold on, and this car doing about fifty miles an hour hit us, knocking us forward a considerable distance. Luckily, the officer had jumped clear; and after a minute or so, we realized that none of us were hurt. The driver of the car came running to check on us. When we got out to inspect the car, we found why none of us were not hurt. When the car impacted our rear, his bumper was higher than ours and hit the spare tire at an angle. This broke all the ropes and threw the trunk lid on the roof of the car and broke the bumper off, which went under the car. The angle of the spare tire had absorbed a lot of the energy of the impact and was actually between the two vehicles. It blew the spare.

The policeman talked to the other man and Coleman, never asking for license or registration. The officer said that he had been working the other accident for about three hours out in the cold rain and was exhausted and cold. He asked the other driver where he was going in such a hurry, and the man said he was from Elizabethtown and had just received a call from the hospital in Louisville that a member of his family was on their deathbed and that he should come quickly. The officer believed him and told the driver and Coleman that if they could resolve the matter, he would not write up a report, and we could both continue on since it appeared that both cars were drivable. The man opened his wallet and had only one bill, which was a fifty. He offered, and Coleman accepted. We both left. It appeared that his car may have had a punctured radiator. We could not verify this because everything was wet, but we agreed to follow behind him for a while to make sure his car did perform.

We continued on the rest of the trip without further problems, arriving at our apartment in late midday. We unloaded everything and got settled in. I had stocked the apartment with food and supplies the week before. We prepared an early supper and then prepared for bed. I had showed Mom and Coleman where I worked as we passed it on the way into town. Before we went to bed, Coleman suggested I drive the car to work because it was really too far to walk.

I continued working, and about two weeks after we arrived, I went to an automobile junkyard on Main Street and found an identical car to ours. It had been wrecked in the front. I bought the needed parts to repair Coleman's car, and we spent our time in the evenings and on Saturday removing all the damaged parts and replacing them. When it was all completed, it looked funny. Coleman's car was a two-tone blue, which I had painted when I worked at the Lincoln Mercury dealership, and the replacement parts were jet-black. I had no access to a large-enough place to paint the car, so I cleaned the car and polished it, and it remained multicolored.

Mom was doing the best she had been in several years even though her speech continued to falter. She was well enough to be left alone during the day. I learned that the mobile home factory one block from where I worked was hiring, and Coleman wanted to go to work now that Mom could be left alone, so I took him there to apply for work. They hired him, so he went to work immediately. I would drop him off in the morning, then drive the block to my work. He got off before I did, and after a day or two, he found a ride home with a coworker so I could continue working as much overtime as I could.

Life was better now. I still missed my friends in Alabama, but I was making new friends in Elkhart. My uncle Leon fixed me up with a sister of one of his girlfriends, and we would double-date. We did this a few times, but I never clicked with any of the girls that I went out with. I had access to Coleman's car at all times since he wouldn't drive, and I had made a friend over the past few months and got him a job where I worked. His name was Bill Birr. Occasionally, I would pick Bill up, and we would cruise the drag downtown. We would meet some boys and girls at a small hangout downtown called the Royal Lunch. We made a number of acquaintances and took the girls to the movies frequently, but we never considered those times to be dates because we went as a group. Sometimes there were more boys than girls, and other times, there were more girls than boys.

In November, I met a boy who had come from my area in Alabama. His name was Wayne Barrentine. Wayne was a senior in high school and drove a new '55 Ford. Wayne, Bill, and I began palling around together, cruising the drag while looking for girls; or sometimes we would take in a movie. Several times, before the weather got too bad, we would go to a miniature golf course and finish the night off with a root beer from one of the several root beer barrels that were in town.

Bill had two brothers. Dick, the older one, had just returned home from military service; and the other one's name was Ron. They lived with their parents and a sister on Division Street. Dick had a car, and frequently, the three brothers and I would mess around town on Friday or Saturday night. I really enjoyed being with the different newfound friends. No one in the group ever drank any type of alcohol when we were out, and none of them were rowdy. It was a pleasant experience.

It was about Halloween, and the weather turned sour. It began to snow; then it would rain, then freeze. I hated it when it started, but little did I realize how much I would hate it until I experienced my first full winter in Elkhart.

Mom and Coleman were getting along fine, but neither of them liked it in Elkhart. They didn't know anyone and didn't go anywhere with an opportunity to make new friends. A weekly trip to the grocery store was about the extent of their travels. I would take them to the A&P store when they needed to go, wait for them, and bring them home. Coleman continued working every day until near Christmas when the seasonal slowdown in the mobile home industry came. My work was going along well because the paint operation was geared more to the requirements of the air force products than it was to the mobile home axles.

Wayne, Bill, and I continued palling around together. Elkhart Central High School, where Wayne attended, had a very good basketball team; and the annual holiday tournament was upon us. The city had just completed the construction of the North Side Gym, which was the most modern and largest gym in the area. The tournament was to be held there, and Elkhart Central was the favored team to win. I had not been going to basketball games because it was a big reminder of what I had missed the past two years by going to summer and night schools instead of the regular session. I knew if I had gone to the regular session, I could have made the team, and I missed not having been able to do it. I loved playing basketball and would have given anything to have been on the floor playing on this beautiful huge floor. The three of us intended to watch the final game, but by the time we were ready to get tickets, they were sold out. We just rode around in the car and listened to the game on the radio.

The game finished around ten thirty, and we were cruising around town. A car pulled alongside us in the other lane that had three girls in the front seat. I was sitting in the middle and asked Wayne to roll the window down. When he did, I got one of the girls' attention and began talking to them as we drove side by side down Main Street. I told them we'd like to buy them a root beer, and they agreed to meet us at the Dew Drive-In just beyond the railroad tracks on Main Street.

The girl sitting in the middle really made an impression on me. She had medium dark hair and a fair complexion, wore glasses, and was really pretty.

On the way to the drive-in, I told the other guys that if they would accept an offer to date us that we would date the one that was sitting in the same position in their car as we were positioned in our car. When we arrived at the drive-in, the girls invited us to sit in the backseat of their car, and we readily accepted the invitation. We ordered root beers and began conversing. As fate would have it, all three of the girls were seniors at Central where Wayne attended school. Even though they didn't know one another, they had seen one another at the school. I thought it strange that you could be in the same grade and not know all the people in the grade with you. As I told them this, they all laughed. There were close to four hundred students that would graduate that year, unlike the thirty-five or forty students that graduated each year at my old school.

The girls' names were Joyce Marcus', who was driving; Judy Kidder, who sat in the middle; and Fran Wright, who sat in the passenger seat. Wayne was our driver, I sat in the middle, and Bill was in the passenger seat in our car. The girls agreed to a date, and we confirmed who would date whom. The girls set a condition that we all go, or nobody goes on the date. We set the time for New Year's Eve and planned to attend the late-night movie at the Elco Theater in downtown Elkhart. We wrote down their addresses and phone numbers and were off to home. I could hardly wait for that night to come. I believed that Judy would turn out to be someone really special. I had already become to like her after the few minutes we all shared together at the drive-in.

New Year's Eve came, and Wayne's new car was not available; so we took Coleman's old Chevy, which did not have nearly as much room inside as Wayne's Ford did. I picked up the boys, then picked up Judy and introduced myself to her parents, and off we went to pick up Joyce and Fran. After we picked up Fran, that made five of us in the car, and it was pretty comfortable; but how were we going to seat six without seating three in the front and three in the back? Surely, everyone wanted to sit next to their date. We'd resolve this dilemma when we reached Joyce's house.

When we got to Joyce's house, she came to the door, and standing beside her was a beautiful little girl about seven years old. My mind raced back to the night I met Vida at the roller rink. She had her little sister with her, and I assumed this girl was Joyce's sister. When Wayne walked to the porch, Joyce told him that she was very sorry, but she was the regular babysitter for the neighbors' daughter and that she got hooked into babysitting while the little girl's parents attended a New Year's party. When I learned what was going on, I got out and approached Joyce and told her the answer to this problem was that we would take the little girl to the movie with us. I asked the little girl if she would like to go on a date with us, and she was thrilled. Joyce called her parents and got their approval.

Now the problem of seating was handled. The little girl would sit in the front seat with Judy and me, and the other four would scoot closely together in the backseat. After some bantering back and forth in the backseat, the four of them found room enough to sit.

We drove downtown to the theater and purchased our tickets in advance. After we purchased the tickets, we realized that this car was just not big enough; so Wayne said that his father was probably finished using his car, so we drove to Wayne's house to check it out. His car was available, so we left Coleman's car there and finished the evening in Wayne's car. I thought that was good. I didn't have to drive anymore. Wayne would take over; and Joyce and the little girl would sit in the front seat, forcing Bill, Fran, Judy, and me to sit really close together in the backseat.

We drove to the A&W Root Beer barrel south of town, and everybody ordered a hamburger basket and a root beer. The little girl thought that was really neat and laughed about being on her first date. Of course, I picked on her because I liked her; and I was glad we had taken her because it would be an experience that she would always remember, similar to my experience when my schoolteacher Mrs. Garrison had taken me to the fair many years ago. We all got along very well, eating our burgers and fries and drinking our root beers. It was so crowded with the four of us in the backseat that Judy and I would feed each other french fries because we had to manage to hold our sandwich and root beer because it was too cold to have the window rolled down, so we had no serving tray to set the food on as we ate. We finished there and went to the movie.

During the movie, we held hands; and finally, I got up enough nerve to put my arm around Judy, and it was all right with her.

When the movie was over, we stopped at another drive-in and got something to drink. All of us were watching the time very closely, and when midnight came and the new year began, I put my arms around Judy and kissed her for the first time. It was very exhilarating, and my heart was racing a thousand times a minute. The others noticed that we had kissed passionately and said nothing. I will always remember the look on Judy's face as we drew back from the kiss. Her head now rested on my shoulder, and she was looking directly into my eyes; then she asked, "Will you marry me?" I was jolted, and everybody laughed. Judy said it was leap year now, and it was the girl's responsibility to ask for the man's hand in marriage. I fell in love with her at that exact moment, and I knew it would last forever.

I silently told Wayne that he should take everybody else home and that I would take Judy home in Coleman's car after we picked it up at his house. He proceeded to do that, and I took Judy home. We sat in her driveway just long enough for me to ask her out again. She accepted, and we began dating regularly.

Wayne, Bill, and I were all having our eighteenth birthdays within a couple of weeks of one another. One of the older men at work, Rollo Stabler, invited us to his house and said we could bring a date. I asked Judy to go, but Bill and Wayne didn't ask anyone to go with them. This was the first birthday party that I could ever remember having, and we all had a great time.

Sometime in February 1956, the factory Shultz Mobile Homes, where Coleman worked, burned; and Coleman was out of work. I had paid almost all the expenses since Labor Day, allowing Coleman to save everything that he had earned, and he had accumulated about fifteen hundred dollars. Under the circumstances of being out of work and having enough money to live on for quite a while, he and Mom made the decision to go back to Alabama.

In the spring, we loaded up the old Chevy, and I drove them back to Alabama and got them settled in an old farmhouse in the country. I knew they would be fine for a while because Mom was still doing OK healthwise, and with the amount of money they had saved, I would not have to send them very much for a while.

I moved them home over a three-day weekend, and when I returned to Elkhart, I spent a few nights in my apartment alone and didn't like it. It was too expensive for just one person. Bill was still working where I worked, and he asked me to move in with his family. He said that he had talked to his parents, and they had plenty of room. I knew they did and that the three boys slept in a huge room upstairs, which contained four ¾-sized beds and their own bathroom, and no one used the fourth bed. The parents and their sister slept downstairs, so it was pretty private for the boys. I moved my meager belongings to their house where Bill and I would walk to work most of the time, but if the weather was real bad, Dick would take us to work.

Without a car at my disposal, I didn't see a lot of Judy. Occasionally, Dick or his brother, Ron, would have a date and take Judy and me along with them. That was strange happening. The first time we went on a double date, Ron borrowed Dick's car and dated a girl by the name of Sandy Krieder. Judy and Sandy knew each other, and we had a good time together. Pretty soon, Dick, the brother, started dating Sandy. Judy and I doubled with them several times, and finally, Dick and Sandy were married.

If I was going to have any life of my own, I would have to buy a car. I had not been able to save very much while Mom and Coleman lived with me since I paid all the expenses. I began scrimping and saving every penny I could and gave up spending money on absolutely anything that I could do without. I still wanted to go back to school but so far was unable to. Transportation had to come first. Elkhart was booming, and work was plentiful. There were a few better-paying jobs available, but I needed the security that I had already established in my job at Leggett's, so I decided to stay there.

Late spring was with us, and I was sure glad to see it. People said that the past winter was one of the worst, and I could believe it. From around Halloween until now, I had not seen the ground. It had been frozen, and snow covered all winter without any letup. In late May, it warmed up very nicely; and at night, the upstairs room where we boys slept would get very warm. One night, we had all gone to sleep; and around one or two in the morning, Dick woke up. He woke the rest of us up and told us that it was too hot and that we were going to the lake to cool off. The four of us jumped in the car and went to Heaton Lake. There was a public swimming area there, and we stripped off our clothes and went skinny-dipping to cool off. This became a habit, and it happened several times over the next month.

I finally had enough money to buy a car and found one I could afford. It was a nice '51 Chevy Coupe that was green with a white top. I paid $720 for the car that had just been reconditioned at the dealership. When I bought it, they told me they had put on a new set of brakes; and after I drove a few miles, they would need to adjust them. As soon as I got the car, I drove to Judy's house to show it off. It was Friday evening, and we had planned to go out for the evening.

As we were ready to leave, her mother asked if we would go to the store for her. We agreed; and Judy, running to the car, was yelling that she was going to drive. She had just gotten her learner's permit and could only drive with a licensed passenger. With her driving, we headed toward the store. We were on solid brick streets and came to an intersection to make a turn. She entered the intersection too fast, and after beginning the turn, she braked quickly while the steering wheel was fully turned to the right. The front brakes locked, and we skidded into a parked brand-new Cadillac. It put a foot-long scar on the bumper of the Cadillac and demolished the front of my Chevy, including bursting the radiator.

I called the police from a neighboring house and located the gentleman who owned the Cadillac. Judy had honestly been going too fast to safely make the turn, but I told her that when the police arrived, she was to tell them she was doing about ten miles an hour. The police came, and two officers began questioning her. She began to cry as one of the officers was real nasty and kept threatening to give her a ticket while the other was playing the good-cop role. I tried to console her, telling her everything would be all right. Finally, when the bad cop asked her how fast she was going, she instantly told him that she was doing eight miles an hour. The cop asked her how she knew, and she told him that she was looking at the speedometer just before the turn.

Judy's uncle Roger was a police officer working the same shift. When the two officers returned to the station, they were telling other officers the story about Judy's wreck and were laughing a lot as they told it. When they told the name of the driver to be Judy Kidder, Roger told them she was his niece. From that day forward until Roger died, many years later, Roger always called her the eight-mile-an-hour kid.

I was beginning to experience some difficulty with my dentures, which were about two years old. My mouth was growing fast, and they did not fit anymore. Someone at work directed me to Dr. Stamp, and he could not reline the old ones because they were too small. He told me I would have to have a complete new set, both uppers and lowers, and that it would cost about one hundred dollars. I told him I guess I'd have to wait because money was tight and my car was being repaired, without insurance. He asked me what kind of work I did, and in the conversation, I told him about working in Ypsilanti roofing houses. He said that he was having a big building constructed just outside of town and had a deadline to meet and wanted to know if I would be interested in helping the night crew, and I could work in exchange for the new teeth.

I started immediately and worked under floodlights until the roof was completed and continued helping finish up the outside. When we were finished, my teeth were paid for. I paid for the repair of the Cadillac that Judy crashed into and also for the repairs on my car.

By the time I paid for the car repairs, I was almost out of money; so once again, I reverted to my "don't spend a penny unless you have to" savings program. Judy was about to graduate and had received a scholarship for college and was aspiring to become a teacher. I had been desperately trying to keep my plan of life going in the right direction and wanted to solidify our relationship, so I asked Judy to marry me. She immediately said yes, and for the following couple of weeks, there was great indecision as to when.

She had planned to go to college yet wanted to get married after graduation. I insisted that she go to college, and she would agree. The next time we were together, she would say she wanted to get married right away; and the next time, she would say she would go to college first. I told her it would be best if we waited, and she should go to school, and I would wait for her however long it took. Once we decided firmly that she would attend college before we were married, things started happening that would affect our choice.

Being of the old tradition, I believed that it was a man's responsibility to ask the girl's parents for her hand in marriage. I set a specific time when both her parents would be home to make this request. Her father was off drinking somewhere at the set time, so the mother postponed it. I set the second time for such a meeting; that one also got set aside because the father, who had agreed to the time, was not home. We all set another time that was suitable for them, and when that time came, her father was out of town at a political convention. I decided to use this scheduled time and simply asked her mother and felt I would have been honoring the tradition by doing so.

When I asked her mother, Betty, she blared out to Judy, "ARE YOU PREGNANT?"

I told her, "Of course not." I further told of plans for Judy to go to college. She settled down, and I left.

When Judy's father came home on Sunday night and Betty told him of my proposal, he blew the roof off.

On Monday, at noon, my friend Wayne drove Judy to my workplace; and she was sobbing. She told me that her father was furious, had called me a number of names, and said he would kill the "hillbilly." I tried to console her and told her I would take care of the situation and that she should not cry anymore and that she wasn't nearly as pretty when she was crying.

I told Wayne to take her back to school and told her I would see her as soon as my wrecked car was repaired, which was going to be that day or the next. She and Wayne left; and I walked into the factory, looked up Mr. Syson, and explained that I had a personal problem that required me to be gone for a couple of hours, but that I would finish my job before the day ended. He agreed, and I left the plant.

I knew that Judy's dad, Bob, spent almost every day in a bar around lunchtime. I had no transportation because my car was in the body shop to have the damage from the wreck repaired. I walked toward town, stopping at four different bars that he hung out in. I did not find him, so I went back to work. Within a day or so, I picked up my car and drove to her house. The father was not home. I told Judy I had gone looking for him the day she came to the plant, but I didn't find him.

We were both very upset because her father thought I was a dumb hillbilly that could not and would not provide for her. Simply stated, I wasn't good enough for her. After living the life I had, going through as much adversity and carrying as much responsibility that I had my entire life, this attitude was totally unacceptable to me; and from that time on, I knew that the only conceivable thing that could keep us apart was God. I knew I could handle the circumstances myself, but I was concerned as to whether Judy could.

At that time, we both concluded that college was out, and we would get married very soon. I told Judy that the only way I knew how to resolve this issue was if she moved out. I told her to think about it, and we would talk again the next day. She was very adamant about our decision and told me we did not need to discuss it further. I told her I would find a place for her to live, and as soon as I had done so, I would come to move her away from her parents. In the meantime, she should see if one of her girlfriends would temporarily stay with her because I did not want her to be alone in an apartment, and it was unacceptable for me to move in with her before we were married.

I was still living with the Birrs on Division Street. When I got home, I found several apartments listed in the newspaper, and one of them was only a few blocks from the Birr house. It was located at 413 State Street, which was the first street south of the Birrs'. I called the number listed and talked to the owner, Mr. Hummel. I told him of my circumstances and the urgency of the matter. He drove over, and I met him at the apartment. I paid him the rent, and he gave me the keys.

The apartment was fully furnished and included some cooking utensils. We had already been buying a few things like dishes, towels, and such without Judy's parents' knowledge. Judy had been leaving those items at her girlfriend Sandy's house. I called Judy, and we set the date and time when I would pick her up, along with whatever belongings she was going to take.

She had another friend, Mary Hartman, that had agreed to stay with her until we were married. Mary and her boyfriend, Eugene, were planning to be married soon; and we four had double-dated several times in the past and knew one another well. The date and time were set for me to move her out, and while we were taking her suitcase to the car, her mother told us we were doing the wrong thing and that our marriage would not last a year. I told her I was extremely sorry that she felt that way and that Bob felt that I was no good. But from that day forward, I would never ask them for anything because I would provide anything we required and, furthermore, that I would never come back to their house nor make any effort to contact them until and unless they initiated an effort to correct their mistake; and she could rest assured that everything I was saying was the way that it would be.

Very soon, it was rumored that Judy's father was attempting to stop us from getting married in some legal fashion. We were both eighteen, and it was legal for an eighteen-year-old girl to marry, but the boy had to be twenty-one. I began to think about all the possible ways he could stop us and decided upon a course of action.

Judy and I went to the police station and walked up to the sergeant's desk. He was a very pleasant officer, and I told him my story and explained that we wanted to get married and would have to go back to my home state of Alabama because at my age, I required someone over twenty-one to sign for me and that I was concerned that Judy's father would try to place some kind of charges against me for taking her across the state line. The sergeant kind of chuckled, then asked us what route we would be taking as we headed south. I told him it would be through Louisville on Highway 31. He laughed and then asked Judy if she could drive (he was probably one of the officers that knew about her being called the eight-mile-an-hour kid). She responded that she could. He said, "Kids, your problem can be resolved very simply." He looked at Judy and told her, "When you get to the bridge at Louisville, which is the state line, you drive across. That'll handle the issue of crossing state lines." We were very pleased and somewhat relieved and left the station.

I had a week off work because another company had contacted me with a job offer. Good painters were hard to find, and most of the good ones were drunkards and weren't very reliable. They offered me considerably more money than I was making, so I decided to make the switch. I was to start my new job about July fifteenth. I was going to leave my old job at the end of the week before the Fourth of July weekend, which would give us time to make the trip, get married, and have a few days to acclimate ourselves with both of us living in our apartment.

Parents Bob and Betty;   Judy, aged eighteen;   Bob, aged eighteen

Chapter Nine

We arrived in Alabama and went to Ella Mae's house. We had decided that we did not have time to wait for blood tests to come back, so we could not be married in Alabama. My brother, Jim, had moved back to Alabama and offered to take us the forty to fifty miles to Mississippi where blood tests were not required; and he and JoNell would attest to our wedding. We were married in Mississippi in a quiet ceremony with the minister, his wife, Jim, JoNell, and Judy and me present. It only took a few minutes for the ceremony, and we arrived back at Ella Mae's house in the midafternoon.

The following day, we left for Indiana and were both as happy as anyone could be. We were filled with anticipation about starting a new life together and discussed how we would do it all the way home. It seemed like the shortest trip I had ever taken because now, I had the start of my own family, and I would take good care of it.

My new job was at Pacemaker Mobile Homes in the paint department. We had a new very modern building that had twelve painting bays and one undercoat bay. Most of the homes were forty-five to forty-seven feet long, which were the largest being made at that time. I frequently worked overtime and made enough money that Judy and I could buy about anything we needed. We continued to provide Mom and Coleman with enough money to maintain them, but at this point in time, they still had money that they had saved.

Things went really well for a while; then the union began harassing everyone. We were a nonunion company, but the AFL-CIO thought they should enter into the representation of factories in the mobile home industry. I have never seen more disruption in a manufacturing process than the havoc they created. Not one of the about two hundred employees wanted or supported the union efforts, so they brought their own people in from outside the area and disrupted manufacturing to a point that the owner decided to build a plant in Florida. The company needed one there to reduce their freight costs, but the deciding factor was the disruption of the union.

During this episode, I grew to hate unions with a passion because all their efforts and disruptions cost all of the employees a lot of lost income. Most employees were on hourly wages, which they continued earning, but a substantial amount of their pay was incentive and based on the count of the taillights that went down the road to the dealer. I would estimate that this union intrusion, which failed for them, cost every employee at least 20 percent of their wages. I hoped I would never see another union in my life, but unfortunately, that would not be true.

My life was progressing toward the plans I had set down in writing when I lived in the single room by myself when I first came to Elkhart. I had reached the point of growth to having a good job, marrying a wonderful girl whom I loved with all my heart, and having a few material possessions of my own. I wasn't lonely anymore but still wanted to see my family and friends back in Alabama. I still had a couple of things that were bothering me, and I needed to clear them up.

Judy and I drove to Alabama and saw the family. I looked up Walter and Ronald and a number of old friends and spent a few minutes with them. Walter had started an automotive service center and had a tire-recapping operation next door. He was doing great. Ronald had married the daughter of the family that owned a trucking company in town, and he was also doing great. I learned where Charles Gibson was working. He had begun work at Jasper Florist when he returned from Elkhart. I went to see Charles; and after greeting each other, I explained to him that as he was leaving Elkhart on the bus, I knew something did not feel right and soon realized that the ring I had given him twenty dollars for was worth much more and was a prized possession of his. "What I should have done was buy your bus ticket in appreciation of our friendship. That's what a true friend would do." I handed Charles his ring and apologized for my weakness of the moment when we made the transaction back in Elkhart. Charles offered to pay for the ring, but I refused.

Judy and I were back in the car and headed to Mr. Burt's house. Burt Richardson and his wife, Ruby, had been almost like second parents to me while I attended school at Farmstead. I wanted to introduce Judy to them and show her what great and caring people they are. We spent a long time with Mr. Burt and Ruby, and they loved Judy. We had made several stops to see friends and family, and I told Judy I had one more stop to make, and this one would be very difficult.

I drove to Lindsey's grocery store at an intersection between the Farmstead school and where I had lived at Walco Lumber. It was called Five Points and was the intersection where a few of my buddies and I would meet and occasionally wait for our ride to the golf course to caddy after school. Mr. Virgil Brown had been running the store for many years, and I knew him well. When we lived at Walco and had no money to purchase anything, Mr. Brown gave us credit. We bought bananas for Mom and things such as flour, sugar, salt, and only the things that were very difficult to do without. When we moved to town, there was some money owing on the account. I had to take care of it because it had weighed on my mind for over four years

I entered the store, and Mr. Brown was behind the checkout counter, and there were only a couple of customers in the store. As I walked in, Mr. Brown loudly called my name and asked, "How in the world are you?"

We shook hands and talked for a minute or so; then I got down to business. I told him where I had gone and how long I'd been in Elkhart and that I knew that when we moved away from the area, there was money owing to him; but until now, I could not afford to pay it. I asked him to look up the amount. He told me he was not going to do it because it would be very little; and besides, it was not my responsibility as it was in my parents' names, and he had written it off. I told him I would not leave until he found it and I paid it.

He reached under the counter and hoisted out a huge metal folding case that opened up like a book with thick pages. On each page were several sections with a small paper clip where tickets were kept. After turning several pages, he found the tickets with Coleman's name on them. They totaled a little over twenty-one dollars. I asked Mr. Brown what the interest was, and he laughed. I handed him thirty dollars, which he was still reluctant to take, and he opened the cash register to give me change. I told him no change was necessary and began to tell him why.

"Mr. Brown, do you remember years ago when Charlie, myself, and some of the other boys would hang around here, waiting for our ride to the golf course?"

He began to smile and said that he did. I was having a hard time, but I had to get this over with.

"We would come in the store and get a soft drink and a candy bar, which together cost eleven cents. You were always busy, and we always waited on ourselves. We had a little trick. We'd immediately eat the candy bar and sneak another one of the same brand and be eating it as we checked out. You always charged us eleven cents because you assumed that the drink and candy bar we had in our hands when we checked out was all we had gotten."

Mr. Brown had smiled all the time I was speaking, and then he sort of laughed. He told me he watched us kids like a hawk and knew what we were doing, but we only did it a few times over the years, and no one ever put anything in their pocket and walked out. He said that we were all good kids; and he was very willing to contribute that candy bar on occasion as long as no one stole something, put it in their pocket, and left the store. He laid the change on the counter and insisted I take it. I picked up the five-dollar bill, apologized for what I had done, and shook his hand; and as I was leaving, he said, "Now you're a real good man." I hadn't felt this good in a long time.

Things were going very well for Judy and me. We were saving a little money and had no debt. Judy had begun work in the office at the Lux Company, which was associated with medical research, and she liked working there. Pacemaker had purchased all of the old airport property in Ocala, Florida, and had been renovating the hangar buildings for mobile home production. There was only one other small mobile home factory in the entire state, and they built much smaller units.

This looked like Pacemaker would advance within the industry by leaps and bounds. The general production manager, Mr. Tom Bathers, was moving to the Florida facility to manage the complex; and he was looking for people to run certain departments. One of my fellow painters was Shorty, who had been with the company for some time and was a real good production man in the paint facilities, and I had painted many thousands of gallons of many types of paint and had the reputation of having a lot of knowledge about the various processes. Mr. Bathers asked Shorty and me if we would be interested in going to the Florida plant. He said we needed to construct a permanent paint facility, hire, and train the people; and during the construction process, we would have to acquire temporary facilities to handle the three-homes-per-day production beginning in January.

Shorty and I discussed it and knew that it would be a difficult task to paint in facilities in Florida in any area that was not environmentally controlled with respect to temperature and humidity because of Florida's climate. I discussed the potential move with Judy, and we viewed it as a good opportunity. We began to set our timetable and schedule. We would move from our apartment between Christmas and New Year's; and Judy would move in with Geraldine and G. A. Scott, a couple that was distant relatives, because I would not go and leave her alone. I felt it would take me about a month to find a house, get everything ready, and get the job going. She would remain working for this month and would live with Geraldine and G. A.

I put the word out that I would be leaving, driving to Florida over the New Year holiday, and would like to have a passenger to keep me company. Brother Jim had moved back to Elkhart; and JoNell's father, Mr. Banks, had been visiting them. He needed a ride back to Alabama, and then a man I had worked with at Leggett called me. Mr. Baker asked if his eighteen-year-old son Chet could ride with me to Lake City, which is about sixty miles north of Ocala. This was working out real well, so we made the plans to leave and would drive at night.

We left Elkhart late in the evening and arrived in Alabama on New Year's Day. For the first 250 miles, roads were intermittently iced over; and in some places, there were stretches of black ice. I reduced my speed accordingly, and we arrived in Jasper just before dark on New Year's Day. I took Mr. Banks to his house; then Chet and I went to Mom and Coleman's house. We got a good night's sleep, visited most of the day, and left for Florida late in the afternoon. Mom and Coleman were doing pretty well, which pleased me.

I dropped Chet off in Lake City and proceeded to Ocala. I went directly to the plant and located Mr. Bathers. Shorty was not there yet and wouldn't be for a few days. When Mr. Bathers saw me, he ran and gave me a big bear hug. "Boy! I'm glad to see you," he said.

The first two homes had been completed, and the dealer who had purchased them had agreed to paint them in his own facilities, but the units had to be undercoated, and no one knew how or wouldn't do it. The two trucks were there to pick them up. The dealer was only a few miles away, and they had promised delivery that day. Mobile homes could not be transported after dark, so I had to hurry.

I went to the locker room and borrowed a pair of coveralls and located all the equipment and supplies for the portable undercoating rig. It was about eighty degrees, but I put the coveralls over my clothes and taped the sleeves and legs real tight to keep the undercoat off my clothing. I put on the fresh air hood, laid on a creeper, and began working. The first unit went well, and by the time I finished it, the truck had hooked up and was ready to leave. I immediately started on the second unit and hurried as fast as I could because I was roasting, and my inner clothes were already drenched in sweat. When I made my last few passes, I had to kick the creeper aside because the asphalt ended, and the creeper wouldn't move on the dirt.

By this time, I'm covered with undercoat and inching myself along on the dirt while lying on my back. I made my last pass and began scooting to the outer edge of the home, and I began to burn and sting as if I had gotten into a nest of hornets. I came out from under the home in a hurry and began peeling off my clothing.

A couple of men helping to hook up the home to the truck saw me and came to assist. They realized what was happening, but I had no clue. When I scooted along the ground, I had disturbed a fire anthill, and they began attacking and stinging. Several had gotten under the tape that was on my coverall legs, and many others were stuck on the outside of my clothing to the fresh undercoat that was all over me. These men helped me remove the tape and my clothing; and in a minute or so, there I stood in nothing except my shorts, with a lot of stinging red spots on my lower body. We made sure that all the ants were off me. I inspected my pants and then put them on. As I was heading to the first aid room, the last mobile home was pulling out.

While my stings were being attended to, Mr. Bathers came into the first aid room to check on me. I told him I was all right. He asked me where I was staying, and I told him I was going to look for a house I could rent for my wife and me. He left; and about ten minutes later, as I was dressing, he came back with an ad from the newspaper. There was a house about a half mile away that had just been listed that day. It was at 1703 Orange Street, about halfway up a hill, and the house could almost be seen from where we were.

I drove directly to the house, which was adjacent to the owner's house. Walt and Ellen Sentels had built themselves a new house on the corner lot and had just moved from this house. The Sentels showed me the house, and I explained my circumstance about my job and that it would be a month before my wife joined me. This little three-room house was clean, fully furnished, and all the utilities were on. They were happy to rent it, and I was elated to have it.

Anyone can say or think whatever they would like to; but without a doubt, God's hand had been on me for a long time, and this was further proof to me. Just in the previous two years, I had gone from a job that paid very little to a good job where I was appreciated. The deterioration of Mom's health had slowed. None of us were hurt when the car hit us at fifty miles an hour. I found and married the love of my life, made the long trip without any mishap, and there's a perfect house just waiting for me. I could go on and on, but I'm sure you get the point.

Shorty arrived a few days later, and we reviewed the plans on the paint facilities and made a few changes that would expedite production, and we had a lead on a facility nearby that we could possibly rent to paint our three homes a day. We made a deal on the rented building. It required some work, but the air compressors and air line piping were already in the building. It was a lean-to attached to the service building of a mobile home dealer and park operator called Wyatts Trailer Sales. One side of the lean-to was open, so we constructed a temporary frame and stretched a tarp. We could get only one home inside at a time, and a lot of the preparation had to be done outside. We paint-finished the homes inside and out. The design was simple, but the exterior took much longer than we were used to because of the humidity.

After a few weeks, we began to learn how to handle this unusual time situation and changed several processes and procedures to get the desired results.

On February 4, my nineteenth birthday, I headed to Elkhart to get Judy. It was 1,103 miles, and driving alone felt like much more. There were much better roads to travel north from Florida than there were traveling from Alabama going north, and if you drove the speed limit and stopped only for gas, you could make it in twenty-four to twenty-five hours. (Today I can drive the same route and make it in about eighteen hours.) When I arrived in Elkhart, Judy had her bag packed. I slept a few hours, and we started back to Florida.

After Shorty and I had been there for several weeks, our new building was near completion, and everyone in the area knew that we were painting. People off the street began to stop to inquire if we could do some painting for them. Some wanted cars painted, and others wanted mobile homes or travel trailers done. We obviously could not do them because we were working many hours of overtime getting our own production out. The facility was just too small. To be efficient, a paint facility for the products we were finishing required at the least one paint bay for each unit that would be done that day, and we were doing three a day in one finishing room.

The last weekend before we moved into our new facility, Judy and I decided to go to Daytona Beach. We had been to Ross Allen's Reptile Institute and cruised the waters of Silver Springs, but we wanted to see the beach and swim in the ocean. It was a beautiful day to begin; as we were swimming, a big rain came. We went into the penny arcade and stayed for a long time until the rain stopped. For the rest of the day, we had some cloud cover. Judy was fair complected and was careful to stay under roof when she could. I had never had more than a slight sunburn because I was dark complected.

Just before we left for home, we meandered out on this long pier where a crowd was gathered. We learned that a swimmer had dived off the pier beyond the fenced-off swimming area, and a shark had grabbed him by his leg. His sister jumped in and managed to get the shark off him. We stayed out in the open much longer than I intended, and I began to feel a slight sunburn while on the way home.

The following day, we had finished our daily production and had started on our first unit for the following day. After Shorty and I had cleaned up and changed clothes, we decided the humidity would be too high the next morning to prime the unit in the shop. If that happened, we would lose all the time we had gained on this unit. We had to prime before we went home. I told Shorty that I would do it, and I didn't want to soil the clean shirt that I had just put on. I pulled my shirt off, cranked up the machines and spent about twenty minutes spraying acid primer bare backed, closed up, and went home.

Judy had supper ready, and as we sat to eat, my back and head began to sting. It got worse and worse. I went to the bedroom and lay on my back on top of the chenille bedspread, slightly moving to scratch my back. That made it worse. I removed my clothing and turned the cold water on in the shower. I almost passed out when the cold water touched me. I then turned the hot water on, which soothed it a little. I yelled to Judy to call the hospital, which was one block away. They told her to get me to the emergency room. I drove the one block to the hospital, and the doctor immediately had me take off my shirt. He rubbed something on my back, and the pain instantly went away and never returned.

Two days later, silver dollar-sized pieces of skin flaked off my body, and my entire scalp peeled. I had to brush the skin out of my flattop haircut with a brush. While at Daytona Beach, I had received a little sunburn, allowing the acid primer to permeate the pores in the skin.

We moved into the new paint facility. By now, we had hired some people and were training them in all phases of the job. We now had people who could do almost every job, except apply the final paint finish, both on the inside and out. One of these employees was a purebred Seminole Indian that drove a pickup truck. He had several small wire cages on the perimeter of the bed with a big heavy wire cage in the middle of the truck bed. He always came to work about thirty to forty minutes before time to clock in.

One morning, he was parked in the lot; and as I drove in, he was getting out of his truck. I noticed that he was barefoot and was starting to put his shoes on. I started talking to him and asked about the shoes. He told me that he would go out in the morning and hunt specific game, mostly wild boar and rattlesnakes, and he did this barefoot because he could sneak up on the game and run better barefoot. I asked how he had done that morning, and he pulled the covering off a few of the small cages, and there were three or four of the biggest rattlesnakes I'd ever seen. He caught them for the Ross Allen Reptile Institute located in Silver Springs. They milked the snakes and sold the venom. The institute paid him a dollar an inch for every snake he could get them.

He showed me how he caught them. He had a long stiff rod with a heavy cord, at the end of which is a loop, with the end of the rope going through eyes attached to the rod the full length of the handle. When he found a snake, he would agitate it until the snake coiled, ready to strike. He quickly put the snare over the snake's head and pulled the rope, closing the snare loop.

One Friday morning, he pulled into the lot and had a medium-sized wild boar in the big cage. It was dirty, muddy, mean, and ugly. I asked how he caught it, and he told me he ran it down and threw a net over it when he caught up to it. Judy and I lived about six or seven miles from the Ocala National Forest where the Indians lived. At about eight that evening, Judy and I were in the yard talking with Walt and Ellen. We smelled a terrible odor that the wind from the east was bringing in. Walt said it was someone roasting a wild boar. The following day, I asked the employee if he had roasted the boar, and he told me that they did it on an open pit. I asked him about the smell; and he just smiled, saying, "It don't smell very good when it roasting."

Things were progressing at work. We had gotten our labor forced trained and were getting our production done in eight hours, so I began to have all my evenings free. I remembered that a number of people had wanted us to paint different vehicles and mobile homes for them when we were in the temporary lean-to. I thought there was an opportunity to make additional money, so Judy and I discussed it and decided to try and rent the facility from Mr. Wyatt. When I approached him, he was elated because he had several customers who wanted paintwork done, and he had no one to do it and told me that the big compressor had been removed. He said if I would furnish my own compressor, he could get some work for me from some of his customers and some of the people who lived in the park.

The deal was simple. If I would paint small emergency jobs for him, he would furnish the paint, and my labor would be sufficient for the rent.

This was a great deal for me. I had no monthly rent, no property taxes to pay, and no utilities to pay. My profits would be everything I took in less the material cost. I only had one problem. I had never established credit and was only nineteen years old. I could not borrow the money for the compressor. I had enough to purchase all the stock and materials I needed, but fell five hundred dollars short of enough to buy the compressor I wanted. It required a special filtering system because of all the humidity.

There was a young couple that lived in the park, and I had met the boy's father who delivered the mobile homes to retail purchasers from the different sales lots in the area. I mentioned to the boy my shortage of the five hundred dollars, so the following day, his father came to me with an offer. As it was, the boy and girl were still in school, and they had just had a baby.

Both of the couple's parents insisted they finish school and had gone together and purchased the kids a mobile home that was set in the park about one hundred feet from the shop. The man, Don, told me he had five hundred dollars that he would loan me at no interest on the condition that if I needed any extra help, I would use his son, and there were no requirements as to how much because I had no idea how much work I could bring in. This was great for me because I had a worker available if and when I needed him. Don handed me five one-hundred-dollar bills and said, "Pay me back when you can." There were no papers signed.

Judy and I began work. One of our first jobs was a fleet of Cudaha Meat Company sales cars. Their entire fleet was red with their name painted on both sides of the car. They were relatively new, but the Florida sun had turned the red color to a powdered pink due to oxidation. I brought several of the cars in and began setting up my process to attack this project. I had to make sure that I got all the difficult things done on each vehicle, which I would do at night; then Judy could do the routine work during the day. My attack plan was all detailed, and I was ready to begin.

I finished my work at the plant at three thirty. Judy would have supper ready at exactly 4:00 p.m., and we would be at our paint shop by five. The first night, Judy did some cleaning on the cars, and I ground all the lettering off and removed any major blemishes that could not be sanded out with the final sanding operation; then I primed the bare spots. We worked until about midnight the first couple of days. A few days, at noon, during my lunch break, I would pick Judy up and take her to our shop, then go back to work. We needed to be making a little more progress and needed a little more daylight to assure that we had all the preparations right before I applied the paint.

We finally settled into a routine where we skipped supper and just had a snack on the run. We would be at our shop near four o'clock. Judy would sand the cars and rough mask them as I was cleaning them, buffing for the final sand job and completing the final masking. She would be working on another vehicle outside the spray room while I painted the car. While the car was tacking up to a dust-free status we both would be preparing another one. By about midnight, we would demask the painted car, close up the shop, and stop at a little restaurant uptown to have something to eat.

During our first month, we had painted several cars and a few small travel trailers, and I had used Don's son several times and paid him. When we tallied the net proceeds for the month, we had made a little over fifteen hundred dollars; plus we also had increased our inventory of paint and supplies. It was a good month. I went to Don and paid him the five hundred dollars I had borrowed.

We continued painting in our shop until about the middle of June. Ever since I had the burn experience, I was losing a little weight and did not feel very well. I was so busy working day and night, my commitments did not allow time for the doctor. Finally, I was sick. On Saturday, I went to the doctor; he drew blood and ran some quick tests and noticed something different, but his equipment for testing blood was limited. He made a phone call, then directed me to a new laboratory that had just opened. When I arrived, the owner was there by himself, unpacking supplies. His equipment was there, but obviously not located where it would be permanently placed. The doctor sent part of the vial of blood that he had drawn, and I gave it to the technician.

As he examined it, he made a loud exclamation; and when I inquired, he said that my white blood count and the red were way out of whack. I asked what he thought, and he said I would have to talk to the doctor. I asked him to let me look at the slide and for him to show me how he made the count. He began to explain, and then he reluctantly told me what he thought the problem was. He stated that what I had was the exact opposite of leukemia, a disease with abnormal high count of white blood cells; but in my case, the red cells were substantially higher than they should be. He named what he thought it to be, using a word that sounded like "ensophelia." I've never seen the word in print, so I can't be sure of the exact word.

The doctor told me the same thing when I went back to him. He said that the possible cause could be overexposure to chemicals. I told him I was a painter, and he advised me to get out of it for a while, at least until I healed.

I had lost almost twenty pounds in a six-week period. My job that I had gone to Florida for was finished. The building was up and going, and the paint crew were trained and doing a good job. Mr. Bathers transferred me to the main plant to the cabinet shop. He wanted me to train to take over the cabinet area. Judy and I discussed it, and it was a good opportunity and a good-paying job; but the truth was that once in my life, I had removed myself from all my friends, and this would be the second time. It was extremely difficult the first time, and I did not want Judy to go through it, and I did not want to do it again.

Concerned about my illness and the hereditary illness my family had, I decided to sell my paint equipment. Don bought everything. He felt like his son could manage to do the paintwork Judy and I had been doing. We both wanted to go back home to Elkhart. We had saved quite a lot of money and decided to purchase a newer car. We had been driving around one evening and saw this new blue-and-white '55 Chevy convertible. We thought we should reward ourselves, so we purchased it. I had discussed this with Mr. Bathers. He was aware that my job at the home plant was open for me to go back after the paint operation was in full swing, and he also knew that I hated unions; so if there still was a union problem in Elkhart, I would stay in Florida. I had to find out for myself. He was agreeable to whatever decision I made.

On Friday afternoon, the day before the Fourth of July weekend began, they delivered our new car to the plant. Judy was all packed for the trip to Elkhart, and we left Ocala in midafternoon. We put on our sunglasses and let the top down.

A few miles up the road, the sky got black, and we stopped to roll the top up. Before it was up, the rain about washed us away for about ten minutes. A tornado was going through the little community of Stark and completely wiped out the town. We were just on the south edge of the storm. We didn't change clothes, so it took a couple of hours for us to dry out.

When we got to Elkhart, we visited family and friends; and on Monday morning, I checked in at the main plant. The owner, Mr. Mort Levitt, told me that the union had cost him a little over a million dollars; and it appeared that he would have to sell the company to stay out of bankruptcy. I left there and drove to Richardson Homes. They advertised for a foreman to supervise the paint operations, which had thirty to thirty-five employees. They hired me as the assistant because of my experience and had me report to the plant production manager. We found a furnished apartment on

Morehouse Avenue and headed back to Florida to pick up the balance of our belongings. We were back in Elkhart the following Friday as I had to start my new job on Monday morning. I wrote down the odometer reading when they delivered our car and read it again as we completed our last trip. We had driven a little over 3,800 miles in an eight-day period and had spent time with family and friends.

Chapter Ten

My work at Richardson Homes was hectic, but I loved it. We were painting thirty-three mobile homes per day, doing both the inside and the outside. We had thirty-three employees and a double straight line. Each line was about 225 feet long, with each holding four full-size homes; and sometimes when we were running smaller units, we could get five in a line. Most of the time, after the daily production was established as to colors and materials, we would replenish all our materials from holding tanks or drums stored in a safe place outside the paint line.

I spent most of my time helping whichever station had the more difficult and time-consuming operations to perform. Each model required a different amount of labor in each station, depending upon size, number of windows, and number of bedrooms. Our complex was strung out over several acres with a number of different buildings, and because of the fire hazard created by the volume of paint we applied daily, the paint building was about three hundred yards from the central plants.

Things were going well, and I worked untold number of hours. My pay was the top rate that was being paid industry-wide, and the amount of the overtime created some really good paychecks. I had to begin sending more and more money to Mom and Coleman as Mom's health was beginning to go downhill. It wasn't a lot of money, but it was frequent. I learned that Judy was pregnant; and of course, because of my changing jobs, we had no insurance in effect even though I had insurance in Florida and had enrolled for coverage at Richardson's when I hired in. Expenses were considerably higher in Elkhart than they were in Florida, but we were getting along and trying to save money for the medical bills that would be forthcoming.

In September, we had a static electricity charge brought about by a combination of the charged air from all the spray guns and the paint creating an electric charge as it came in contact with the aluminum metal that was used for siding on the homes. The homes rested on their own rubber tires, so there was no place for the stored charge to go until someone or something that was grounded touch the metal to release the charge. The static sparks began bouncing around among the steel girders of the building framework. The sparks arced downward from the underside of the steel roof and traveled down a couple of four-inch steel posts in between the two production lines. As it reached the top of the paint barrels, the dust that had accumulated blew like gunpowder, spraying sparks everywhere. The building was concrete and steel, and the only part of it that was wood was four overhead doors and three rows of benches that we walked on to reach the roof line of the mobile homes while painting.

We cleared the employees, and on our way out, we manually pushed three of the homes out of the building. Within ten minutes, the overhead doors were falling, and the explosions were tremendous. Every fire truck within miles was on the scene. Everyone escaped without injury, but the problem was where one can paint thirty-three mobile homes a day. A shop on the south side of town took half the production, and we rented a building close to the main plant to do the other half. I went to the latter. It was a rough winter that year for the industry, and my hours were reduced. We were building a new modern paint facility, but it would require the entire winter to complete and equip the structure.

Our oldest son, Randy, was born in March; and when we paid the doctor and hospital bill, I thought we had purchased him from the hospital. The bill was double what it should have been, and we weren't prepared for it financially. We soon learned that the apartment we were in was way too small for the three of us. I was making good steady money, but the cost of our first child was more than we had planned for.

The Simpson Memorial Methodist Church was at the end of our block. Judy had been a member of the church long before we had met. Now that we were back from Florida, we began attending services there. We were going to have to find a larger place, and we didn't want to move too far away. Work was close, the church was close, and Judy's parents lived about five blocks away.

Judy's uncle, who was a lawyer, had possession of a house that was in an estate. The house was run-down and needed substantial repair. Her uncle Dick had become a friend of mine and offered us this house on a work trade out instead of rent.

In the late summer, we cleaned the house up well enough to furnish it and move in. We had to buy all our furniture since we had never owned our own. The only thing we had was a television set and kitchenware. By the time we purchased all the appliances, bedroom suite, dining room table and chairs, and furniture for the living room, we were broke. I refinanced our car to settle all debts, but we had a large car payment. I wasn't accustomed to having to make monthly payments. I preferred to pay as you go.

To honor my part of the agreement on the house rental, I had to construct a new rear porch completely, repair the front porch, replace numerous exterior siding pieces, and paint the house. I had plenty of time to do it, but I wanted to get it done so my obligation would be satisfied and over with.

Our son was about five months old, and we learned that Judy was pregnant again; and the same month, I received a delinquent notice from the IRS, stating that I owed them $272. Upon inquiry, they had disallowed the deductions that I had taken for the keep of my parents, including the medical expense. They said they had sent several notices to which none got a response. I told them I had been in Florida and had never heard from them. Since I had not responded, they turned it over to the delinquent accounts department run by a Harry Habel, who was an unadulterated jerk who was trying to play the role of this really big powerful man. I told him I would take it to court, and he laughed and told me that no court would take a delinquent case and that I had to pay the bill to make it legally acceptable for a court case.

About a week later, Judy got a postcard, which anyone could read, in the mail from the church. It was a direct message that said, "If you don't pay you're 10 percent tithes within the next fifteen days, your membership in Simpson Memorial Methodist Church will be canceled." How's that for a lot bad news all at one time?

All of these things had to be handled, but the one that made me extremely angry was the postcard. I jumped in my car and drove to the parsonage. When I arrived there, a large building crew was putting on about a one-thousand-square-foot addition to the parsonage. It was already four times the size of my house and on the market worth ten times my house in dollar value. Of course the pastor wasn't contributing a red cent for its construction. They were reroofing the entire house, including the older section, which had almost new shingles already on it. He just wanted to change the colors at the church's expense.

The pastor was on the sidewalk talking to two men. I waited until the men drove away and approached him. I told him I would like to discuss an issue with him, and he replied that he didn't have time because he had to try out the new car that the two men who had just left brought to him. Another big cost for the church. The car he had before that belonged to the church was less than three years old, the one he just traded in.

Obviously, this person was driven by pure greed and could care less about the real church. I left him standing there and would never set foot in that church again. A few years later, the church had severe financial problems and was forced to merge into another one down the road. How in the world could this so-called man of God be so selfish and arrogant and still stand before the congregation and attempt to preach God's Word? Self-serving interests without consideration for anyone else—that IS NOT God's way. I have never gotten over this incident. It had no influence on my relationship with God, but destroyed my confidence in "man's" church.

The IRS had threatened to garnish my wages if the delinquent tax was not paid within ten days. After moving, buying new furniture, and paying the hospital bill, we were virtually broke and now had a big car payment. I knew Richardson's, where I worked, had a policy of firing employees rather than complying with garnishment orders; and I had to do something fast. I was embarrassed about the situation even though I had done nothing wrong in my tax filing. I had even employed the services of a tax accountant to prepare my return.

The following day at work, I discussed this situation about the garnishment and my current financial condition with my boss so if and when it came, at least he would have advanced knowledge of the circumstances. I had a good job and was frightened that they would fire me.

The following day, I heard my name paged, which was not unusual because people were always paging me to come to a particular line station, but this page requested I come to the main office. I jumped in my car and drove to the office. When I entered the receptionist area, the lady directed me to Mr. Bob Richardson's office. Bob's father, Cliff, had started the company; and Bob had become the number one man in the company. I was scared to death, but if they were going to fire me, the production manager or the superintendent would have handled it. I was confused.

When I walked into Bob's office, he stood up, walked around his desk, introduced himself, and then got right to the point. He said, "Son, I hear some real good things about you and your work, and we're very glad to have you as an employee. It has come to my attention that you have a tax problem." While he was speaking, he reached for his wallet and opened it. He pulled out three crisp one-hundred-dollar bills and told me to go get the problem taken care of and pay him back when I could. I profoundly thanked him and told him I would not disappoint him. I later learned that the company had a policy of no cash advances nor loans to employees.

The company was growing, our new paint line was complete, and I began working fifty to sixty hours a week. We needed more people in the main plant, so I contacted Ella Mae and brother-in-law Jack and told them. The company Jack had worked for in Jasper had moved away, and he was out of work. They moved to Elkhart, and my company put him to work in the metal department. They had two children when they arrived in Elkhart.

I paid the IRS, tried to put the church thing behind me, and repaid Mr. Bob for the three-hundred-dollar loan. I had insurance in force to help pay for the new baby that was coming. I still had to scrape every penny I could to help Mom and Coleman.

The second week of March was real hectic at work. We were getting really organized in the new facility, but production took a leap. We were starting to build larger mobile homes and increase production quantities at the same time. I had worked over fifty hours by Thursday night. Judy was beginning to have labor pains, and I took her to the hospital. I told her she'd best have the baby soon because I had to be at work by seven and couldn't afford to miss the overtime. Our little girl, Teri, was born early in the morning on Friday 13. I made it to work in good time and finished the week with about seventy hours.

Teri looked like an Indian papoose with her real dark hair and crumpled face. When I went back to the hospital to see Judy and the baby, Betty, Judy's mother, was there. She and I walked to the nursery to see the baby. Betty had been there already, so when the nurse saw us coming up to the glass window, she started to pick up my daughter so we could clearly see her. I was kidding around with Betty and told the nurse, "No, no, the other one," pointing to the baby next to Teri that was real pretty.

Betty said, "No, this one's Teri," pointing to the baby the nurse was picking up. I said, "It can't be. She looks like poor, pitiful Pearl." (This was the most popular doll of that time and carried that exact name).

After a few hours, Teri's crumpled face that had looked like an old person with weather-beaten skin changed, and she was a beautiful baby.

By this point in time, Judy and I had become very close to her parents. After we had been married a short period of time, the wounds created just before we were married were completely healed. They had accepted me and supported me in every situation; and most times, if Judy and I viewed something in a different way, both Betty and Bob would support my view. This became somewhat of a joke over the years. Until the day they died, I never let Betty forget her comment as I was moving Judy out of her house where Betty had exclaimed that she'd give our marriage a year. By the time she died, we had been married for thirty-one years.

Soon after going to work at Richardson's, I bought a '51 Henry J automobile from one of the employees for fifty dollars. The engine burned about as much oil as gas, and pieces of the body would fall off as you drove down a bumpy road because the body was rusted so bad. I needed work transportation because I was ruining my convertible with the paint residue at work. I cleaned, polished, and waxed the convertible and left it home. The Henry J needed a lot of work and became unreliable, so I parked it in the driveway and returned to driving the convertible.

I could never sit still for any length of time and needed something other than work to maintain me mentally. One day, I started working on the Henry J. I repaired the engine and muffler system and got it running very good. I picked up parts at the junkyard for less than twenty dollars. After the mechanical parts were in good order, I decided to cut the body down and make a little sports car convertible. I used a big hammer to knock out all the glass, then used a metal hacksaw to cut all the pillar posts, removed the entire metal roof, and junked it. I shortened the body a little, welded the doors shut, removed the trunk, replaced the rear body area with formed sheet metal, and cut a circular radius on the top of the two side doors to allow stepping into the car with no doors. I upholstered the entire interior with red vinyl, painted the car white, and installed a speedboat windshield.

Judy and I would take our two kids and ride around the area when the weather was nice; but when the third child was born, we didn't have enough room, so we stored the car.

'51 Henry J. that I customized

Soon after Teri was born, Richardson's began a policy of no overtime, and we could not survive on just forty hours of pay. I began to think about the paint shop we owned in Florida and firmly decided that I was going to own my own business where I had a better control over my destiny. I decided to get an additional job and found a night job at Excel Corporation. My work shift at Richardson's was from seven to three thirty, and the shift at Excel was four till eleven thirty with no supper break. I began working this fifteen and a half workday and began meeting all my financial obligations.

I ran a punch press, piercing the metal tracks used around the windows of school buses; and some shifts, I ran a forming press that made the metal part of the wing windows that were used on almost all automobiles in those days. At Excel, we were paid based upon piece rates. After two weeks on the punch press, I was producing 130 percent of the rate. I was not in the union and, of course, never would be. The union steward came to me and told me I had to slow down because I was ruining the rate. If I continued producing 130 percent, the company would establish that quantity as the rate, and everyone would have to produce 130 percent just to make the base rate.

I needed the money, I hated unions, and I was going to continue working as fast as I could. The quality of my parts was within tolerance, and my scrap factor was almost zero. I believed everyone should work to the best of their ability, and I wouldn't change. The union had a stronghold on Excel; and it was a closed shop, meaning that to work there, you had to join the union and were supposed to after your thirty-day job trial period ended. I managed to stay about two months, and they kept pressuring me to join. It was obvious I could not succeed there and had no chance to bump or bid on any higher-paying job as they became available. This was how every union I ever knew worked. They control their members' output to about 75 percent of ability and set their rules so if you're not one of them, you either won't work or will have to do menial jobs forever. I told them they could take their union and flush it down the toilet because I refuse to be a kept man.

While I was at Excel, the grandfather of a friend of mine was the area manager for Electrolux vacuum cleaners. We had purchased one from him, and at the time we made the purchase, he told me if I were ever interested in selling Electrolux to contact him. The day after the union steward had talked to me, I was uncertain about the future of my job there; so I called the Electrolux man and said I'd like to learn the ropes, but I was working two full shifts. My plan was to make one appointment each night, Monday through Thursday night, with people who worked the night shifts and got off work at eleven thirty. I took a one-hour lesson from him, picked up my sales kit, and demo and began to make appointments.

For about six weeks, I had up to four appointments per week and sold six vacuum cleaners. They paid me twenty-five dollars commission for each one. I didn't like sales work and chose a different course.

The owner of a travel trailer-manufacturing company contacted me and offered me a job running his paint operations in Marcellus, Michigan. This was Cree Coach and was thirty-five miles from my house. I looked at the job; and they had only three people in the paint department, which meant that if I took the job, I'd do most of the work because their problem was the painters spent over half the workweek repairing bad paint jobs. I discussed this with the owner and gave him a bid to contract all his paintwork to me on a per-foot basis. It was about 30 percent less than it was costing him then. He was to furnish everything, position the units the way I directed in the paint department, and maintain the inventory and supplies; and I would provide the labor with a guarantee of acceptable quality and timely performance, and all would be subject to his approval. Any unit that was not acceptable would be repaired at my cost, or he would not have to pay for the paint job. I believe that's the way work should be done; then half of the management and supervision of an operation will be eliminated, with huge savings.

The workers' pride is on the line, which forces him to find a better way of completing a job and allows management to utilize a lot of hidden talents of most employees who, by management's choice, supervise them and instruct them on every move they make. When your operating procedure allows for the daily input, correction, and selection of methods used to get a job done, the most difficult job is to provide them with enough work because their production will increase 25 to 30 percent; then the quality will go up while scrap goes down. Don't do this with the worker at the very end of a production line because he'll suck the line dry and wait for the product to come to his station. Do it with all the employees starting at the beginning of the line.

I continued working at Richardson's and got home just before four. Judy would have food ready, and I would eat my food on the long drive to Marcellus. During the transition to my starting the painting, they had several units waiting. They were producing three a day, but there were about ten ready for paint. Five of them were positioned in the paint room the way I had instructed. I worked as fast as I could, and about one o'clock, I finished these and left a note for them to put five more in position for the next night.

The following night, the owner came to the shop as I was preparing to tackle the next five. He thanked me for trying to get the units caught up and asked me how many workers I had. I told him one—me—and that if things go smoothly that night, he would have five more before daybreak. Things went well, and I was home around one thirty in the morning. I worked all day on Saturday, and after about a week, all the units and the daily production were caught up. The pay from Cree and my wages from Richardson's coupled together was the largest I had ever earned in a week. It was five times what I was used to.

By Saturday night, I was beat and could hardly stay awake. Judy was taking our baby somewhere and wanted me to look after our less-than-two-year-old son for a couple of hours. She left Randy with me, and I just couldn't stay awake, which wasn't good. I put a blanket and pillow on the floor along with some toys; and using a soft rope, I tied his leg to mine so it would wake me if he tried to leave the area. I dozed off for a few minutes; and my leg would jerk, then get settled back in my chair, and it happened again. I got through it, but I guess I needed a longer rope.

I had no time to spend with friends or family, except on occasion, we would see Ella Mae and her family. Judy would go to see her parents, or they would come to visit us for an hour or so; and sometimes on Sunday afternoon, we would see Ginny and Dwayne Curtis, who had been friends for a long time. Mom's health was sliding downhill, and their needs were becoming greater; and still, no one else seemed to care. I'd taken care of them for so long that it appeared like everyone just thought, "Everything's OK, Bob will take care of it."

Brother Jim had returned from the service and was working in Elkhart. He did not have any children, but still provided no help to Mom. Ella Mae and Jack had three children, and the fourth would come soon, and they were struggling. My sister Shirley and her husband, James, had two children and were struggling to make ends meet. Shirley lived in the area where Mom lived and would visit and do things for them, but they were not financially able to help.

By now, we had paid off all our debts, and I had completed all the agreed-to repairs on our house. The kids had nice clothes, and I was beginning to save a few dollars. I was going to start a business soon. Work at Richardson's was booming again, and Cree Coach had upped their production to seven units a day. They had built a new paint facility and wanted me to run it. The painting contract with them would end, but I had the opportunity to work all the overtime I wanted at Richardson's, so I declined Cree's offer.

From the end of May 1959, I worked forty-nine days without a day off. I was making what they called rate pay, which was the highest hourly rate in the company, and I averaged working seventy hours a week for seven straight weeks. We had gone to all prefinished materials on the inside of the homes and were running thirty-three a day. The process for applying the wood grain panels had just been developed and was called roller coating. The raw wood panel was filled with a white pasty filler, which reduced the natural grain pattern of the wood. It was sanded, and a big drum with a reverse photograph imprinted the wood grain on the filled panel. The process was completed by applying a very thin coating of clear material and force-dried. The coating was real brittle, which resulted in dozens of scratches to the walls of the mobile home during construction. While the deficiency of the coating process was being corrected by the panel suppliers, we had to live with it and had to change hundreds of panels. The homes came to the paint department with numerous scars and scrapes in every unit, which had to be repaired. This required a true artist to patch the scratches by filling them and smoothing the surface and then matching the numerous colors and repainting with various artist's brushes all of the grain lines through the damaged spot.

We hired a worker by the name of Joe Pitz. Joe had a lot of talent and did excellent work in repairing these damaged areas, but it was far too much work for one man. We could not find another artist, so I had Joe teach me how it was done. To begin, he let me do the filling and sanding; and afterward, I would apply the base coat, which was the same color on all the panels. Joe would then paint the appropriate design matching the various colors and grain. The artist paint tray contained several colors and mixes from white to black, including raw and burnt forms of umber, sienna, and such. You had to have a good eye for color to match the dozens of different colors and shades imprinted on the panels.

When Joe came, we had about fifty homes in the paint parking area, with thirty-three a day adding to it. It took a few months for the panel producers to resolve their problem. We were desperate to catch up the damaged backlog, and both Joe and I worked the forty-nine days in a row. On the Fourth of July weekend, the company was having its annual company picnic on Saturday. I told the production manager that Joe and I would work until noon and then go to the picnic. All the rest of the plant was closed, including the offices. The manager told me we couldn't go and that he would send someone over later to bring us a food basket.

We barely got this problem under control, caused by switching from raw wood to prefinished materials, and now the whole industry was changing the exterior from aluminum to steel metal siding. Steel is far more difficult to get a quality long-lasting paint job than aluminum is. It requires a much different kind of primer and a few other applications because steel siding retains oil residue that slowly seeps, whereas aluminum has some processing oil on the surface, which can easily be removed in the cleaning process.

Richardson's went to the steel siding. I refused to apply the same primer coating on the steel as we had been using on the aluminum, and working with Lilly Industrial Coatings, they quickly formulated our requirement. The result was that out of the first five hundred steel homes we painted, we had one spot on one unit that failed. I believe it to have happened because of improper cleaning rather than being caused by the fact it was steel.

The industry as a whole began to experience major numbers of paint failures in the field. Customers would have a home that was only a couple of months old before the failure occurred. Richardson's never had a single failure in the field. Skyline, Redman, Buddy, Homette, and twenty others that I personally knew of were experiencing these failures.

I knew I was going to start my own business, and I was very close to having enough capital to do so. I wanted someone to enter into business with me as a partner. I had mentioned this to my brother, Jim, in the past; and he indicated he might be interested. When this condition of paint failures in the field began, I realized here was my opportunity to get a jump start. I found all the equipment I would need and had enough money to make the purchase with some left over for supplies and family needs while I was starting. I discussed the program with my brother. He didn't have any money to put in the capital fund. I told him I would purchase and own all the equipment, and we would share equally the net proceeds.

The work required being on the road for a few days at a time, so he declined. Field refinishing of mobile homes required a lot of ladder work and at least two people. I could not interest anyone to go into business with me, and I was not going to pass up this opportunity. I knew the roadwork would be temporary and high dollar return, but I was not going to stay away from my family for long periods of time.

I got a contract from three major manufacturing concerns, one of which was the largest mobile home company in the world. This was Skyline Corporation. I knew the owner, Mr. Julius Decio, and his son, who was beginning to run the company. His name was Mr. Art Decio. Their record of paying their bills was 100 percent, so to do business was not a risk of not getting paid as it was with a majority of the companies in the industry. No one would go with me, so I set out on my own.

My equipment included a big panel truck, a two-hundred-pound-capacity sandblaster, several types of blasting heads and spray guns, and all types of supplies that would be needed. I headed toward Detroit with enough signed orders between Elkhart and Detroit to last for two weeks. Every place I went, they greeted me like a long-lost friend and were glad that the company that built their home was standing behind its warranty.

I did one home each day for five days and came home for the weekend, leaving my trailed air compressor at the next job site. I was back on the job at daybreak on Monday and repeated doing one unit daily. Most of the units were two-toned, but on occasion, I would have a three-colored unit. I had quoted for the extra color, but the dry time for masking caused me a lot of extra hours on these units. I finished all the units contracted for and returned home for a couple of days. I talked to Ron Birr, one of the brothers that I had lived with before I married, and Ron was going to come to work with me. He was in the process of having dentures made and could not join me for two weeks. Ron was temporarily out of work and expected to be called to work at the post office in a month or so.

I scheduled my trip based on doing one unit every day. My schedule was to begin painting units east of Chicago, working myself into Iowa and then back toward home. Dick was scheduled to meet me in Iowa City. Because the sand for blasting was so heavy, I would locate sand sources in the area I was heading to before I left. I knew all the colors of the units on the schedule and took adequate paint and supplies so I did not have to buy anything on the road, except sand and gasoline for the equipment.

The job was really hard for one person. My routine was that I would start at daybreak and prepare the unit, covering all that need covering, mask the unit, and begin sandblasting using a ladder. Once the blasting was done, I blew all the cracks and crevices, removing any sand residue, then final mask for spraying. After the primer dried, I sprayed the base color, masked it for the design of the paint colors, and sprayed the color. After the area was cleaned and all the sand washed away, I would wash up in the truck, change my clothes, drive to a lumberyard, replenish my sand supply, and drive to my next location. I had a cot in the truck where I slept.

I had been on the road for some time and was doing a home in line with the end of the runway at O'Hare Field in Chicago. The park owner kept coming out because he was afraid I was going to get paint on all the vehicles and other homes in the park. He interrupted me four or five times, but I finished. I was on the roof, making my final inspection, and was almost blown off by the wash of a huge jet that was taking off. All day, the turbulence was so great that the home shook, and the windows rattled. That's a lot of movement to get mobile home windows to rattle.

The park owner was satisfied that I had not painted anything other than what I was supposed to and asked me if I would sandblast his trailer, which he was using for an office. I looked the unit over and found that it had very thin aluminum on the exterior and was painted red, which had faded badly. This would be a difficult task to remove the red paint without overheating and stretching the aluminum. The owner said he would paint it; he just wanted me to blast it. I had about two hours before dark, so I'd have to hurry.

I masked the unit and began blasting. The paint I had been blasting on steel came off in sheets. This paint that Shultz had put on aluminum years before was real stubborn. After about three hours and having to hook up my lights, the job was done, and I had about had it. The job was too hard for one man; it was hard on the equipment, starting and stopping it so often to do other minor procedures another person should be doing, and I missed my family.

The park owner paid me, and I borrowed the use of his phone. I called Judy and told her to turn the covers down. I'd be home in about four hours. The decision was easy because one of the fellows that I had worked with a couple of years back had declined to come into partnership with me, but stated that he and his father would love to buy the equipment and my contracts.

I got home around one o'clock, and Judy had a big meal waiting for me. The following day, I called the man that wanted the equipment; and the following day, we went to the Burr Oak Bank in Michigan, and they cut me a check for the purchase of everything. I assigned the contract to them, and they hit the road to complete it.

I called each of the companies I had contracted with and told them I had exercised my legal right to assign the contract, and as we were speaking, the new people were on their way to begin where I left off in Chicago. I told all of them that I would be back in the paint business in the near future and would appreciate it if they kept me in mind. The next time my operation would be located in Elkhart because my time on the road had come to an end. I had never had a close-knit family, but I was going to build one.

I called brother Jim and told him I had sold the sandblasting and painting business and was going to start an operation in Elkhart. I told him he was welcome to join me if he cared to. He wasn't sure at that point in time and gave me no further response. When I was at Richardson's, the head painter,

Don Gardner, and I had become very friendly. We had discussed starting a business, but nothing came of it. Don had left Richardson's and was now running Jeff's Paint Shop, which was in the reconditioned building where Coleman had worked a few years before. Don wanted me to come and help him for a few days. I helped him get the line caught up, and winter was upon us. We talked about starting our own business, but the wintertime slows the industry down, so we decided to wait until near spring. He told me I could stay and work through the winter, helping in the shop and transporting some of their mobile homes that they were painting. I stayed, and it was the easiest job and the most consistent work hours I've ever had. I worked eight hours a day five days a week and felt that I was only working part-time.

When I left Richardson's, I lost my insurance coverage and had not yet replaced it. So during the few months before the spring of 1960, our family medical expenses were paid out of pocket, and we had a number of visits to the doctor's office; plus we continued to help Mom and Coleman. Mom was getting worse all the time and had gotten to where she could barely eat, except for baby food or finely ground foods. Her expenses had increased, and they still lived in the little old ramshackle farmhouse and probably were about freezing in the wintertime. Coleman could not work and really didn't look for work because Mom could not be alone for any extended period, and there was no one to help look after her.

My Chevy convertible was manufactured to be a Florida car and did not even have a heater in it. It was too cold to transport the kids. I had previously installed a small generic one, but it did not do the job in real cold low teens temperatures, plus the fact that convertibles in those days were made for summer cars. I decided to trade the '55 Chevy for a cold-weather car that was a '55 Oldsmobile, with much more space inside for the family. I paid five hundred dollars' difference and made a mistake of financing the entire amount. This was the only debt as we had paid off all the materials that were used to repair the house, which we had contracted to do, but working forty hours a week barely handled our living expenses; so the extras such as medical bills, Christmas, and winter utility bills ate up the savings we had.

Chapter Eleven

By the end of February, Don and I had solicited several manufacturers to build a base of customers for the business we were about to begin. We wanted to make sure that we had enough in savings to handle food and shelter for at least thirty days because it would take thirty days to start the flow of cash. We knew that we would not be able to take any salary from the new venture for at least a month. For me to get in that position, I decided to basically forfeit a lot of equity in my Oldsmobile, and I treaded back to the dealer for a '47 DeSoto and five hundred dollars, which I used to pay off my loan at the finance company. Don had gotten his financial affairs in order, and when we pooled our remaining resources, we still needed six hundred dollars to begin. We went to a finance company and borrowed three hundred dollars each, with monthly payments of $27.50.

We had found a building where they were doing the same type of work that we were proposing to do, and he was about to go bankrupt, but still had about a month's supply of some materials and a contract to fulfill. Then he was closing the doors and selling the property. The building owner, Eldon Ferm, rented us one bay that was attached to the main building and said we could rent more space later up to the time the building was sold. This bay was seventeen by fifty-one feet, barely large enough to get started, but we rented it. And while we were still employed elsewhere, we set the bay up and got all the material and equipment installed in late February.

On March 1, 1960, we started B&D Paint Inc., sharing ownership fifty-fifty. Don was going to remain working at his then-current job until I had to have his help. The phone had been connected in February, and I had lined up some small jobs and required that the customers transport their own goods to and from our place until we could afford a delivery truck. I made an agreement with Skyline Corporation on special terms of payment. They were the best in the business to pay, and they had a need for our services.

So they agreed that any products that were delivered to them by noon, that between one and two in the afternoon, every Friday, we could hand carry a billing for the week's work; and they would cut us a check.

The first few days of operations I had enough room to handle the work with the paint area and storage racks we had built. I was painting molding, passage doors, and some small cabinet parts; but a problem arose. A couple of the customers could not pick up their goods before midday following, and I would not be able to begin painting until the finished parts were gone. I couldn't get them in my car, so I called Don. He had a station wagon that had a removable rear seat. I told him the problem, so he came right over and made the deliveries.

This became a regular routine every day. Customers would deliver OK, but could not guarantee the time they could pick up. I had to get everything out of the shop before starting the final finishing of dissimilar items. By the end of the second week, the adjacent bay of the same size became available, so we rented it. I was working twelve to fourteen hours a day, and Don would come in the evenings for five or six hours.

On Friday, during the second week, Skyline called and said they wanted to send a full truckload of louvered closet doors. I had no idea how many doors were in a truckload, but they needed to deliver the following morning, and I was happy to tell them that it was OK. It took over an hour to hand-unload the truck. Don came in to help me on Saturday morning, and this semi rolled in, bringing seven hundred doors. We had to unload by hand and were happy to do it. Don contacted the owner of the company he worked for, met with him, and gave his two weeks' notice that he was leaving. When Don told him we were starting a paint shop without asking what we were going to paint, he fired Don. Much later, he told Don that he thought we were going to go into competition and paint mobile homes.

We immediately hired another employee by the name of Ray Roderick, and by the end of the month, we had five employees working these two small bays. Don and I were able to draw twenty-five dollars a week and pay our bills on time.

Another couple of weeks went by, and Mr. Ferm was vacating the main building, and I went over to talk to him about renting the whole building and the parking lot across the street. He said there was no way we would ever get enough wood parts to fill the building, and I told him we were going to start painting travel trailers, which is what he had been painting. He asked how many a day, and I told him I had sketched out the layout, and it looked like we could run about thirty-five a day on one shift. He belly-laughed and told me he had been all around in different shops before he started his own business, and he felt he had reached the capacity of the building and had been painting up to fifteen a day. He said the business was too competitive, and he could not make it. I signed a lease with him with an option to purchase the property, and Mr. Ferm went down the street and started a used car lot.

I made a few phone calls to the same people I had dealt with during the sandblasting and repainting venture, and within a week, we were painting ten a day; plus we tripled the volume of wood parts we were doing. On the Friday before the Fourth of July weekend started, we had thirty-three employees and were painting fifty-five travel trailers a day, working the crew ten hours a day and half day on Saturdays. We had five vehicles on the road, picking up and delivering trailers, which included our fourteen-foot box truck that we picked up and delivered our parts in. We turned business away on a daily basis and recorded all the requests that we turned down because expanding was already on our minds.

There were three banks in town. Two were very large and catered to the blue bloods, but one was small and still operated like a small-town consumer bank instead of the pure commercial attitude of the two large ones. This was the First Old State Bank, whose president was Mr. Clifford Martin. When Don and I were getting our financial affairs together immediately before we started the company, both of us had gone to both of the large banks and tried to borrow three hundred each. They denied both flat out, and we both were excellent credit risks.

We did not talk to the First Old State; instead, we went to a local finance company where we borrowed the three hundred. Without knowing anything about the First Old State, we chose to set our checking account with them; and by now, they were very familiar with our operation and our cash flow. They had voluntarily asked us, on a couple of occasions, if we would need operating funds; and we declined to set up a credit line. Our office secretary had made the daily bank deposit and had cut checks paying off the balance of all the financing we had done in purchasing our five trucks and the yard tractor. All our equipment was paid for, and Don and I go to see Mr. Martin at the bank and hand him our lease with the right to purchase the entire property from Mr. Ferm. After paying off our entire debt, we had enough to pay the down payment on the property and enough operating cash in the bank to run our business. The paperwork was finished on the property a couple of weeks later.

From that day forward, Mr. Martin handled our financial affairs, both personal—and businesswise, and would not delegate our account to any other officer in the bank. We still had not set up a line of credit, nor had we borrowed any funds until late fall. Accounts receivable were exceptionally slow for a couple of weeks, and we had some bills that were due. We waited until the last day, thinking enough money would come in, but it didn't.

I called Mr. Martin and told him we needed some money to pay our bills. I expected him to tell me to come down, and we would fill out all the paperwork. Instead, he asked, "How much do you need?" And I told him in order to get my discounts, I needed to pay now and needed ten thousand dollars. He instantly said, "I'll put the money in your account, and when you have some free time, come down and sign the paperwork." I realize that mode of operation is not the best, but it worked for him, and it certainly worked for me because I was busy trying my best to figure out a way we could increase our production in these facilities.

There was a residential house on each side of our property, but we had enough land to expand the building, but Don and I felt it would put us too close to the houses with respect to dust and odor. So expanding was out of the question, and neither neighbor wanted to sell at that time.

Typical trailers that we painted.   **Busy Bob, 1961**

Wintertime in Elkhart is a tough time for the painting business, especially if vehicles that must be painted that day spend the night before outside in rain, sleet, and snow; but we made it through the winter. We took on the job of painting a few mobile homes because we had enough room as the travel trailer business took its seasonal downturn. Winter turned to spring, and that brought on the stormy season and another difficult time when you're painting as many units a day as we were. You have to be careful how they're parked, and the dolly wheel must be removed. Otherwise, the wind crashes them all together and poses a huge problem as it dries the ground, throwing clouds of dust in the air, which filtration systems cannot fully remove.

One of our large customers opened a plant in Hemet, California, and needed paint services. We sent our first hired employee to Hemet to set up the building and train the employees. We operated this plant for about two years, and it was barely profitable, so we elected to sell it.

Judy was expecting our third child, and on May 22, Michael James was born. We gave him his middle name after Coleman, whose last name is James. Mom was still getting worse, and something had to be done real soon. I began to inquire through the medical profession as to what type of doctor would be the very best. No one had any idea, but they suspected that what she had was a neurological disorder. I learned that two such doctors would be in Birmingham at a particular time and made arrangements through a number of people for one of the specialists to examine Mom.

They ran their examinations and could not conclude what she had, but they wanted to perform some extensive tests. I had made arrangements to pay for their services. They suspected that she had St. Vitus's Dance, a neurological disorder, but to confirm it would require some very intricate surgery in the nerve lobes near the temples. The risk was extraordinarily great, and Mom absolutely refused to proceed. It had become quite obvious that she would not live much longer, so I wanted her to be as comfortable as possible during her latter days.

Our second son and the third child was born on May 22, 1961. He was a robust baby and immediately took to his grandpa Kidder even before he could walk. Bob thought that he was the greatest thing in the world. He loved to be with all three kids, but Mike was the apple of his eye. I'm sure it was because soon after Mike was born, we put in a swimming pool, and Betty and Bob spent a lot of time watching the kids swim. Teri received a lot of playful attention from Grandma Betty. Randy was not nearly as active when he was between three and ten years old because of an accident. He probably got more attention from both Bob and Betty than the other two kids, but it was a somewhat different kind when all three of them were under five years old. They were the only grandkids that Bob and Betty had.

When Michael was about a month old, Judy and Betty took all three kids to the Pierre Moran Mall, located on the south side of town. Judy had Mike in her arms and had gone inside the bank while Betty took Teri and Randy past the bank and into the Mode'Da dress shop. They were inside the store, looking around and killing time while Judy did her banking. Randy had turned three in March and was at a stage that he was always full of energy, but he was still a very disciplined child as he was taught to be.

As they were leaving the store, Randy ran in front of Betty and Teri to be the first to the door; and when he reached what he thought was the door, he put his hand up and pushed, trying to open it. This was not the door, but a plate glass window a little larger than nine by eleven feet. The window broke in half from side to side, with the bottom half falling to the outside and shattering on the sidewalk. The top half fell inward and hit Randy. As the glass made contact with his face, this piece broke in half from side to side, and one of the pieces put a big slice by the side of his nose and continued downward into his chest.

The ambulance was called immediately and took a few minutes to respond. When I received my call, the secretary paged me since I had walked out of the building. She said, "Come quickly, we have an emergency!" I ran to the office, and she told me Randy had been hurt badly, and I was to get there right now. I ran to my car, which was a new Thunderbird convertible, and headed toward the mall. The roads were actually small county roads, with about four stops between me and the mall. I turned south for two blocks, then east for another ten blocks; with my lights on and my hand on the horn, I once looked at the speedometer, and I was almost pegged out at 120 mph.

As I turned into the mall drive, I saw an ambulance coming from the direction of the town with red lights flashing. I jumped out of the car by the time it stopped; and there was a man sitting on the curb, holding Randy in his arms, and he had a wet barber's towel covering Randy's chest. I reached for my son, and the ambulance EMTs forced me aside and began to work on Randy. They looked under the towel and put it back on his chest, and while one of them was starting medical procedures, the other was on his radio to the hospital. They loaded him into the ambulance, and I jumped in beside him. He was in total shock, his eyes were open, and he showed no signs of pain. I don't think he even knew I was there. I kept talking to him all the way to the hospital, which took less than fifteen minutes.

As we exited the ambulance, Randy's pediatrician, Dr. Campbell, and a surgeon, Dr. Finfrock, were standing in the emergency entrance door and hurried to meet us. Both began examining Randy as they walked alongside the gurney. The EMTs rolled him directly to the examination room, and I was told to stay until they came for me.

I knew both of the doctors really well and was so glad they were both there. Both had the reputation of being the best in their fields, and thank God, both of them were in the hospital when the EMT made his radio call. Neither doctor was on call, and both had their private practices. An eternity passed, and then the doctors came to me. Dr. Finfrock looked at me with a somber look and said, "Bob. It's pretty bad. I can fix the cut on his face with very little scarring, but the chest is torn up quite a bit. We are taking him to surgery now, and I'll talk to you the minute we're finished." He took me by the hand, and we walked back into the examination room.

Randy looked exactly the same as he did in the ambulance and was unresponsive to anything. Dr. Finfrock gently lifted the towel from his chest, and I almost passed out. Dr. Campbell had his arm around my shoulders and steadied me, or I would have fallen to the floor. The glass had taken some pieces of bone from the collarbone and ribs, and a gaping hole was in his chest. The pectoral muscle was gone. His heart and lungs were slightly exposed, and with every beat of his heart, the cavity on the edge nearest to the heart would spill over. The towel was the only thing that kept him from bleeding to death before we got to the hospital.

They asked Judy several questions and when he had last eaten. He had eaten lunch shortly before the accident, so they would have to wait a while before performing surgery. They took him to the operating room; and both doctors stayed by his side before, during, and even after surgery until they were confident that he was going to be OK.

Surgery lasted about three hours. Plenty of time to do a lot of thinking. I thought about what he said about the towel keeping him from bleeding to death and remembered that there was a man with Randy on his lap, holding pressure on the wet towel. I remembered that his pants were covered with blood as were his hands and white shirt. I thanked God for this man and had to learn who he was.

Over three hours had gone by, and the doctors came for us. Dr. Finfrock explained the extent of the injury and that surgery had gone as well as expected. He took us to the intensive care unit; and there was Randy with a big bandage on his face and a plaster cast encasing his entire right shoulder, arm, and most of his chest. He was asleep. The doctors hugged and assured us that he would be OK, and they would see us in the early morning. Judy and I sat by his side in the ICU.

A nurse offered us a drink and something to snack on and told us we really should go home because Randy was very stable and would not be fully awake until morning because they were continuing to sedate him. We needed to get the other kids home, and I needed to clean up and change clothes. I smelled like a paint shop. Judy took me to get my car, and while she picked up the kids at Betty's house, I drove home and changed. When she got home a few minutes later, I spent a couple of minutes with the kids and returned to the hospital where I stayed until midmorning on Tuesday.

Sometime in the morning, Randy woke up. He had no idea what had happened and was frustrated with the bandages and especially the cast. He'd best get used to it because it was going to be there for the next three months.

In midmorning, I went to the plant to check in. Everyone was concerned and inquired about Randy. I had a regimen that I followed the best I possibly could because I thought it was extremely important. If I was at the plant, I would always take a break or have lunch with my employees. That's where you really learn if what you're doing is right or if you should change it. At lunchtime, I sat with everyone and told them the story and then discussed activity with Don.

After spending a few minutes with them, I went back to the hospital. Randy was wide awake and was very talkative; and I explained to him, once again, what had happened to him. He stayed in the ICU for maybe another day and then was taken to a room where he could have visitors. In those days, visiting hours were set; and except under critical conditions, visitors cannot come except during the set hours. At visiting time, there was a steady stream of friends and relatives.

Finally, we got to bring Randy home, and we were all very glad. Teri had missed him terribly. Now we would begin a rehab program as soon as the doctors allowed it. He had to do everything with his left hand because his right side was totally immobile. We were starting to get back into a daily routine. I finally found who the man was that held Randy at the accident, but could never learn his name. No one knew, or if they did, they wouldn't tell. I put together a lot of pieces from people who witnessed the accident and know what happened, but I concluded that because of who this man was, no one would confirm that he was there at that time or who he was.

When the glass fell on Randy, this man was coming out of the barbershop next door. While getting a haircut, he had told the barber that he was a detective from Gary, Indiana. When he saw the glass hit Randy and all the blood was gushing, he turned back and asked for a wet towel and then ran and picked Randy up, placing him on his lap as he sat on the curb. Randy did not have a shirt on, so the man could see the gaping hole in his chest and attempted to stop the bleeding with both his hands. Someone brought the wet towel, and he forced the towel into the wound and kept pressure on it until the EMTs took over. In the confusion, the man must have just walked away. No one saw him leave. I have thanked God numerous times for this man's actions and asked God to greatly bless him for his good and kind deed.

Thank you, sir, wherever you are.

When we filed the insurance claim against the Mode'Da Dress Shop, their insurance company refused to pay on the grounds that Randy had run into the glass. I had enough bad experiences that I was not going to leave anything to chance. After the accident, I immediately researched the entire situation and obtained documents confirming all that I had learned. On my way back to the hospital the day after the accident, I took a camera and photographed the store from top to bottom.

By this time, the glass had been cleaned up, and some of the blood was washed off the floor and sidewalk, but my pictures and documents would prove my story and display the facts. Judy's uncle, who had become my best friend, was a lawyer and would handle the case when I was ready to collect from their insurance company.

On the Friday before the accident, a tornado had ripped through the area and passed our plant to the south about two blocks and continued directly to the Pierre Moran Mall. The mall had been under construction for a long time, and only three businesses had moved in and opened for business. From the dress shop on down the strip, the buildings were in various stages of completion, with the last one being a huge structure of concrete block, which was to be a Kroger grocery store. A bank occupied the first building on the corner, then the barbershop, and then the dress shop. The bank and the barbershop had no damage from the storm, but it took out all the large plate glass windows in the front of the dress shop and leveled the block walls that were ready for roofs the next three hundred feet to the east.

A local glass company had worked around the clock replacing glass in the path of the storm and had replaced the dress shop glass on Sunday. They installed the glass in the old metal coping that was twisted and bent as the glass blew out during the storm. Burnstine's, the glass company, had scheduled to return at a later date to replace the damaged coping and then would seal the glass. Their main objective was to get the building closed up.

The store employees had removed their display from inside the window and had taken the damaged display platform away. This raised platform is required by law to prohibit anyone from attempting to use the window as a door. The store had a triple glass front, and from the inside, each of the three sections looked about the same when no display was present. Randy had mistaken the window for the door; and without a raised platform, which would have stopped him, he continued and pushed on the window.

Mode'Da's lawyers were from California, where they were headquartered, and were a very belligerent group and were very adamant they were not paying. Two of them were in Dick's office and had no knowledge that he was Judy's uncle and my best friend. They began to belittle our family and told Dick that their investigation showed that I was a painter working in a factory and certainly could not afford to pay legal fees and that if he took the case to court, he'd probably never get paid. Dick responded that he was taking the case pro bono and gave them a deadline in which to pay all the medical bills, and additionally, it would be an open-end case for damages since it would be some time before we would know the extent of Randy' disability. He then physically escorted them to the door.

Within a week, they paid everything, including the legal fee; and Dick prepared the documents providing for compensation for Randy for his injuries sustained once the disability could be determined by the doctors.

The cast was removed in late summer. Randy had little use of his right arm and hand, but the injury to his face had healed with some scarring. His care had been turned over to a specialist, and therapy was ongoing. Randy began to get a little use from the arm, but it hang at his side most of the time, and he used his left hand for everything.

The therapy sessions were completed the last week of September, and the doctor called me into his office. He made Randy sit in another room. He told me Randy would never use his arm again; the pectoral muscle was 95 percent destroyed, along with damage to the surrounding area of his shoulder and chest. I refused to believe him. From the day Randy was born, I—like most fathers with a son—wanted to see him become a good athlete and live a good productive life. This news from the doctor had to be wrong. The doctor was going to confirm to me what he had just said and called Randy into the office.

As he walked into the office, the doctor tossed a small object at Randy; and he reached out with his left hand, attempting to catch it. The right hand did not move. The doctor said, "See, no response." I was never so angry in my life. I got up and took Randy to the therapist and discussed the situation with her. She told me that the best possible thing I could do was to keep him in the water, swimming as much as possible, and there might be a chance that he could train other muscles to do the job as he grew.

Now I knew what I had to do. We had just purchased our home a couple of weeks before Mike was born, and now we had to build a swimming pool for Randy. We arrived home in the late afternoon, and I opened the phone book to the yellow pages. There were several pool companies listed in the area; and I began to call, telling them I needed a pool, and I needed it now.

It was at the end of the season, and most of them were booked; but finally, I talked to one in South Bend, which is near Elkhart, and discussed my need with the owner. He came to my home that evening, and we contracted to build the pool.

The pool was finished near the end of September and normally too cold for use, but we had put a huge heater in the system and could keep the water temperature up to ninety degrees if we wanted to. When the water was warm enough, I took Randy to the pool; and I got in the water, then reached for him to bring him into the water. He was scared to death and backed away, crying his eyes out. I didn't really know what to do because I didn't want to force him and scare him further.

I brought Teri and Mike to the pool. Teri was two and a half, and Mike was only four months old. I put Teri in, and she liked it as I swirled her around while Randy was watching. After a few minutes, I walked the steps into the water with Mike in my arms. When we touched the water, he became the happiest baby I ever saw. He was an instant water bug. Randy saw that his little brother and sister had no fear, so reluctantly, I got him in the water. This was the beginning of a long therapeutic venture.

We lived on Crawford Street in a three-bedroom house with a very small garage and had a newer building adjacent to the pool. I purchased the house next door, removed the old garage, and concreted a large area where we could park up to four cars between the two houses. We built a rear patio with a huge brick grille, fenced the backyard in, and converted the remaining building into a pool house where we would spend many hours over the next few years.

Winter came and went, and I couldn't wait to get back to the pool with Randy. He had shown some minor progress, but still could not use his right arm. We were working an untold number of hours at the plant and were bursting at the seams. I had to find time to work with my son. I came home every day and would work with him in the pool. He was beginning to get over his fear and showed positive signs. In the evening, we would spend an hour or so working out; but it would be a long, hard trek.

Mom was not doing well, and the old house was terrible for them; plus it was some distance from other family members. In late spring, I purchased a mobile home; and my brother-in-law Jack and I hauled it to Alabama, set it up, and moved Mom and Coleman into it. We set it on Grandma's old property where Mom was born. This would be far more comfortable for them because it had all modern facilities, two bedrooms, and was small enough that Coleman could take care of it since Mom was unable to. We hired a cousin to look in on Mom and help Coleman maintain things.

Back in Elkhart, Ella Mae had begun showing similar signs that Mom had, and I became concerned. I was twenty-four years old, and believing that my productive life would end at around fifty, I had to make sure that my family would be taken care of financially. I still wanted to retire at age forty-seven; but instead of having our fourth child, which we had planned early on, we decided that if we could do a good job raising the three we had, that would be enough.

We only took enough salary from the business to pay our way. All of the earnings of the company were put back into the company. It still took a fair amount for us to live on. We had paid for the trailer for Mom and Coleman and still provided them with some money. We took out insurance on both of them, knowing that Mom would not live much longer. I had bought Judy a new car because she was always having to go somewhere, and since she was raising the kids pretty much by herself while I worked all the time, I made sure her car was in excellent condition.

Even though our company was doing very well, I believed there was something out there that I could be better at doing. I had finished my high education and received my GED from American School. I remembered that soon after Judy and I were married, her uncle Dick had offered to pay my way through college and fully support us until I got my law degree and come into law firm. I couldn't accept such a generous offer. I had to make it on my own because I refuse to be a kept man. More importantly, I had the obligation and deep burning desire to help Randy get to a point that he could lead a normal life physically.

If I were going to succeed in life, I would have to have further education. I enrolled in the night session of Indiana University extension in South Bend. I studied business management and accounting and over a period of time began in the prelaw classes.

It was difficult. I worked the plant during the day, coming home once a day to work with Randy. Judy would bring my supper and the kids to the plant every evening, and at six thirty, I would head to school in South Bend. My class finished at eleven, and my home studies ended at about one. In the morning, at six, Judy would bring me breakfast on a tray and lay out my clothing while I ate in bed. In the wintertime, while I was dressing, she would scrape the ice and snow off my car and start it to allow me as much rest as I could get.

Business was still good, school was tough, and I wasn't getting much time with my family. I usually worked most of the day on Saturdays and spent most of Saturday afternoon and evenings in the pool with the kids and some neighbors.

This was beginning to be too much. When I started back to school, I had no specific intentions of getting a particular degree. I wanted to learn accounting, some law, and the general principles of business. I had some pretty good street knowledge by experience and wanted to supplement and increase it. After almost two years, I felt I'd had enough. It was too hard on the family.

I returned to my old routine of working the plant and spending more time at home. Randy had continued to improve and had regained some use of his right arm and hand. We began training him how to eat holding the fork in his right instead of left hand. He had turned six and was about to enter school. He resisted us in every way he could, and it became almost funny. I began playing games with him at the table. I'd challenge him to use his right hand, and I would use my left to eat. Then it would be awkward for both of us. That helped a little, but in furthering the games, I tied his left hand behind his back and rewarded him when he ate with his right hand. He progressed very well. God, he was going to be all right.

Teri was four, and Mike was two. Both of them loved the water and had become excellent swimmers. Mike had started swimming before he learned to walk, and by the time he was two, he could swim the forty-foot length of the pool and always swam underwater. He'd swim to one end, gulp a breath, and under he'd go swimming back to the other end. Bob and Betty were always scared for him; and on several occasions, one of them would jump in the pool intending to help him, and I would call them to leave him alone. "That is the best way. Let him do it himself."

Teri was Grandma's baby, and Betty spoiled her rotten. She developed a bad habit that really scared Judy and me. In the summer of 1963, Mom had taken a turn for the worst, and we were leaving for Alabama. Betty was keeping the kids. We said goodbye and headed for the car. When I got in, I remembered that I had all of my partner Don's keys lying on the dash. I promised him I would leave them at Betty's.

I returned to the house, and as I handed the keys to Betty, Teri wanted them. They were dirty paint shop keys, and I said no, handing them to Betty. Teri started screaming at the top of her voice; then her face began to turn solid dark blue. She turned a full turn like a dancer would do, fell to the floor, and passed out. She was lying perfectly still on the floor unconscious and was breathing so lightly that you could barely see her chest move. I thought she may have swallowed something. I grabbed her up and threw her over my shoulder, beating on her back while Betty called the ambulance.

As the paramedics were approaching, I was standing at the edge of the street and rushed her to them. For the first time, she moved, and the blue face subsided. The medics worked with her for a while and communicated with the hospital and her pediatrician, Dr. Campbell. After a few minutes, she was up and running around in fine condition, and the medics said that she had passed out from holding her breath in anger.

Judy and I left for Alabama, and the kids were all fine while we were gone. Mom was in really bad condition, and we knew there was nothing more anyone could do for her except make her as comfortable as possible. We returned home.

The business had accumulated some surplus cash, so Don and I purchased a little new house near the plant and rented it to an employee. Don lived in Nappanee, about fifteen miles south of the plant, and he became aware that there was a restaurant and tavern downtown that was for sale This particular business was quite profitable, but would require daily hands on management.

Don and I agreed that we would purchase it, but would need another invested partner to give us good administrative control. We took in a man by the name of Warren Burke. Don would take over the overall management and run one shift while Warren would run the second shift. We were open eighteen hours a day, from 6:00 a.m. to midnight. We changed the name of it to Burke's Bar. I would remain and manage the paint operation. We had outgrown our facilities and barely kept up with required production. We were transporting over twenty-five units a day from the east side of town; and our largest customer, who had been close enough to us to haul the units to our plant with a farm tractor, was moving to that area. We found a huge paint building right in the center of the area and leased it.

We had just gotten our production under control in the new facilities, and the travel trailer industry was converting from unpainted aluminum siding to a factory precoated aluminum. Even though there was still paintwork required on every unit built, the amount of work was far less. We were still painting the inside of all of them, but the per-unit income was less.

I began to see the trend that was developing. The next major move in the industry would be to use prefinished interior panels the same as the mobile home industry had done. If this were the case, there would be a tremendous market for cabinets and cabinetry parts. We had a second building on-site that had not been completed. I made an agreement with the landlord to finish the building, and once done, I started a cabinet shop called Mobilcraft Wood Products.

Our first day of production was November 22, 1963, the day Kennedy was assassinated. Immediately, we were covered up with more work than we could handle in this facility. We still owned the factory building where we started B&D Paint and were using it for some special off-line operations and had been phasing it out. This building would be perfect for our cabinet operations.

I decided to sell my interest in the B&D Paint and Burkes Bar. Don and I agreed that we would work a sale and exchange of stock from our holdings where I would own the old building property, and he would own 51 percent of B&D Paint, and we would both sell our interest in Burkes Bar to Warren.

Within two months, we had the deal completed. Don now owned 51 percent of B&D and had a new partner, Lionel Smead, who had purchased enough stock from my shares to give him 49 percent. Warren purchased all of the Burkes Bar stock, and I owned 100 percent of Mobilcraft. Don and I sold the house to the employee that had rented it. We parted company as partners, but remained friend for many years.

Chapter Twelve

Randy was still progressing, Michael was growing like a weed, and Teri was still pulling her "I'm gonna pass out if I can't have my way" action. We had taken her to the doctor several times, and the doctor said she was perfectly healthy. Every time she did it, I was scared. Her face got so blue, and she'd lie so still. The doctor had no idea what we should do about it, but assured us that it was impossible for her to hurt herself by willfully holding her breath, even to the point that she passed out. We had to get this situation under control.

The kids and I were in the living room while Judy was in the kitchen preparing a meal. I had ordered Teri to do something, and she rebelled. I told her again and proceeded toward her. She did her little "turn around in a circle" move, her face began turning blue, and she collapsed to the floor. I'd had it with this program. I ran to the refrigerator and got a glass of ice water while she lay on the floor with her face turning bluer and bluer. I dashed the entire glass of ice-cold water in her face, and instantly, she spat and sputtered but was wide awake and alert and began to cry. I picked her up and quietly explained that she should not do this, and if she ever did it again, I would use more than a glass of ice water. That ended it forever . . . She never did it again.

In February, I moved Mobilcraft into our old building. Business boomed, and we needed more room. I purchased the residential property next to the plant and converted it into offices and added a huge showroom on to the building. I worked more hours at Mobilcraft than ever before, and most weeks turned into seventy to ninety hours that I was away from home working.

Judy and I owned the house next to ours, a big duplex on the south side of town, and a four-unit apartment building uptown. There was always something that needed to be cared for with the properties, which required my time even though I had a couple that lived in a unit at the quads that took care of most everything there. I began a major effort to relieve myself from this hectic pace. I desperately needed a plant manager because we were growing.

Brother Jim had moved back to Alabama some time back but called me one day, asking how jobs were in Elkhart. Jim and I had never been close; but he was a good worker, smart, and dependable. I offered him the job, and he came back to Elkhart, which relieved me considerably. I rented the house next to mine to the Hartman family. They had three girls, ranging from eleven to fifteen years old, and Mr. Hartman hired in as our deliveryman. That solved the maintenance time I had to spend on that property.

In November, Mom died. She was little more than a skeleton covered with skin. The death certificate listed the cause of death as a stroke. I knew it was not, but did not yet know the name of the disease. Since sister Ella Mae was showing some early signs of the illness, Jim, Shirley, and I shared a concern for our well-being. I began an in-depth investigation of this disease and concluded that it was called Huntington's chorea. There was no known cure, and very little was known about the disease.

Over the recent years, several of my relatives had developed symptoms; but all were in denial, which is one of the characteristics of the disease. The victims don't really know that their communications skills are waning and pay little attention to the involuntary jerky movements of their limbs until the disease progresses for a few years. I detected the signs early in its stage because I had lived with it all my life. As far as Ella Mae was concerned, Grandpa got hurt when the limb from the tree fell on his head and certainly did not pass on a bad gene.

Mom had been buried a couple of months, and I was still thinking of all her misery and suffering but honestly felt that she was far better off now than before.

Our work came to an abrupt halt for a number of reasons. It was industry-wide and only about three weeks before Christmas. I had to do something to keep our people busy because under no circumstances would I lay them off just before Christmas. I couldn't get any orders from within the industry, so we took on a couple of custom jobs and whatever came along.

We needed a project to keep our people going. I talked to some people at the church, and they told me they had several families with kids that were really down and out and would not have anything for Christmas—even food. I asked them to make me a list, which they did. I took the list to the plant, and at break time, the employees and I discussed what we could do. We got a few ideas, but I wanted us to do something that would keep the people busy until Christmas. There were twenty-two children's names on the list, so I decided we would design a huge toy box and fill it full of groceries for the families. We got the input from everybody and decided on a design. These boxes were large, heavy, sturdy, and gorgeous.

We were in the middle of the project and sitting at break time when it dawned on me how stupid I was to decide to make toy boxes. This was not going to work. Giving a family with kids some food could be delivered in a bag. If we gave a toy box, they would expect a toy to be in the box. I apologized to the employees and told them my motive was to have something they could do so their pay would not be affected just before Christmas.

Some of the employees came to me later and said they had an idea. We had about eight ladies and about fifteen men in the plant. The women said their plan would be that some of the men and some of the women do all the normal production, and the rest of them would finish the toy boxes and provide presents for the twenty-two children. The ladies collected dolls and little girl toys while the men made toys for the boys. Our truck driver began soliciting money and goods from every customer and supplier that he came in contact with.

After a few days, many people heard what we were doing, and they all gave something. All of a sudden, we had about five thousand dollars in cash. The ladies washed and cleaned all the toys, bought new clothes for the dolls, and made sure all twenty-two children had at least two nice toys. Then they started shopping. They went to the supermarket and told the manager what they were doing. He pitched in and sold them two for one on anything they wanted. They got canned ham, sweet potatoes, cranberry sauce, cakes, cookies, bread, and on and on. The service station that serviced our vehicles called the wholesale candy store and bought two hundred dollars worth of candy.

Near Christmas, the chairman of the board from Patrick Industries, Mr. Mervin Lung, called me. He had learned from our truck driver that one of the families on the list was a man who worked for him. He was a new employee that had moved here from West Virginia. His little boy had just started school, fell, and burst his kidney. They had no insurance because he had to wait thirty days to be insured under the insurance company's rules. He sent a five-hundred-dollar check. I told Merv we would give this family special attention.

Two days before Christmas Day, I happened to walk by the time clock. All the time cards were gathered in one spot. I pulled them out of the rack, and no one had clocked in, but they were all there. I went to the plant, and everybody was laughing and carrying on and busy as a bee. They were counting the goods and checking them twice and having a real good time. I asked them what the meaning was for not clocking in. They told me I had let them work long enough without much work and that this day and tomorrow was the employees' contribution to Christmas for these families, and it was unanimous.

On Christmas Eve, we finished getting everything ready to deliver to the families. We cleaned all the equipment and the plant, and I had made arrangements for a small catered party for the employees which, we finished around two in the afternoon. Everyone had the name of the family where they would deliver, the directions on how to get there, and the names of all the kids. Most cars had two people in them and delivered to two families. Our foreman and the office lady took three in our pickup truck, and when all the employees were set to go with their companions and toy boxes, there were five left. We loaded these five on the delivery truck. Paul, our truck driver; Dick, the plant superintendent; and myself headed out. All the boxes were packed to the brim with food and toys. The girls had put the toys right on top so when the lid was opened, they were readily in sight. There were three big shopping bags of food left over after filling the boxes based on the number of people in the family. We placed those groceries on our truck.

We made our first stop at an old boxcar that was on a spur line, which had been long vacated. As we drove down the dirt drive, a car followed us in. We stopped in the yard, and a man got out of the car. A small boy, about ten, was standing in the cracked doorway of the boxcar; and I could see a fire burning in an old potbellied stove behind him. When the man walked to us, the boy came running. We talked to the man and boy for a minute and told them we had a Christmas present for them. We took the box into the boxcar and walked out. The man reached under the seat of his car and pulled out a bottle of whiskey and, while thanking us, offered us a drink. "No thanks, have a Merry Christmas," I declined; and we drove off. I thought, *What a shame. No food but a jug in the car.*

Our next stop was very much the same, but the residence was a little dilapidated old house in the slum district and was so filthy, it was pathetic. I felt sorry for the two kids that lived here.

I would see something I'd never seen on our next stop. We drove into the old county landfill; and looking around, we thought surely, no one lived here. Out pops a little black old lady, and she began chewing us out, telling us that we were supposed to be there yesterday and that she and the kids were real hungry. We explained that we had food and toys, but she would have no way of knowing we were coming. She called out a name, and we said,

"No, ma'am, we are not those people." She invited us in her basement house. It had sticks stuck in the ground around a dugout and oilcloth covering everything exposed to the weather. They had a little wood-fired heater and hand-dug shelves in the dirt walls where a straw bed was made. I was glad to leave because I was having a hard time with what I was seeing.

The next stop was awful. These three kids were the rowdiest and most undisciplined kids I'd ever seen. They about had the toy box ripped apart before we set it down, and the mother never said a word. She'd been drinking and offered us a drink. Merry Christmas and goodbye.

I told the other men, "Let's hurry and get this last one delivered." It was getting late, and I still had to assemble the kids' toys. Almost all the toys my children were getting for Christmas would require some assembly; and Judy had bought Teri a full kitchen set, all of which had to be put together, plus the bicycle for Randy and only the Lord knew what else. My mood wasn't the best, and I'd surely better change it before I got home.

The last stop was at the home of the young man that worked for Mr. Lung, the man who had given us the five hundred dollars. Paul had met him when he was picking up material at their warehouse. We knocked on the door, and both the man and the lady came. The man recognized Paul and was very friendly. We told him who we were and that we heard that their son had a serious injury and inquired as to how the boy was. They had brought him home from the hospital that day, and a nurse was with him at the moment. The lady was a very pretty, kind, but a simple woman. Both of them were scrubbed as clean as one can get, and standing behind them were two of the prettiest, most well-behaved little girls I had ever seen—one about three and the other about five. We told them our story, how we got their name, and that our employees wanted them to have a good Christmas. We also told them we had three grocery sacks full of food in the truck. Both of them began saying they just couldn't take them. But we convinced them it was the right thing to do.

We asked if we could bring the things in, and they agreed. Paul grabbed two grocery bags, and Dick and I carried the box in. The box had to weigh a hundred pounds. Paul returned for the last grocery bag, and the lady set the bags on the table.

The toy box was sitting against the wall, and the two girls were standing about five feet away, staring at the toy box with a quizzical look on their pretty faces. I opened the box, and on top were the two most beautiful dolls I had ever seen. Both the dolls had blonde hair, and both the little girls were blondes. When they saw the dolls, their eyes became huge, yet they just stood there. I looked at the mother and told her it would be all right for the girls to go to the box and see the dolls. The mother told them it was OK to look, and they walked to the edge of the box, and both kept their hands behind their waists.

I looked around the apartment, and it was old, but crisp and very clean. They offered us a cup of coffee, but we declined since we needed to go. We were ready to say our goodbyes, and there were small tears on both their faces. I felt a tug on my pant leg and looked down. The mother looked at the three-year-old and very quietly said, "Don't do that," then continued looking at us again.

I felt the little tug again and looked down at the little girl. She had her hand up and in front of her, motioning for me to bend down. I bent over, and the three-year-old put her arms around my neck and, holding on tight, whispered in my ear, "Mister, thank you for a good Christmas."

The parents weren't the only ones with tears on their cheeks. The girls hugged all of us, and we shook hands with the parents, wishing them the best for their son. "Have a good Christmas," we said and left a very nice and thankful family with lumps in our throat.

Our neighbors the Hartmans moved out of the rental house next door, and there was a young couple that was renting one of our apartments. Bob and Clare Sheldon needed more room, so they moved into the house. They had two children, Brian and Denise, and both were younger than our Mike. They only had one car, and Bob had it at work. Judy was keeping two children for a friend of ours, and all the kids were playing in the yard. They had found some firecrackers and were laying them on the concrete, hitting them with a hammer, and one of them popped.

Little Brian liked it; so he ran in the house and got a .22-caliber rifle shell, put it on the concrete, and hit it with the hammer. He was barefoot, and the shell casing blew into his foot, causing a big slice. He began screaming, and while Denise ran to tell their mother, Judy got there first. Brian's foot was bleeding badly, so Judy rushed him to the bathtub and cleaned the wound and wrapped his foot in a towel. The mother held him in the backseat as Judy drove to the hospital. Brian was scared, and all the way to the hospital, he would keep asking if he was going to die. The girls thought the bullet had hit his foot, but it was the casing and left only a shallow, long cut.

Denise was a cute girl, but she had a habit of pulling her clothes off and running down the sidewalk. She was about three; and several times, I would see her mother chasing after her, and Denise was running around bare bottomed.

They became real good friends and also became good friends with Keith and Marilyn who were very close friends that lived two houses away. The three families had a total of ten children, and there was only one that was over twelve. Many times, all three families would spend hours around the pool. The girls would prepare snacks; and usually, when the kids tired of swimming, the six of us would play cards or some other game in the pool house. We gave a key to the back gate to Keith and Marilyn; in the event we were gone, they and Bob and Clare could enjoy the pool.

Life was getting back to normal; even though I really did not know what normal was, I felt that it was. The business was going good. Judy and I could get away a few hours at a time, and Randy was doing great as I continued his activity in the pool. Our pool had become the attraction for all the kids in the neighborhood. We had so many that I had to put a rule in effect to make sure they were always supervised. No child was welcome unless accompanied by a parent or an adult that brought them.

The Raders across had three kids; our very good friends Keith and Marilyn Bates, two houses away, had five kids; and the Sheldons next door had two. Put a few adults in the pool with this gang, and you have a crowd.

Our three kids

Left to right

Michael, Teri, Randy

Jim was doing a good job, which I knew he would. When I hired him, I told him if he was interested in owning part of the company, I would make some stock available to purchase at whatever the book value was at the time of purchase. Further to this, for every share that he purchased, I would give him a share up to a total of 24 percent of the company. I was reserving 25 percent for my kids, and I would retain 51 percent, which was controlling interest.

After he had been with me for over a year, he had not mentioned purchasing any stock, but I was pleased with his work; and to show my appreciation, one evening, after a long hard day, he and I were in the building alone. Jim was sitting at his desk, and I walked in. We talked about the production and did our planning for the next day, and I told him how much I appreciated his efforts and results. I had paid him exactly the salary that I was taking, and the year-end W-2 tax statements bore this out. We finished our meeting, and I went to my office and returned to Jim's and handed him a stock certificate for 24 percent of the entire company. He casually thanked me and left for the day.

About four months went by, and Jim informed me that he was moving back to Alabama because his wife, JoNell, had some emotional problems that they had been treating her for at the local hospital. We discussed the issue, and he wanted to know if I wanted to buy his stock. I was somewhat shocked and had not expected it. Even though he had not acted in any way upon the offer I had originally made him, I had, out of the goodness of my heart, given him the stock thinking he would continue and have an opportunity to make a fair amount of money.

We set a price, which was several thousand dollars, and terms of the payments. I did not have enough cash to pay him in full, so we had the company lawyer write a sales/purchase agreement setting forth all the terms and conditions. I would have to sell the rental properties in order to pay him. I wrote him a check for one-third of the amount and followed up in three months with another third. As the date for the last payment was approaching, I sold the quad apartments and hoped we would close in time that I would not have to borrow money or take money from other investments to make the payment.

The weekend before the last payment was due, I had a very important task to do regarding family records, and I drove to Alabama. I arrived there on Saturday morning, picked up the information I needed, and learned that Jim was building a new house. I drove there to see him. We began talking, and I helped him string electric wiring for a couple of hours. I reminded him that the last payment was due on the following Friday and that I was cutting the time close because I wanted to wait for the closing of the property I had sold and it might take a couple days after the due date before that happened. But if he really had to have it, I would borrow the money and send it out as soon as I returned home. He assured me he did not have to have the money, and I could take whatever time I needed to make the payment. I returned to Elkhart and arrived home midday on Sunday.

The following week was hectic. I still had not replaced Jim's position and was, again, trying to handle it myself. I stopped by the office late Sunday evening to look at some paperwork, and when I left, I turned the light off and locked up.

The following morning, I arrived at the office at six o'clock, and the lights were on. There was no one scheduled to be in that early, so I was surprised. I entered the office, and there stood brother Jim. I greeted him and asked if he just drove in and how he got into the office, thinking momentarily that I had not locked the door. He had gotten in the night before, and I asked why he had not come to the house. He said he still had a key and was here on business, and that business was to retake possession of his interest in the company because I had not paid on time. Jim was always a prankster and joked around all the time. I laughed, and then he said it was no laughing matter and that he was serious.

I instantly changed from being a brother to being a businessman. I told him I had sent a certified check by registered mail and had mailed it on Thursday, which was postmarked before the due date, and I showed him the postal receipt. He said, "Well, I was supposed to have it in my hands on Friday." I wasn't about to argue the legality even though he was incorrect, so I reminded him that on Saturday, the week before when I stopped at his new house, he approved—allowing me extra time to get the money to him. He responded that the date was in writing within the contract and that what he told me was verbal, so it did not count.

I was livid. Anger was going out the top of my head, but I wanted to handle this the right way. I said, "OK, Jim, get your work clothes on and be ready for work at seven."

"No," he said, "I'm not coming back to work. I just wanted you to know that I still own 24 percent of the company."

I said, "That makes the resolution simple. The corporate charter (the minutes) states very clearly that all stockholders must be full-time employees of the company, and you'll be working for me. I'm sure that won't be easy."

He began crying and said nobody except Mom ever loved him, then left. Later, I learned that the check was delivered to his house on Saturday.

I had made the same stock offer to Ralph Crosby, who was a plant manager in a mobile home plant, but he chose to accept another plant manager position in a company that was a customer of mine. When he began at his new job, we worked together a lot, designing cabinets for the new models he was producing, and developed a good relationship, which would turn into a lifelong friendship.

After several months, Ralph asked me if my job offer was still open. I told him that it was and made him a deal, which—if he accepted—would give him a true opportunity to see if my company would satisfy him. The deal was simple. He was to be the plant manager and have full control of the plant, and he had to follow me in the work routine for thirty days. I wanted him to see how difficult it was, but I was only going to give him about half the normal salary for those thirty days. At the end of thirty days, he was to make the decision as to whether to stay or go.

His thirtieth day was on a Thursday, and this had been a big production month and required a tremendous number of hours to do. That evening, as we planned out the next day, I walked by Ralph's office; and as he sat behind his desk, he had his hands cupped around his face with his elbows on the desk. He was tired and appeared to be whipped. I walked into his office and commented on the fact that this was graduation day, and he wanted to know if he had passed. I answered, "Yes, with flying colors." Then I praised him for the fine job he had done and asked what his decision was.

He answered by telling me that I had almost killed him and that he had not worked this many hours since he left the farm, but that he loved it. He said he liked what he saw and the way I ran my operation. "I'm here for good," he said. I walked to my office and handed the 24 percent stock certificate to him. I never discussed what had happened with brother Jim.

We diversified the company and installed a urethane forming line and several large glue presses. I attended school at Dow Chemical in Midland Michigan for a week to learn how to make Silastic rubber molds that were used to pour the urethane and had an automatic eight-stage rotating pouring machine. We engaged the services of wood-carvers to make our prototypes and could duplicate with exactness every detail of the prototype with our process. Our panel glue machines could produce several hundred panels per day. We had two separate paint finishing operations. The main shop painted all the cabinets and parts that we produced while the secondary paint facility was finishing about seven hundred closets and passage doors per day.

I loved to be with my family, but I worked so much, I was tired while at home. Judy was the strength in raising the kids, but we shared the job of discipline. Teri was more afraid of any discipline I might hand out than she was of that her mother would render.

Mike was the easy one. When he was little, he never lied about doing something he wasn't supposed to do. When he was confronted with an issue, he would immediately own up to it. He learned very quickly that by being truthful, any discipline given would be much less than if he lied.

Randy was different. He had gone through a lot of pain and misery, and I was always proud of him; but without a doubt, we pampered him during the worst of the rehabilitation process. When he was being disciplined, he would stand in front of me or his mother and quietly listen. The instant we finished, he was off as if nothing had happened. Teri would get scared and begin to cry. But little tough Mike would come completely clean and tell you the whole story, regardless of the consequences.

By now, we were learning what it really meant to be a parent, and we thought we did a pretty good job of it. Our kids were happy, were never in serious trouble, and got along real well with one another. I had told each child many times, "You're only on this earth for a short period, and while you're here, you only have two things. First and foremost is God and your personal relationship with him, and secondly, your name. You are known by your deeds and not the words you speak. You must honor both of these to live good and full life."

The kids certainly weren't saints and did a lot of things they should not do. My most favorite story to tell about their discipline is when Mike was about six years old, they and several neighbor kids had written on the brick front of a building and continued writing on the sidewalk about a block from our house. The building housed a company called Smolers. The family was sitting at the dining room table eating as soon as I got home from work. Randy finished very quickly, asked to be excused, and went to his room. Teri followed very close behind Randy to her room. Judy began to talk and said that the kids had gotten in a little trouble that afternoon and had written on the walls and the sidewalk at the Smolers building. I turned to Mike, who had just finished eating. "Son, were you involved in this?"

"Yes, sir," he replied.

"Who else was there?"

Then he began to name all the kids. He had named his brother, so I told him to run upstairs and get Randy to come back to the table with him.

Mike came running back, and Randy moped all the way to the table. I began to question Randy, and he would not admit to his full participation, but admitted he had done a little. This was Randy's way so it would not be a complete lie if the full story were known. He would say that he forgot.

As I questioned Mike, I asked what they had written, and he said that he did not know what the word was. I asked if he could spell it. He looked at Randy and began to spell f—. I asked where he learned to spell the word. Guess what? His brother Randy had taught him. I asked what they had used to write with, and Randy replied that they had used some chalk stone that they found. I pondered the situation as Randy squirmed in his chair. "Ok, boys, here's what you'll do tomorrow. When you get out of school, take your allowance and go to the drugstore (right by the school), and each of you buy a toothbrush and a bar of soap. Take buckets from the pool house and go to Smolers with your buckets of water, your soap, and toothbrush and don't come home until the lettering is all gone. If Smolers is open, walk in and apologize. Any further punishment will depend on how good a job you do removing the writing."

It rained all the next day, and the boys came home with the new toothbrush and soap. When they got to Smolers, they were closed, and the rain had washed the chalk completely away. On my way home from work, I inspected the area, and it was clean as a pin.

I had still been working with Randy, and he was getting a little more use from his arm as time went by. Mike had started Little League Baseball the year before, and I was trying to prepare Randy to play. Randy was ten by now and could throw a baseball about the same distance with his right arm that Mike could. No one ever believed that Randy would ever use his right arm, including Bob, his grandfather.

A couple of years before, Bob bought Randy and Mike a baseball glove, and they were very glad to get them from their grandpa. I looked at Randy's glove, and it was a right-hand one made for those who throw left-handed. I adamantly told Bob I appreciated the gifts for the boys, but under no circumstances will I allow Randy to wear a right-hand glove. "If you want to give him a glove, it will have to be a left-hand one." Bob exchanged the glove for a left-hand one and brought it to Randy.

We kept working, and when Randy was eleven, he started playing competitive baseball and after a while turned out to be a really good player. He and Mike both continued in baseball for many years. My fears about his physical being were over. He had recovered.

When he was about eighteen, he was playing fast-pitch softball and was in right field. The diamond he was on was the longest in the city and was used for traveling teams who were top-shelf players and included a few ex-pro baseball players. With a runner on second, the batter flew a ball to deep right field, which Randy caught on the fence. The runner tagged up and was heading from second to home. Normally, the throw goes to the cutoff man, and you would rarely get the runner out because it takes about two seconds for the normal transition from cutoff to the catcher. Randy fired the ball home, and the catcher caught the ball one foot above the plate, and the runner was out. He did this right-handed, and less than one out of ten healthy players could do it.

Michael was a pitcher, and the best junk pitcher that I had coached in the thirteen years I coached in Little League. Both Randy and Mike made the all-star team within their age group most every year. I was real proud of both of them. They were disciplined young men who loved to participate in sports and knew how to win. Michael and his team were one run away from going to the World Series when he was sixteen or seventeen. He was pitching relief even though he was put in the game before any outs were made. The opponents had scored four runs and had the bases loaded when Mike relieved the other pitcher. Mike gave up one hit, and the fifth run scored. For the rest of the game, not even one player ever set foot on first base. He completely shut them down with knuckle curves and junk they had never seen before. Our team manager made a big mistake in the fifth inning that cost us the game. Mike went on to pitch at his first year of college.

My favorite story about Mike and his baseball pitching was when he was about ten. We had two good pitchers, Mike and Nick. This was the all-star game at season's end. I put Mike in to pitch, and for the first inning, everything was fine. During the second inning, he had a full count on the batter, and the next pitch broke so much that the catcher had a difficult time just stopping the ball, and it had split the plate for a called strike. I called time and went to the mound and asked him what kind of pitch that was, and he said it was a fastball. I said, "Baloney. I do not want to see another curve."

A couple of batters later, he got a full count on the batter and threw the same curveball again. I walked out to the mound and took him out, bringing Nick in. "But, Dad," he said, "I struck him out."

I told him, "That's not the point. The point is I told you not to throw *any* curve." It reminded me of when I was removed from a basketball game after I hit a beautiful hook shot after the coach had instructed the team that there were to be no hook shots.

Teri had played some softball, and several times at the ballpark, we had three different games to watch at one time. Mike in the minor division, Randy in the senior division, and Teri in the girls division.

The economy was way depressed, and the industry was suffering. Jack, my brother-in-law, was still working at Richardson Homes, and for the first time since he worked there, he got laid off. He tried working in a car wash that would only open on nice days, and there weren't very many of those in the late fall. There were six in his family to feed, so he and I made a deal. I bought him a new Bronco with a snowplow so he could have an income during the winter months. The mobile home industry would be back strong by spring without a doubt. Jack maintained snow removal at my business and stayed busy all winter.

Ralph and I had a good relationship and became lifelong friends. We operated Mobilcraft very successfully and sold the company to Patrick Industries in May of 1968. The new owners were a public-held company and requested that I stay with Mobilcraft for a period of sixty days to train two new managers that they had hired. Ralph took an extended and well-earned vacation in Canada. The new managers were very good and efficient, and after thirty days, I really had nothing important to do at work. I discussed this with the president of Patrick, and he agreed. He asked me to come and work out of the corporate office where I would become the vice president in charge of acquisitions.

I moved into the corporate offices and immediately found an operation in Valparaiso, Indiana. They manufactured post-formed countertops. This product would certainly enhance our ability to compete because we then could supply all the countertop needs to our customers, particularly the cabinet customers. What we really wanted was the equipment and the technology to manufacture a rolled-edge cabinet door where we could match with absolute accuracy the grain pattern and colors of wall paneling used inside mobile homes. We purchased the plant in Valpo, and because of union problems, I moved it to Elkhart.

When I made the announcement to the employees that we were moving, the union began to fight it because they would be losing some revenue. Any employee was given the right to make the move with us, but only two of them made the move because it would be about one hundred miles from where they lived. I needed help to phase out the plant, so I called Ralph and told him I had another challenge for him that was bigger than the one he had when he came with me at Mobilcraft. Ralph came immediately, and we made our plans.

After a few days of phasing out the operations, it became obvious that the union officials would go to any extent to keep the plant there. I told Ralph we'd nip that in the bud, and I hired two bodyguards from Elkhart who would be by his side day and night while he was in Valpo. We made the physical move of all the equipment and set up the Midwest Plastics facilities in Elkhart. Once again, Ralph had successfully done a very difficult job and could go back to some well-deserved leisure time.

Ralph and I had been on a couple of fishing trips together, and both loved to spend leisure time with each other. We had gotten to know each other's habits so well that we could collectively tell a yarn about fishing, without rehearsal, and knew exactly what to add to or take away from the embellishment while telling the story to make it entertaining for the listeners. Ralph bought a twenty-one-foot Starcraft boat and took it out with another friend to learn how to handle it on Lake Michigan. He called me and invited me to go fishing, which I quickly accepted. There were five of us: Ralph, his stepson Jim, and his friend Ken, a much older fellow (whom I had never met), and myself.

We got to the lake early and made our plans. We intended to perch fish, but for the few previous days, they had not been schooling in the area we were to fish until early afternoon. We had two gas tanks, and one of them had not been filled yet, but we decided we would take a tour over toward the Chicago side of the lake. We had put in at New Buffalo, Indiana. The water was uncharacteristically calm. Lake Michigan is known for its rough water, and it happens in a hurry.

We rode around toward the west for a long time; and in the calm water, I saw something far off, lying in the water. I jokingly said that it looked like a man's head for the benefit of the two young boys on board. We approached the object, and it was a basketball. I fished it out of the water with a long net, and we decided we should head back to shore. We were going to have lunch, gas up the boat, get our bait, and head for the fishing area, which we planned to be fishing around two in the afternoon. We had been offshore about twenty-five miles and were at full speed heading back.

This beautiful sunny day began to cloud up, and the wind came up. By the time we could see the shore, the waves were pretty high, and we slowed accordingly. We looked onshore for our landmark so we could go directly to the harbor, but we were too far out to spot the harbor. Our landmark was the power plant stack at Michigan City, and New Buffalo was only a few miles north. We decided to turn north and veered closer to the shore. We still could not see the entrance to the harbor, and the waves were too rough to continue in shallow water, so we headed back toward deeper water.

I was looking ahead of the boat, keeping a careful watch for huge waves since we were cornering the waves. I spotted something in the water and told

Ralph that I thought it was a body. Ralph eased over to the spot, and it was a body. I asked the young boys to help me, and we would pull him in. They were scared and refused to help. Ralph had his hands full handling the boat, and the old man was hardly able to walk. I would have to do this by myself because no way were we going to leave him out there. Ralph handled the boat real well and got close enough that I could reach the body with a boat hook that had a rubber snubber on the end. The waves were tossing both of us around, and the snubber would not go under his belt. Ralph threw me a new ski rope, and I hurriedly opened the package I made about a ten-foot loop and threw it in the water around the body. When I retrieved the rope, it didn't catch on to the body; the waves would take it under, and the rope would wash over the top of it.

I tried this several times, and Ralph began to tell me that we were very low on fuel, so I had to hurry. Finally, after several tosses of the rope, as I was retrieving it, the loop caught on the arm of the body; and I quickly tightened it up. I barely could drag it to the boat, and the boys still refused to help because they were frightened by the weather and the dead body. I got the body to the side, and using the boat hook, I wove the rope around the body several times and tied it off to the side rails.

During the long time we were doing this, we could hear a faint noise that sounded like someone talking on a loudspeaker; and soon, it faded away. But looking on shore, we could see tiny red flashing lights. We began moving toward the lights very slowly, and it seemed to take forever. The wind had pushed us north and to the west during the time it took, and we were five miles offshore.

After a very long time, we were approaching shore and knew the water was too shallow for the boat to reach the beach, and we could see the police cars. There were two policemen making their way down the vertical wall on a stairway that the bottom few feet of which had been washed away earlier. They were now within yelling distance and were going to take the body. I tied two large lead weights to the end of the rope and threw the rope to them.

We asked them what they had been saying on the loudspeakers while we were getting the body. They said they could not see us clearly and were telling us that if it were a body to please pick it up. I told the officer I didn't understand why he would ask such a thing, and he explained that they had several cases of drowning every year, and boats would actually pass a body and knowingly leave it out in the lake. We gave them our names and address and asked them which way to New Buffalo Harbor. The officer pointed north. They thanked us, and we were on our way.

We rode for a while and came to the harbor and were very glad because the gas gauge was on empty. We pulled up to the dock, and it was dark. The place was closed. Someone saw us pull in and talked to us. He went and got the man who ran the pumps; we gassed up and were on our way home. After gassing the boat, we had to turn around and head south to New Buffalo. The officer had directed us to St. Joe, which was north.

A few days later, we were going to try perch fishing again and stopped by the bait store on the dock. We learned that the body we had pulled from the water was a twenty-eight-year-old and had been in the cold water for thirty-three days. The water had warmed, causing the body to rise to the surface. The man recognized Ralph and handed him a letter from the father of this man. He and his brother-in-law had been fishing in a small boat; the winds had come up so abruptly that they could not outrun it, and the boat capsized. The brother-in-law made it to shore. The letter expressed sincere appreciation for what we had done. One of the young men on board that day ended up being my barber, and I kid him about that day and being so scared he couldn't help. I'll probably see him tomorrow, and I'll tell him I've written the story after all these years.

Once we got everything rolling at Midwest Plastics, I went to Fort Lauderdale, Florida, and purchased an automatic Bechtel forming line. Once we got the line installed, we began producing one full semiload per day of rolled-edge cabinet doors. We had the plant in full operational order before Christmas and were producing a profit. I decided to leave and go to the next phase of my manufacturing life.

Chapter Thirteen

When I had started B&D Paint in 1960, I hired an independent accounting firm to do our bookkeeping and accounting. The gentleman who came to our office every month was Mr. Don Winkler, who was a member of the Thomas A. Houlihan firm in Fort Wayne. Don had been with me from the day I started, and he and two other accountants purchased their firm and changed the name to Carrol Deal and Winkler. Don was a brilliant accountant and had an uncanny ability to direct me in the right direction in business based upon his knowledge, experience, and trends of the economy.

Ralph and I decided to start a manufacturing plant building travel trailers. We would need an engineer, so we invited my neighbor and a very good friend Keith Bates to join us in the start-up. I insisted that we would need Don, and the others agreed. In December 1968, we started Brentwood Inc., and began building trailers under the brand name of Continental. We would later change the corporate name to Continental Trailers Inc.

We rented a building on Elkhart Avenue downtown, and by March, we were producing three units a day. We continued growing, and early in 1969, we had to start a second plant where we built campers for pickup trucks. We had prototyped a full fiberglass-bodied motor home and were growing so fast that we could barely keep up.

Ralph was one of the best, if not the best, production managers I knew. Keith had great skills in drafting and engineering and material procurement, and I ran the business end and was president of the company. Don guided us in every respect regarding financial matters. We had a sales manager experienced in the industry, and each person did their job very well. Manufacturing and outside storage space were limited as was operating capital. We established controls that would optimize our production and limit our unsold finished products based upon the space and capital available.

To assure a positive cash flow and that units flowed in the delivery process, we set parameters and limits of the number of units that were allowed to remain in line and in the storage lot. The minute that limit was reached, production would cease, and the employees would have to go home until sales reduced the number of units in inventory. This happened one time in the first two years. It made no difference as to whether all the units were sold or not. This put the burden and responsibility on the sales department to perform and get the units shipped on time. Our attitude was very simple. We didn't get paid until you saw the taillights go down the road.

By late 1969, we were producing seven units a day in the downtown plant and three truck campers a day in the other plant. In our camper plant, we began building jigs and fixtures to begin another plant, which would be in Pennsylvania.

When all the jigs and fixtures were complete, we rented a building in Hamburg, Pennsylvania, and transported several loads of equipment to the plant. We rented an entire small motel nearby and sent a crew who would live there until production was going. Keith went to Hamburg to manage the operations.

Soon after getting the Hamburg plant going, we purchased a large building in Elkhart and moved the Elkhart plants into the one building. We were gradually increasing production in both our locations and were displaying our units at all the major trade shows throughout the Midwest and the East.

We immediately outgrew the plant in Hamburg and purchased land at the intersection of the east-west toll road in Shartlesville, Pennsylvania, a few miles from Reading, and constructed the most modern travel trailer and motor home manufacturing plant in the industry. The travel trailer production was in line, but the motor home line was an automatic line where the units traveled sideways through all the workstations with automatic scaffolding that folded into place as the line moved, driven by underfloor cable systems.

We were making some inroads in the industry and were becoming a viable competitor in the marketplace, but to continue growing and being competitive would require plants in several geographical locations. Our master plan was to have five plant locations, which would be Elkhart, Shartlesville, Pennsylvania, one in the southeast, one in the northwest, and one in Canada. Freight was very expensive, which was the underlying reason for locating in these areas.

We found a suitable location for a plant in Elberton, Georgia, and rented facilities. In about two months, we had this plant running three units a day. It had become a hectic world, but we were doing pretty well considering all the fast growth.

Keith was doing well in Pennsylvania running our most profitable plant. Ralph was vice president, in charge with all engineering and production. Don still ran his accounting firm in Fort Wayne, but spent a lot of time analyzing and monitoring our financial position. I was going crazy keeping up with new products and overall management and decided that we needed something that no other manufacture had. I discussed this with my partners, and soon, Ralph came up with a product that if done right would set the industry on its competitive heels.

After we moved into the new plant in Elkhart, brother Jim called to inquire as to how jobs were. He had, once again, moved back to Alabama, but now found that he needed a better-paying job. I asked Ralph to interview him, and Ralph hired him to work in the purchasing department. Jim had been there a few months, and Ralph had promoted him to plant manager, which freed some of Ralph's time. Now he could pursue the new product idea that he and I had discussed.

We rented a large enclosed bay in a huge building to prototype the new product, which no one was to see except Ralph, the on-site engineer, and myself. Ralph had off-line production construct the running gear, frame, and general outer shell, which looked very much like any other unit on the market, and transported this shell to the rented building where Ralph and I worked on the design every chance we could and spent a number of nights with unusual tools, which included chain saws, big chisels, contouring tools, and some big sanders. We cut, formed, and fitted every conceivable angle, securing them together to make a mold that would form a complete body about thirty-two feet long for the most modern fifth wheel in the world. After we polished every square inch of the mock-up, we had a company make a fitted canvas covering so no one would be able to see the profile until we were ready to show it. To keep anyone from seeing it, Ralph and I towed the mold unit to the plant that produced the Corvette body, and the project was rolling along.

This type of project was very expensive, and before we would even get the molded body, we had over a hundred thousand dollars invested in this project. We were growing fast, but sales expense for travel was very high, and the cost of freight was making it difficult to compete in certain markets. We decided that our next plant would be in the southwest.

So in preparation for that potential move, we rented space at the rail yard in Irving, Texas, as the FOB point and put in a fair-size inventory so we could compete in that general area.

The move after this would have to be Canada. My partners and I discussed this many times, and during the general time that the subject was hot on the burner, we received an offer to sell the company. We weighed the situation carefully and knew that in order to continue our growth, we would have to make a huge investment in the millions for two more new plants, or we could negotiate the offer that we had gotten. The interested company was very heavily involved in the automobile industry, providing stamping and metal forming equipment to the big three. They also were the largest manufacturers of steering wheels and manufactured ambulances and hearses, and they were also the largest school bus manufacturer in the world.

We decided to take their offer, which was to be a tax-free exchange. I would be required to stay with the company for ninety days, and my stock was lettered and could not be sold for one year. The other three shareholders were under no constraints regarding selling their stock and had no requirement of employment. The day we closed the deal, we had 262 employees in our three plants.

The new owner was Sheller Globe Corporation, who had its home offices in Toledo, Ohio. It was a rule of thumb in those days that the administrative personnel represented about 10 percent of the total workforce in our industry. When Sheller Globe did a detail analysis of our three companies, they found that we only had seven nonproduction people, not including the sales force. They came to me to learn how we were doing it. They had given their word that no changes in basic operations would be made and that internal organization would be unchanged.

Before my ninety-day workout period was finished, my boss came to me and asked me to stay with the company. They would give me a vice president's position, and I would be in charge of four of their twenty-two divisions, and my salary would be almost double that which I had been making when we owned the company. I became a member of the corporate acquisition committee that met frequently at the corporate offices in Toledo and served on the products manufacturing committee, which met once a month in Lima, Ohio, to review and evaluate the merit of any new product that the corporation would enter into production. I would report to the senior group vice president, Mr. Dwayne Shields.

I had attended a few meetings and gotten to know several of the officers of the company, and Mr. Shields showed an interest in me. He wanted me to attend a special school, which was the American School of Management, which was holding a special session in Boca Raton, Florida. I had been in management a long time, but Mr. Shields wanted me to bring myself up-to-date with the current accepted methods of management that had proven to produce the highest level of productivity and how to maintain the best relationship with the employees of different levels, working in an environment much larger than the work environment that I was accustomed to. My secretary set up the schedule, and after just under two weeks of ten-hours-a-day classes, I passed the examination and received my certification from the ASM.

I have always been a planner and diligently try to prepare for any meeting that I attend. The last thing I want to do is waste someone's valuable time with superfluous or meaningless information.

Late one evening, I got a direct-line phone call from Mr. Chester Devenow, who was president and chairman of the board of Sheller Globe. I had been in his presence several times and liked him. He asked if I could be at the corporate boardroom in Toledo at eight the next morning. I asked him what the purpose was for me being there and how I could prepare for it. He told me there was nothing I needed to prepare for but to just be there. Toledo was an hour ahead of Elkhart, so I had to leave around four in the morning to make sure I was there on time.

Dressed in my very best suit, I arrived there about seven thirty and went to the Ivory Tower, as it was referred to. I checked in with the receptionist and saw a large number of people milling around. I knew the boardroom only seated twenty-two people, and there had to be forty there already. Some workers were bringing in chairs and lining the walls on both sides.

Shortly before eight, Mr. Devenow stood at the head of the table and directed everyone to take a seat. As they began seating themselves, I waited at the entrance door. I was thirty-three years old; and most of these people were considerably older and included the past president of Ford Motors, Mr. John Filstra, the chairman of the board of Westinghouse, the president of General Electric, and a list too numerous to mention. I was not about to mistakenly take one of their seats.

When about all of them had sat down, Mr. Devenow motioned for me to sit at his right hand. I was a little nervous because normal protocol in the corporate world considers this seating position to be "the hot seat," meaning simply that the primary business to be taken up will involve the one in this seat.

I still had no idea of what the meeting was about nor what was expected to be accomplished at that meeting. Mr. Devenow opened the meeting and gave a little institutional speech, telling those present in general terms that the company had entered into the recreational vehicle industry through the acquisition of my company and continued speaking about Superior's new entrance into the motor home field with a plant in Mississippi. All of the people there sitting around the walls and several at the board table were taking notes. It then became apparent what we were doing. This was a hype session to glorify the company's being in this new field and showing the world that the company had great expectations of future profitability.

The RV industry was the hottest thing going from a stock market standpoint, and all the major news media were represented. The *Wall Street Journal*, *Time*, *Life*, *Field & Stream*, and all the big magazines and newspapers had a representative there.

Mr. Devenow ended his talk and offered to answer any questions. After answering a few, he introduced me as the previous owner of the RV companies they had acquired and instructed me to speak to the point of who we were, where we fit within the industry, and what our future looked like. I gathered my thoughts and began to speak, describing our operation, the number of plants and their locations, number of different models and quantities of each that we produced, the number of employees, our gross sales each year, the percentage of growth per year, and our profits. I ended speaking after about ten minutes and offered to answer any questions that I could. There were several, which took another ten minutes or more. When the news media questions stopped, an officer of the company asked me a question.

Mr. Hahn—the corporate executive vice president, second in command—was seated directly across the table from me and said he had a question. Mr. Hahn was a Jewish man, whom I had seen only on a couple of occasions. I knew little about him, including that the majority of the other officers in the company felt he should retire as he had long passed the normal retirement age of sixty-five.

Mr. Hahn made a particular move, which I knew was considered as the Jewish power move. He leaned forward in his chair as far as the table would allow, placed his elbows on the table, and clasped his hands, one over on top of the other, and looked me straight in the eye. His voice was gruff, and he began to speak in somewhat of a curt manner. "Well, Bobby, you're a young man of thirty-three now working in this great company, Sheller

Globe. Tell me, on a personal level, what is it that you personally expect for yourself in the future?"

First, I was offended by his gesture; and second, my personal aspirations had nothing to do with the profitability of Sheller Globe. Being offended, I sat in silence for quite a long time and silently asked God for help in formulating my answer. It was so quiet in the room, you could have heard a pin drop. Instantly, the answer came to mind. I leaned forward as far as I could, placed both elbows on the table, and clasped my hands. Looking Mr. Hahn directly in the eyes, I responded, "Mr. Hahn, I believe that the normal response to that question from an average thirty-three-year-old man would be that they would work hard and show great diligence and aspire to holding Mr. Devenow's position as chairman. But, sir, that is not what I want . . ." Every page on the reporters' writing pads could be heard as they turned them. "Sir, I want your job."

There were smiles all around the room. The meeting ended; and as we were leaving the building, Dwayne caught up to me, put his arm around me, laughed, and said, "What a great job! I'm taking you out to breakfast."

Getting acclimated to my new position was difficult. I had to spend some time at all the different divisions that I was charged with to familiarize myself with their products, processes, and procedures while researching new companies for potential acquisition. We had two corporate planes; and for the first three months, I used them a lot, traveling to California, Canada, Pennsylvania, Georgia, Mississippi, and Ohio. Life was hectic, and most days required a lot of extra hours to stay abreast of business. We had our own internal security and legal staff and a huge engineering staff from which to draw personnel that could be assigned to different divisions as the need arose.

I was at a point that I could spend some time in our Elkhart plant where we were going to manufacture the new fifth wheel that Ralph and I had prototyped. The fiberglass plant in Michigan was ready for us to make the final inspection of a finished body and needed to have final confirmation for the precise locations of all the cut and trim lines. Corporate engineering had become involved and decided that the job was too complicated to follow the procedures of assembly with this product as we did with all other vehicles and brought five automotive engineers in, three from Ford and two from General Motors.

We had another new product under way, so Ralph and his staff were so busy that they left the final decisions of all the cut lines to this group of engineers. This new product was an ambulance or rescue vehicle that had the same chassis and body, but was outfitted differently. We took a full-size Chevy van and sliced the entire body in half from the front bumper over the hood and roof to the rear bumper and then widened the entire vehicle by fourteen inches. We put extenders on both bumpers, rebuilt the hood, installed a new windshield and new rear doors, and installed a formed top that raised the roof, which provided enough room to stand. The interior was equipped according to the order, and the exterior was finished in white and red; and pretty soon, we were seeing eight a day rolling down the line.

We had purchased a mobile home plant that was going bankrupt. I closed the operation for thirty days, reorganized the management, and modified the product line. After thirty days, we began production; and by the third month, we were producing three top of the line homes a day.

About the time we purchased the mobile home company, my boss, Dwayne Shields, had come to see me. Dwayne was a wonderful man, a great person to report to, and had become a friend. We had lunch, and Dwayne asked me if I would object to temporarily reporting to a different person and proceeded to explain why. On the organization chart, my position—in charge of one-third of the now twenty-two divisions—would fall as the fifth one from the top of the corporate structure, and his was number three. The fourth position was in finance and not directly involved with manufacturing. There was a major union problem at one of the plants outside my jurisdiction, which involved about four hundred employees. The plant was in Iowa and was one of the biggest profit centers within the corporation, and this union issue would have to be resolved quickly.

Dwayne proceeded to say that they had found a man who was working as the general foreman at General Motors who they felt could resolve this problem. But for him to have the influence that would be acceptable to the union during negotiations, he would have to hold one of the top positions in the corporation, and they wanted to give him the title of group vice president. The four vice presidents, of which I was one, would have to report to this position; but it would be temporary.

I did not understand why this was necessary because titles never indicated to me what a person's ability was, but it was acceptable because Dwayne asked me.

The new group vice president was Dale Wonus. He was hard-nosed, didn't care about anybody as to what they thought, and insisted you do everything he wanted even when he was wrong. I met him during his orientation time and then did not see him for a while since he was occupied with the union problem in Iowa. He had not been in Iowa for more than a month, and the Teamster union officials showed up at my Elkhart plant with the intent to organize our operations. I told them to leave the property, and they told me I'd best call my lawyer. I called our legal department and found there was absolutely *nothing* that I could do. They were entitled to be in my plant, disrupt production, hold meetings with the employees, and do *anything* they wished to do.

I hated unions with a passion. Two years before, these same people hijacked one of our travel trailer toters, threatened the driver, demolished the three trailers on the lowboy, and did several thousand dollars' damage to our truck. The next day, they fired a huge-caliber bullet into the hood of a contract driver's tow truck, disabling the engine, and kidnapped the driver and his girlfriend. The driver's name was Ben Wilder. The Teamster people held the couple for four or five days. The first event happened in Ohio, and the second in Michigan. The police, sheriff's department, the FBI nor any other agency would take no action of any nature. I talked to John Brademas and Birch Bayh, who were congressmen from our area, and even they would take no action.

I was at the end of my rope. I had our shipping manager set a meeting with all our drivers and sales department personnel and ordered anyone who towed one of our vehicles out on the open road to attend this meeting. I told them of the situation and that for safety's sake, we would stop all shipments until further notice, which would mean we very soon would have to close down production. Everyone to the last person objected because they had to have an income. I told them unemployment compensation was available, but that was still not acceptable. They wanted to continue and needed to work. We collectively devised a plan.

My private secretary—I lovingly called her Sam—prepared a written statement, collected all the phone numbers we would need, and, from my office on my private phone, called every law agency on a state and federal level. When Sam got the person on the phone that I wanted to speak with, we turned the speakerphone on and advised the listener that they were on a speakerphone, that only the two of us could hear the conversation, and that the conversation was being recorded.

I told the listener that I had a prepared statement to read and proceeded to read it. It was about the union activity, what had happened to our drivers, and that our people had to make a living. Further, that no law agency would do anything about the lawless actions the Teamsters were engaged in; therefore, in self-defense and to protect our interest, we would have an expert shotgun rider in all our delivery vehicles. Their response was varied, but ineffective.

Every unit of ours that went down the road for the next couple of weeks had an armed person in the passenger seat. This was a terrible way to get a job done, but when the greedy union officials who care nothing about their members can do violent acts and remain untouchable, enough became enough.

The Teamsters were in my Elkhart plant for about thirty days. Production had fallen by 25 percent as they rallied the new employees around their doctrine. I was not allowed, at any time, to talk to the employees in a group meeting. I needed to assess where this thing was going and had to do it by happenstance. I decided a simple course of action was in order to negate further influence by the Teamsters. My plan was to get a less-powerful union in the other plants, and if I was successful, all the orders would be filtered to one of these plants and eventually close the Elkhart operations if the union won the vote.

I drove to Reading, Pennsylvania, and met with officials of the Textile Workers Union of America, who were a recognized union. I handed them a contract proposal for the Pennsylvania plant, and within an hour, they agreed. The following day, the personnel department hired a young blond man off the street, and he began advocating the union. Officials came, the employees voted, and now they were represented by the Textile Workers Union of America.

I flew to Georgia and met with the Granite Workers Association and did the same thing.

Back in Elkhart, the day to vote to accept the Teamsters came. The union was defeated. They spent many hours going over their records, recounting the vote, and wanting to take a revote. The moment the votes had been counted, all of the legal restrictions that had been placed on me—prohibiting meeting with employees and restricting where I could be in the plant at certain times—were lifted.

I was given the news and learned about the officials not willing to accept the results. I called my brother-in-law Jack, who worked for us, and asked him to the office. I told Jack to get three other employees and himself and meet me where the two union officials were still trying to figure out a way to set the vote aside. I approached the two union men and told them that it was time to leave; that they had cost me and my company many hours of work, anguish, and hundreds of thousands of dollars in lost production; and that I had absolutely no use for the union officials. Then they began to give me all the reasons and rights they had to continue.

I pulled my coat back, exposing a .38 automatic, and very sternly said, "Let's go." Along with the four other men, I escorted these terrible greedy people to the front gate. They kept threatening me all the way to the gate, but when we arrived there, I told them I had one very important thing to say to them. "Hopefully, our paths will never cross again. I want you to go back to your—organization and tell them that from this day forward, if any Teamster official sets foot on my property, they will not leave."

Things were going well at the new mobile home plant. We had made a profit in our full second month of operations after restarting the plant and were on track to earn a better profit in December. Christmas was near, and I received a phone call from my new boss, Dale. I could hear a lot of partying going on in the background, and Dale had been drinking. He and his staff were holding their Christmas party. He was very direct. He said, "Dutton, close down the mobile home plant."

I told him, "We are making money. Why should we close it?"

His answer was, "Because I said so. Close it today."

His curtness upset me, and I responded, saying, "It's holiday time, and there's no way that I will close the plant during the holidays. If you want it done, come on over and do it yourself. I will confirm this order with corporate headquarters and proceed accordingly."

After the holidays, I met with all the employees at the mobile home plant and advised them that we were getting out of the mobile home business, but every employee could transfer to one of our other plants since we were upping production. I had not closed a plant before and referred to the corporate policy manual for instructions. I called security and requested they send two guards to monitor the closeout.

Sam made reservations at the Holiday Inn for the guards, and they were to call me on Sunday by noon when they arrived. I had received no call, and no one would be at corporate on Sunday, so I had no way to communicate with the guards. Late Sunday evening, they called me from a little motel on the east side of town. They told me they had gotten lost and were late getting there and took the first place to sleep that they came to. I felt something wasn't right, but would not learn the facts until later. I gave them directions and their instructions and met them the following morning where I was to inform the employees of the closing. The guards set their schedule, and the employees began finishing all the units that were in the line. I monitored the situation very closely because we wanted to make sure we retained as many of the experienced people that we had for the other operations.

Late Wednesday night, I received a call from the fire department advising me the plant was on fire. I drove the ten miles to the plant and watched as it burned out of control. Years ago, at Richardson's, I had seen our paint facilities burn; but this building was ten times larger, and the fire raged out of control. It was a total loss.

The next morning, I talked to security at corporate and advised them of the fire and discussed the security guards. The guards were not part of our security team; they were hired by Dale Wonus from General Motors' security pool. Obviously, he knew them from when he was at GM. Security sent a full team of investigators, and, along with the local authorities, determined that the fire was arson; and needless to say, everybody included me was a suspect.

As the investigation proceeded, the local law enforcement had a tail on me everywhere I went. Finally, I tired of being followed and went to Michael Cosentino, who was the assistant county prosecutor and a friend of mine, and discussed the matter. They made a close investigation of my activities and cleared me.

In the second week of the investigation, they solved the case. The guards had set the fire and let it burn long enough to be out of control, then called the fire department. All that was left of the building was a section of the offices, and three of them were usable. The investigation team was sitting in the first office and heard a gunshot. They ran to the office where the shot was fired, and one of the guards from GM shot himself in the toe. They took him to the hospital, and after treatment, he said he could not help guard the premises any longer and was going back to Detroit. The investigators knew he had been involved in setting the fire and called the local sheriff's office, and both guards were arrested and charged with arson. Within two days, both were out of jail and gone, never spending any more jail time nor ever had a trial.

The facts were that Dale Wonus had not sent our own guards who were available but, for some reason, had sent these two. They burned the place down, resulting in my division losing somewhat over a hundred thousand dollars after all the insurance was settled, and that did not include the building that we were leasing from a Mr. Roy Beck. They were not prosecuted, and I never understood the reason; however, I would not remain with Sheller Globe much longer.

By this time, Dale had virtually tried to take over manufacturing throughout the corporation. I had no use for him because he was dishonest and treated everyone very poorly. He had been successful in causing our Elkhart plant to be in a bad position where we could barely make a profit. He increased the monthly fee we paid to corporate just from the Elkhart plant to about twenty thousand dollars a month, removed sales from my people's control, loaded the plant with a major excess of people who were supposed to report to him but were placed on my division payroll, and ordered thirty-seven new offices to be constructed at our site. While waiting for the new offices through corporate, he purchased a huge mobile office so he could have one of his cronies, Ed Woodward, on-site to tell him every move that was made daily. Ed did nothing. He was supposed to be in charge of sales for several divisions, but never sold one single product while he was with us.

We had taken the first new fifth wheel to the Louisville show. Word had spread within the industry and dealer network about this new product, which up to now only our employees had seen. We continued to keep it covered with the custom-fit canvas cover. We had advertised for a period of time and had a huge sign at the display that we would only take the first thirty orders and that a deposit of two thousand dollars would be required, which would be forfeited in the event of cancellation.

The announcement came over the loudspeaker that the show was officially open at precisely 8:00 a.m. The signs stated that we would unveil the unit at show opening time, and the crowd was big. A long line was forming. We lifted the canvas, and the line proceeded through the unit; and within an hour, we had written thirty orders, with deposits, and had set up a waiting list.

This fifth wheel was so different in construction and had electronic, I should say electrically operated, controls because this was long before computers and small circuit boards were readily affordable. We had automatic sensors everywhere, which switched about everything. When the door was unlocked and someone approached the door, the step would be activated and slide out. The lights and entertainment center could be remotely operated. When a towing vehicle backed under the front end to hook up, the connector plate on the fifth wheel would automatically align with the hitch plate on the towing vehicle; and when you parked the unit and set it up for an extended stay, there were four automatic leveling jacks, which leveled perfectly and would also level the refrigerator, which was a requirement for continuous operations of refrigerators in travel units at that time.

We had tested the unit extensively and had engineers on the project every step of the way, but anything that is new and different would expose the company to possible major warranty costs, and we limited the exposure to thirty units. We had orders standing with the body manufacture for a large number of bodies, but would not put them in production until further field tests were made on the first thirty.

The engineers from Ford had made a major change in how the front colored glass windows would be installed, which delayed our colored adhesive design strips from 3M Corporation. Our first of the new fifth wheels had rolled off the production line, and we were anxious to finish off the exterior accent stripes, but we had not received them from 3M Corporation. We decided to use a paint application on the first unit.

It was about noon, and I spent a few minutes at the lunch tables with some of the employees, and they told me they were having trouble getting the paint to adhere. The unit was all masked and ready for etching, so I volunteered to help resolve the problem because of my paint experience. After a few minutes, I found the problem, corrected it, and told the worker that was to paint it to let me do it. It was not going to be a messy job and would only take about ten minutes to apply the coatings. I jumped on the scaffold and painted the unit.

Then I left that area and had a discussion with Ralph; then he and I went to the assembly line to talk to brother Jim, who at this time had become plant manager and was monitoring the new assembly processes. We took about twenty minutes or so, and as I was returning to my office, Ed Woodward met me in the hallway. He told me that Dale had been there and saw me out on the scaffold painting the fifth wheel and was really angry, so angry he immediately got back in his car and headed back to Toledo.

I laughed, making a comment to Ed that we had to do whatever it took to get the job done, and it wasn't about what Dale Wonus liked or disliked. I went into my office, and minutes later, Sam entered. She spoke very softly while standing in the doorway and said that Mr. Wonus was on the phone, calling from the service plaza on the toll road at the Indiana-Ohio state line, and he was angry. I told Sam to put the call on my regular line and for her to listen on her phone and record the conversation by shorthand.

I picked up the phone and said hello. From that point on, Dale did all the talking, except for two words. He said, "Dutton, you are an officer of the 384 largest companies in the country. And as such, you will act like one and dress like one. Stay off the production line. And furthermore, from this day forward, you and every employee in your divisions will wear suits and ties."

I answered, "Yes, sir," and hung up.

Sam walked in, and we discussed the conversation, and she had it pretty accurate. Sam was maybe ten years older than I, but we had almost a mother-son relationship. I have been a Dr Pepperholic for years, and Sam kept a supply in the refrigerator in the conference room adjacent to my office.

She had a keen sense of when I really needed one; and frequently, when she would see me drive in from a job she knew would tax or upset me, she would have a Dr Pepper on my desk by the time I reached the office.

I thought about my brief conversation with Dale and made a decision. Upon firmly deciding what course of action to do, I buzzed Sam to come to my office. Within seconds, she entered with her steno pad and a cold Dr Pepper, smiled, and sat on her chair to the side of my desk. We discussed what we believed would happen if I ordered all the people from line foreman up to wear a suit. In the recreational business, a leisure time product, very few people wore suits. I only wore a suit when at corporate and other times when it was appropriate. Sam and I knew there would be a great resistance from our people. I asked her to get a current listing of all the employees, which she did, and we determined by name those that this asinine order would include.

Sam made a list and worded the order very carefully. I approved the message; and Sam gave it to the office girl, who was in charge of our TWX system, which was our communications device at that time. I had a phone fax in my office, but could not handle conference calls and was real slow and expensive to use. The girl would type the message on a TWX perforator and feed the punched tape into the TWX machine, which would be received by every plant at the same time.

I instructed Sam to not include our Shartlesville plant, for I would call Keith and personally talk to him. I called Ralph to the office and told him what Dale had ordered, and he should immediately enforce it in this plant. Ralph said that we may as well close down the operations because we could not continue producing twenty-seven units a day and contend with such a rule that prohibited people from getting their job done. The people that this would affect were highly productive people who did numerous tasks daily that required getting in under and over materials and finished products. Their wearing suits would certainly not be appropriate.

I made the call to Keith, whose division was the most profitable of all the remaining divisions under my control. Keith did not hesitate with his response and said that he wouldn't do it, and if anyone forced him to, he would leave and take most of the employees with him. I had done a job I did not agree with and disliked a lot; now I would do a job that I would take extremely great pleasure in. I called Sam back into my office.

For several weeks, Sam and I had been sharing information and opinions about work and where it was going. I had told Sam that if I could not get a number of changes made with respect to the authority and command,

I would be leaving. Dale had continued working my divisions behind my back to a point that we were earning much less than before he came; and at corporate, every chance he could, he would place the blame on me. Dale had not been on any committees or any boards, and I served on two of the major ones and one minor one. He was jealous and tried, unsuccessfully, to remove me in the hopes he could replace me in these committees. Now the fun would begin.

Sam sat on her chair with her pad. I told her she really would not be needing it anymore since I had made the decision to leave the company. She said, "I'm going with you wherever you go."

I told her, "I really appreciate you and your work, and now I want you to write a simple formal resignation letter for me. Find some palatable words to say why."

She was eager to do this because we both saw some time back that our actions this day were inevitable. Sam left for her office.

I made a few phone calls, then called Ralph, brother Jim, and Jack into the office. I told them I was leaving and cleared all my personal things from my car and sent it out for a thorough cleaning. I proceeded to clear out my desk and left instructions for the night cleaning crew to do an exceptional cleaning job on my office. I called Judy and asked her to make arrangements to pick me up at five in the afternoon and that I would have to use her car to come to work the following day.

Sam returned to my office, smiling. She was pleased with the words she had used in writing my resignation, and so was I. I asked her to get Mr. Wonus on the company phone and turn the speaker on so she could hear the conversation. When Dale answered his phone, I began speaking very softly and very slowly. I was going to savor this moment.

"Dale, this is Bob Dutton. What I have to say will prove to be very important to you and your future, so I want you to listen very carefully because I will not repeat myself. You made a big mistake today and have made many other ones with me during the time of our association. I passed over all the others, believing what I was told before you were hired that you would be temporary, but you have gone well beyond your authority today.

"You are the poorest supervisor I have been associated with, and your greed and selfishness show in all your actions. Your actions have created a breach of contract between Sheller Globe and me, and according to my contract, my remedy is to call in everything that the company owes me. I've had enough, and here's what you are going to do. You and the corporate secretary will be in my office tomorrow morning with the balance of money that is due on my contract, a check in full for my accumulated bonuses, and my salary in full. I will hand you my written resignation and will leave the premises.

"If you need transportation from the airport, call Sam. If you are not here by eight o'clock, I will be in my lawyer's office by nine, and you can't count high enough to the amount of damages I will file for. Goodbye."

I put the phone back on the cradle and felt good for the first time in months.

Sam left the office, and I called my old boss Dwayne Shields and told him what had transpired. Dwayne and his family held the single largest block of stock in Sheller Globe since they had exchanged shares for their Superior company in Lima, Ohio. They also produced ambulances and hearses. I knew a lot of people there because I had served on the products committee, and we always met at Superior's corporate offices in Lima. He was sorry to hear the news and asked if there was room to reconsider. I told him no, and then he said confidentially, "I'm about ready to leave myself."

The following morning, slightly before eight o'clock, Dale and the secretary, John, entered my office. John began the conversation, telling me that we could work this matter out and that my leaving was not the way. He went on to say that corporate had been very pleased with my performance and wanted me to reconsider. I told him there was no way I would spend another day as long as Dale had anything to do with my divisions because he knew nothing about any of the various products we produced, thought they sold themselves, and had created a corporate charge to my Elkhart facility that was far greater than normal and that he had severely hampered our ability to prosper and grow. I further told him that if Dale remained with the company in such an authoritative position, Sheller Globe would be reduced to half what it was when he came.

Dale made no comments. He was quiet all the time, standing in my office. John handed me three checks, which were payment in full for contracts, bonuses, and wages. Dale spoke for the first time. He advised me that it was company policy according to the policy manual that he would have to supervise me clearing out my belongings. I handed him the keys to my furnished automobile, shook John's hand, and walked through the office and plant, telling everyone how much I had appreciated their work and association and that our paths may cross again. I went back through the office on my way to my car, hugged Sam, and said, "I'll see you soon."

When we had first considered selling Continental, Ralph and I took in a partner and started Travelers Recreational Sales lot in Elkhart. The third partner was Benny Holt, who had a lot of experience in the travel trailer industry. Sales were going very well. I was a silent partner and only invested in the operation; in the event we sold Continental someday, I would have a place of business to hang my hat. When I decided to stay with Sheller Globe, this operation would be considered as a conflict of interests, so I sold my interest to Ralph and Benny.

Within a few months of my leaving Sheller Globe, Ralph left Continental and started working the trailer sales business with Benny. Ralph would continue in the RV sales business and eventually become the largest dealer in the area. The year that Ralph retired, his company sold eighteen million dollars of trailers and motor homes.

Jim and dozens of the top employees left Continental, and the plant slowly faded into oblivion.

Within a year, Sheller Globe closed the Georgia plant; and soon thereafter, they closed the facilities in Pennsylvania. The entire loss for Sheller Globe was created by one man by the name of Dale Wonus.

You must treat people with respect and dignity if you expect to get the best they have to offer. Dale Wonus believed his voice was so powerful that he could shout it into existence. He never knew that only God has the power to do that. If corporate would have gotten rid of Wonus, Keith Bates and his team in Pennsylvania would have been contributing five times the profits per employee that all the other divisions combined were producing. Don Winkler remained with his accounting firm and would remain my company accountant in the future. Don and I, along with a gentleman who Don knew in Fort Wayne, started a publishing company. We sold advertising, which was included in the books, which were special-purpose school books we provided to the school system in Indiana without charge.

I liked the potential of what I saw in the short period of time that I had my investment in Travelers Recreational Sales, so soon after I left Sheller Globe, Don and I agreed to open a sales lot in Fort Wayne. We did not open in Elkhart because Ralph was already active in that business; and we certainly were not going to, in any way, do anything that might take sales away from his operation. One of our salesmen, Joe Montalone, who had also left Continental, ran the operation called Parkmaster; and after a couple of years, Don and I sold the business to Joe. Neither Don or I really got used to retail sales. I had produced things, and Don determined what they cost.

The following photos represent our product Line.

We had a total of twenty-one different models.

Our ultramodern new transcontinental fifth wheel

Sales managers from each plant (Bob is second from the right.)

You knew **CONTINENTAL** *would do it !*

Introducing our beautiful all-fiberglass body, steel welded frame, luxury motorhome.

How can you top beauty, safety, luxury and economy?

You can't! That's why your best buy in the exciting motorhome field is Continental. The all-fiberglass body means no rust, corrosion from road chemicals, color fading or dents. The comparatively light weight of fiberglass also helps gas economy. Safety and ruggedness are assured with welded steel frame, extra duty brakes and unobstructed vision. All the fine standards you are used to with Continental are included, and a wide range of optional equipment is available.

See your Continental Dealer or write direct.

Specifications subject to change without notice.

CONTINENTAL TRAVELER
Post Office Box 786 • Elkhart, Indiana 46514 • Phone AC (219) 293-2559
Hamburg, Pennsylvania 19526 • Phone AC (215) 562-3021

6360-3-70

DEALER:

Our first motor home, 1969

**Dealer opening, with Keith, Ralph, Bob, and movie star
Rory Calhoun**

Ambulance and emergency vehicle outfitting line

Chapter Fourteen

It was midyear 1973, and I had taken a little time off after leaving Sheller Globe. I was getting my affairs together. Judy and I had purchased twenty-seven acres at Simonton Lake, five miles north of town, and only a forty-acre field was between our property and the Michigan line. We had built a beautiful big two-story house with all of the exterior being Indiana limestone. It had a mansard roof, a huge garage for two or more cars, and a lot of space where the kids could entertain their friends.

Each of the kids had their own room, and there were three baths. We had to have that many because Teri needed two. She had to get up an hour earlier than the boys because it took her so long to shower. We had a very large recreational room that had a fireplace and a wet bar with a pool table sitting in the middle of the room. We used this room often.

We built our house on the lakefront, and the street ended at my property's edge. Our driveway was 330 feet long and was landscaped the entire length with burning bush. I had constructed a turnaround in the front of the house so the school bus could drive around the cul-de-sac without having to back up as the driver had done before we built the house. We installed a pier and docked our boats and pontoon there.

As we were ready to decorate the house, I had my designer who worked for me at Continental do the job. Louise Shibelhut was her name. Louise and Judy did a great job. The house was colorful and cheerful and had good natural light. We sold our house on Crawford Street and were moving to the lake because it was in a school district of our choice. Randy and Teri would be going to the new high school at Memorial, and Mike would attend Brookdale. We moved into our new house in August 1973 just before school started.

We were just settling down in the new house, and Dwayne called me, asking how things were going. He said he wanted to talk to me and that he wanted to know if it would be permissible for him to meet with me at my home. Dwayne lived in Lima, which is quite a hard drive to Elkhart. He came to my home on Saturday morning; and after discussing our experiences at Sheller Globe, Dwayne told me he had left Sheller Globe and was taking over as president of Blue Bird Bus Company, which had a huge plant, and their corporate offices in Richmond, Indiana. He would be starting the new job very soon.

He and his family had owned Superior in Lima and had grown to become the number one school bus manufacturer in the world. Also, they were in the top three of ambulance and hearse production in the United States. They had sold Superior to Sheller Globe before Sheller Globe had purchased my company. After Dale Wonus got a foothold in the company, Superior was starting to wane, and Dwayne saw an opportunity to take over Blue Bird's management. He asked me to come with him as the number two man and offered a huge salary and benefits program. What a great opportunity, and I would have loved to do it.

There were numerous considerations to be made. I didn't have to have the huge salary; we had just moved into our beautiful home, our kids were starting at new schools, and I was in the process of attempting to get another new venture started. I told Dwayne how much I appreciated the offer and would love to again work with him, but I had to respectfully decline. I wanted to stay and let my family grow up in Elkhart.

Since leaving Sheller Globe, two other gentlemen, Bob Pickrell and Ted Coleman, and myself started a consumer bank in Elkhart. We had known one another for many years, and they had just taken their company public. They made enough money on the public offering that to celebrate the event, they hired a limo to drive them to Chicago to the brokers to collect their money; and on their way home, they were lighting their cigars with a hundred-dollar bill.

The First Old State Bank that I had done business with in the sixties was the only consumer-oriented bank in Elkhart. One of the commercial banks acquired them, leaving a void in the financial community. The two big banks had become huge banks over the years and catered to big business, making it difficult for the average wage earner to borrow for small appliances, automobiles, and small loans; and their interest rates were somewhat higher for these people than bank rates in surrounding towns. We had been quietly working to obtain a charter and knew if the big banks learned what we were doing, they would block our getting the charter through political means. No one knew about our efforts, except our families and our lawyer, who was a friend and assistant county prosecutor. We would enter the lawyer's office uptown through a doorway in the alley; and if we went out to eat, everyone knew that we were friends, so there was no suspicion of anything going on.

We had a huge financial concern that was owned by a man that had been President Kennedy's financial advisor during the early sixties. His name was Mike Carmichael, and he wielded a lot of power in the state. We followed the rules to the letter and qualified for the bank, but at our final hearing, Mr. Carmichael blocked it by his influence. He called our lawyer and said we could get the charter if he could own half of the bank.

We discussed it and agreed that we would agree to a counteroffer. We offered to allow him and his family to purchase up to 10 percent, but no more. He agreed on the condition that we hire one of his financial people to oversee the bank. We hired his man and made him chairman of the board, and I held the position as vice-chairman.

We put a group of eleven investors together to form a company called Group Eleven. The sole purpose of this corporation was to own the property. I was president of Group Eleven. We purchased the old Hotel Bucklen on the corner of Main and Jackson streets, demolished the hotel, and constructed a new bank building. We wanted to open real soon, so we purchased an old bicycle shop, which was across the alley from the new bank building site. I took a crew in and reworked the old bicycle shop, and in late 1973, the Citizens Northern Bank was opened. I had never realized the extent of politics that were involved in banking, and the more I learned, the less I liked being in the banking business.

In July of 1973, before we moved into our new house, a group of men came to me and wanted to start back up building travel trailers. I called my brother, Jim, to see if he would be interested. The group met, but Jim decided not to come into the business because one of the fellows had been known to drink more than he should. This guy had been my in-house controller at Continental and had not missed a day's work nor drank on the job in the two years he was there.

Four of us decided to start. I would own 51 percent, and the three of them would own the other 49 percent. We rented a building and started Chevron Corporation. There was an extra large room in the building that we did not need for building trailers. They did not need me in the daily operations, and my children were growing up, so I wanted to start some kind of operation where I could teach the kids how to work along with some of the ropes in the workplace. Secondly, the company could not afford four administrative salaries; so everyone's choice was either work on the line in production part of the time, or I would drop any daily involvement and do my thing.

We all agreed, and I rented this large room from the company. I set it up and hired a few people, and we began making cabinetry for mobile homes, travel trailers, and the van industry.

In the meantime, a cabinet-manufacturing business became for sale and had a very large complex. They were going bankrupt, and I wanted the building. I put a fifty thousand deposit into escrow at the bank to apply either to the purchase of the entire business or to the real estate, depending on whether the company was bankrupted or not. Our contracts were all signed, so my crew and I moved in. We inherited several employees from their operation. We had a customer base within two months of start-up to warrant this move.

We were in the building about two weeks, and the plant burned. Everyone believed the previous owner burned it, but no proof was ever gotten. We had already outfitted another building on the premise, which would be large enough to get by, but costly to operate in. I immediately had an addition built, and this building would be the home of Dutton Industries Inc.

Once again, I had my hands full. Our crew and I had outfitted the temporary building to house the bank since it would take six months to construct the new bank building. I was building an addition to the property I had purchased on Johnson Street, and Chevron was starting to take off.

On the home front, the kids were acclimating themselves to the daily routine at new schools and a new neighborhood. Life was hectic, too hectic. Judy took good care of the family during these hectic times.

When I would have a trying day at work, I would come home about an hour before dark and take one of the small boats and go fishing. Mike loved to fish and would frequently go with me. This time was very important. I got to spend one-on-one time with Mike, and being on the water was relaxing.

I spent a lot of time with the boys, helping them develop skills they would need in sports. They began playing basketball, so we poured a concrete court at the side of the lake side yard. I still loved basketball, and for several years before we moved to the lake, I rented the gym at the elementary school where the kids attended; and one night a week, several dads would bring their boys.

This activity helped Randy in his healing process. Due to his injury, he could shoot the ball with his left hand as well as he could with the right. Both the boys were good players and very competitive. As they got older, the game got a little rougher when we played. They were good enough to block the old man's shots, so I reverted to my style of play that I had done as a kid when all the players were bigger than me—I'd drive to the basket with my left elbow extended forward and the ball in my right hand, above my shoulder. When I left the floor for the shot, the left knee would also be extended. As they attempted to defend the shot, all they came in contact with were knees and elbows. Randy would yell at me, saying, "DAD, you're nothing but elbows and knees!"

The new factory building was completed, and I outfitted it with a truckload of reconditioned machinery that we had purchased from a GM plant. They were going to build a completed van, but after setting their plant ready for production, it proved to be a conflict of interest for them. They never turned the machines on. We were building a few cabinets for travel trailers, which included supplying about six sets a day for Chevron.

The new bank building had been completed, and we moved in and used the temporary building for storage. The politics of banking was taxing on my nerves. Every politician associated with the banking industry had his hand out, including the state attorney general, who had guaranteed that we would get our charter if we made a huge contribution to his campaign for office. This made me sick to my stomach, and I refused to do it.

Mike Carmicheal's man who we had made chairman was worthless and knew less about banking than I did. The situation was becoming intolerable, so I fired him and took over as chairman of the board.

Dutton Industries was booming. Sam was back with me running the office, and we had more work than we could get done in one shift and put on a four-hours-per-night shift. Randy was old enough to do some light work in the plant and began working after school, helping keep the plant clean and handling finished parts; and in his spare time, he would help in the paint department.

We had added another addition to the building, constructing a paint facility, storage, and shipping room. Randy helped in those areas as time permitted. He was learning all the phases of the operation except those in the mill room, where he was not allowed to run any machinery because he was too young.

We continued growing, but I was limiting the amount of production to a point that required no more than twenty-five employees. We had reached that point. Brother Jim had moved back to Alabama and called again, asking how jobs were. I told him that the cabinet operation could use him if he was interested. He moved back to Elkhart and took the job running production. Having gone through the experiences of having worked with Jim in two other businesses, giving him stock, and immediately having to buy it back, I was going to approach this association differently. The only conditions of his employment were that he had to perform to a point of maintaining reasonable profitability, and he would receive a fair salary. I paid him the exact same salary that I was earning.

I had reached a financial point in my life that I really did not have to work every day, but refused to retire because the kids were too young, and Judy and I were too young. Many nights, I would lie in bed, thinking how tired I was. The Chevron start-up had required some of my time, and getting the charter for the bank was a very time-consuming job. Starting the Group Eleven Corporation took some time, and reconstructing the old bicycle shop to temporarily house the bank took day and night for a couple of weeks.

I had supervised the construction of the new bank building on a daily basis. It was expensive, and the code required by law had to be met to assure future security of the bank, so I could not afford to make a mistake in its construction.

Dutton Industries was very time-consuming. I ran the entire operation and worked on the line most of the day. My original purpose of starting a new business was to provide a place where my children could be taught what it takes to succeed and how to work. This whole scenario was not leading toward that objective. The bank was profitable, but I did not like the business. Chevron was earning good profits, which I did not need for my family and felt that the boys working Chevron were more entitled to its profits.

Group Eleven had reached a point that there was nothing to do except collect the rent on the two buildings it owned. Dutton Industries was my primary concern, so I convinced Bob and Ted to sell the bank. We immediately sold it to a group of people who owned a large bank in Fort Wayne. They also purchased all the assets of Group Eleven. I sold my interest in Chevron to the other three investors under the condition we would continue selling to them their cabinet requirements. I sold a building I owned on Middlebury Street, a ten-acre parcel of land on a little lake north of Goshen and a rental property on Michigan Street. Now I was free to concentrate on more important things. I wanted to prepare my children for the future and spend some time with the family.

My mom had died in 1964 with what we later learned to be Huntington's disease. My birth father had died in 1967. I never got to know him well because of how he had left us when I was five. I went to his funeral for the sake of my half brother and sisters, whom I had gotten to know. Mom was fifty when she died, the same age as her father when he died. By this time, I was seeing several relatives, who were offspring of Grandpa Duncan, developing Huntington's; and not even one of them would admit it nor talk about it. This disease was horrible and caused untold suffering to its victims.

I was very concerned. Ella Mae had the symptoms; and one day, I noticed a very slight twitch in the eye of her son, Dennis, who was a young teenager. When I discussed this with Ella Mae, she got mad at me for the first time in our lives. I would not discuss the matter with her again for several years. Having seen this, I was really disturbed and concerned, not only about myself, but also with the possibility of my children having the gene that caused the disease. Very little was known about Huntington's at that time. The doctors knew that those who had it usually began showing symptoms near the age of thirty and usually lived to be about fifty. I kept monitoring this condition of my extended family and relatives, but could do nothing but worry and make sure that if I were to have it and die at age fifty, my family will be provided for. I began to sense that I would not have it because I had never had even the slightest indication, and neither had brother Jim or sister Shirley.

The first two years we lived at the lake, we had constant problems and never knew why. It was as if we had been targeted by all the rowdy people on the north side of town. It began soon after we moved into our new house. The yard was not complete, and there was a small pile of baseball-sized limestone rocks at the side of the house. There was a forty-acre forest next to the house, and a motorcycle gang rode into the yard, having taken a path that went through the woods to another road. They broke out every window on the east side of the house, throwing these pieces of stone. Teri was fourteen, home alone, and scared to death.

When I received a call from her, I took a car full of employees there to confront these people. By the time we got there, they were gone, and we never learned who they were. We posted No Trespassing signs throughout the perimeter of our property, but it didn't stop anyone who wanted to come in the back way. I completed my 330-foot drive from the dead-end street to my house and planted burning bush along the entire length and a landscaped area about five feet wide and filled the entire strip with bark.

One night, a carload of people set off several railroad flares in the stretch of landscaping and caused two thousand dollars in damage. We did not find them. Soon thereafter, they stripped my pontoon boat of about everything that was removable. This went on with many other visits from vandals, and we could not catch any one of them.

By this time, I had developed a "shoot first and ask questions later" attitude. While I was firmly committed to doing whatever it took, including stopping this at gunpoint, I learned from a local police officer's nephew that there would be a large group coming that night to do damage. I called the sheriff's department and discussed the situation with them and told them how I had learned of this. They contacted the policeman whose nephew had contacted me, and the policeman called me. I told him that I'd had enough and had enough weapons to ward off whatever size group that would come and would not hesitate to shoot if confronted with such a gang.

No one came that night, and the word was out on the streets that it was not wise to mess around at my house again. Several kids around the neighborhood and at school relayed this information to my kids. Things settled down for a couple of years but eventually would return, and when it did, I would be ready.

I had taken up golf when I was eleven, but had not played very much. I might play five or six times a year with Dick, my lawyer and best friend; but now, when there was no conflict with the kids' sports schedule, I would play. I was getting in about three rounds a month on the weekend. I concentrated my efforts at the plant and made a one-acre garden across the street from my house.

The garden was sprinkled, and we grew enough during the season to last all year. We had three freezers that we would fill with about any type of vegetable that we ate. In one of the freezers, we kept our meat. We would purchase half of a beef or a whole hog when friends of ours would be slaughtering. We ate like kings—a big difference from the way it was when I grew up. It pleased me that I could do this for my family. Even though the kids would sometimes help me in the garden, I never required them to do so.

Some years after Randy's accident, after we learned that he could overcome his disability, Dick had gotten him a settlement for the accident. The court ordered the money be placed in an account until Randy was eighteen years old. We knew that when he was ready to begin college, he would need those funds.

As time passed, we were doing well at the plant. We had started a Western furniture line; so I built a nice building at the front of the property to be used as a showroom, retail sales, and our offices. Teri had come to work for us part-time and worked in the office. Mike and a friend, Brad, would come to the plant after school and clean the plant. By now, Randy was running the paint operation and was in charge of quality control and shipping. Randy had been with the company since we started and was almost eighteen. He absolutely refused to go to college. He had been living at home without any expense, other than his own personal expenses, and had saved some money. He wanted to move out on his own. I went to the courts and got them to release the funds from the accident to him. He purchased a new car, put a down payment on a little house, and furnished it with his own money. I hated to see him go, but was proud of him for wanting to make his own way.

Sam got remarried and moved out of state. Teri finished secretarial school and came to work full-time running the office. All the kids were smart and innovative and could find ways to get the job done faster and with better results. Mike continued his education and worked at the plant after school. He was too young to operate any machinery, but would work wherever his supervisor directed. He amazed me with his ability to lead the people in the group that he was working with as young as he was and obviously had no authority. Teri reported to me in the office, but the boys reported to the plant manager, and "nepotism" was a word you never heard in our company.

Time passed, and Randy had been dating Jean Raber for quite some time. They decided to get married. The first time I had met Jean was unusual. Judy and I were sitting in the family room downstairs, and this girl came to the door. She was very pretty, and when I went to the door, she asked if Randy was there. I told her no and that he was out somewhere. She said, "That's good because I want to talk to you and Mrs. Dutton."

I invited her in, introduced Jean and Judy, and we sat down. Jean began to explain that she was the daughter of Paul Raber, who owned a sprinkling company, and her grandfather had built the Raber golf course. She stopped and paused for a moment and said, "I'm gonna marry Randy."

I laughed and began to joke around with her, telling her how pretty she was and such. Then I asked, "Does Randy know this."

She said, "No, but he will very soon."

When Randy got home, we told him of this visit. He just laughed. They continued dating, and one day, Randy told us they were getting married. I really liked Jean, but both she and Randy were different and were as compatible as oil and water. I sat both of them down and explained their personality differences and impressed upon them that marriage was for a lifetime. If they were going to make a marriage work, each one of them would have to give 95 percent because of their incompatibilities. They were always courteous and respectful and acknowledged what I had said, but made plans for the wedding. I told Randy to take a week off work and go somewhere where he knew no one and away from all his friends. "Think about what you really want to do. Make a decision, and whatever your decision is, Mom and I will honor and support it."

He wouldn't take the time off work, and soon, the wedding day came. I prepared a stock certificate in his name for 25 percent of the company and gave it to them for their wedding present.

In 1977, Coleman died. It was in January, and the roads were terrible, slick with ice and snow. We drove to Alabama for the funeral and, because of the road conditions, arrived there after the private family viewing. The funeral home was filled with people, most of them I did not know. When I walked in and stood by the casket, a man came to me and introduced himself as being Coleman's best friend. I recognized his name as Coleman had talked a lot about him. He told me that Coleman knew he would not be around too much longer and had left his prize possessions with him. He said that he had all of Coleman's guns and his two purebred hunting dogs. He told me the guns in their cases were in his trunk wrapped in a blanket and that he had the two dogs at his house, caring for them.

I asked him if he would put the guns in the trunk of my car, handing him the keys and describing the car and its location. In a few minutes, he returned and asked what he should do with the dogs. Each of the dogs was worth about a thousand dollars, and it's all that Coleman owned. He told me stories of Coleman and him hunting, and he really loved to hunt with these dogs. I asked him if he wanted the dogs, and he said they were the best he had ever seen, but no way could he afford the thousand dollars each. "How much do you want for them?" he asked.

I said, "They're not for sale, but if you'll take good care of them, they're yours. Coleman would have wanted you to have them." Tears ran down the old man's cheeks; he gave me a hug and thanked me.

After Mom died, Coleman went to live with his aunt and moved the mobile home and parked it near the farmhouse. The aunt had died, and Coleman was living alone in this crumbling old farmhouse. I remember when I was a kid, we would visit there. This old house had been used by the Yankee army as they pushed the Confederate army to the south. I spent many hours when I was about seven or eight years old searching through the many acres of scrub-land surrounding the farm, looking for Civil War relics. There was a pile of metal near the house that had been there for over fifty years, which had old cannonballs and broken rusty metal pieces that came from weapons or wagons used during the war. These were found as they plowed the fields years ago. I never found any, but it was exhilarating to hunt for them.

Coleman had died from a heart attack while sitting near the wood-fired heater. Apparently, when the attack happened, he pitched forward and struck his head on the heater. The coroner's report indicated there was a small amount of blood on a scrape on his forehead, but this small scrape was a result of his dying and did not, in any way, contribute to his death.

At the funeral home, while Coleman's friend was putting the guns in my car, Coleman's brother Leon came to me and said that we would have to delay the funeral time by a day or so. I asked him why he thought so, and he said that a sister, Eddis, who lived in Florida about five hundred miles away, could not get there before the funeral's set time, which was two thirty the following day. My response was that brother Jim and I had driven 650 miles over ice most of the way, so if Eddis wanted to attend the funeral, she could have been here at noon that day; and further, if she left her home at the current time, she could still make if she wanted to.

As we were speaking, the funeral director came and told me I had a phone call. It was Eddis on the phone. She said that we could not hold the funeral because it sounded like foul play and thought that someone had hit Coleman in the head since someone had told her about the scrape he had on the forehead. I told Eddis that this was certainly not the case and that the funeral was going to be held at the scheduled time the next day.

Leon had heard my conversation with Eddis, and when I put the phone down, he began to get hostile with me. The funeral director was present as this was his office. Leon raised his voice and told me that I had no right nor authority to make any decisions regarding Coleman because he had never adopted me. This made me very angry; and when I get angry, I get pretty quiet, contemplating what my next action should be. The longer I stay quiet, the more violent I might become based upon the circumstances.

I responded to Leon. "You've got a lot of nerve and a warped sense of facts as to who has the authority! You're right, Coleman never did adopt me. But he was my dad, and I was his son. As his son, I've done everything in my power to see that he and Mom had a decent life. And I started my contribution when I was a kid, giving them most of all I earned while you, on the other hand, would only come to see Coleman when you wanted to borrow money, drink some home brew, or needed something he could do for you!"

I faced the funeral director and asked who was paying for the funeral, and he responded that I was. I turned back to Leon and told him two things. "If Eddis wants to attend the funeral, you should call her and have her young son drive her, and they can make it by nine tomorrow morning. And secondly, I've already heard you and other members of Coleman's family talk about going to his house tomorrow and split up his possessions, so I want you to pay close attention to what I'm telling you. Tomorrow when the graveside services are finished, and we leave the site, my brother, both sisters, and myself are going to the house and get a few personal things that Coleman still had that belonged to Mom. Please understand that my car will be the first one there, and we four will be the first ones to enter the house with the key I hold in my hands. If anyone dares enter before I get there, they will not leave, guaranteed."

When the services were over, we four kids headed for the old farmhouse; and when we got there, two other cars had beaten us there. One of the people was Leon, but all of them remained in their cars. When we got out, they exited from their cars and were going to enter the house immediately behind us. I turned around and told them we needed ten minutes in the house, and then the rest of its contents were theirs. Leon insisted on going in, and I reminded him of what I had said at the funeral home, and he knew I was dead serious, so he stopped.

We four kids rummaged through drawers and such, and each kept some small thing that belonged to Coleman, and the girls took a couple of very small framed pictures from the top of a nightstand. I opened a drawer in a small stand by Coleman's bed and was about blown away by what I saw. There in plain sight was the Scout knife he had bought me when I was eight years old. It was in its scabbard. Tears came to my eyes as I remembered what happened.

Coleman had given both Jim and me an identical knife, and as he handed them to us, he said there two rules: be very careful and don't throw them. Within minutes, Jim and I were near the firewood chop block, and Jim threw his knife at a tree, and it stuck in the tree. He retrieved his knife, and then I threw mine. Coleman walked behind me. We thought he was in the house and would not see us. He had not seen Jim, but did see me. He walked to where my knife lay, picked it up, asked for my scabbard, and never gave it back.

This was the way he was. You could count on his word because he always honored it, and he thought this would be the proper punishment, which taught me another great lesson. He only took the knife of the one he saw disobey him. Now in the drawer in front of me was my knife, which I had not seen in over thirty years. The knife is in a drawer at home as I write these words and is one of my prized possessions.

After a few minutes, we walked outside, and I told the people standing there that everything in the house was theirs for the taking. They rushed over one another, getting through the door. We were saying our goodbyes when Leon came out. I told him I was going to disburse the four guns that had belonged to Coleman, which were in my trunk, and that I felt he was entitled to one since he was the closest blood relative there; but because Jim was older than I, he got first choice. I opened the trunk, and Jim chose the single-shot .22 Remington that Coleman had taught him to shoot with and the one that Coleman chose for all his fine target shooting.

I chose next and took the .22 Remington repeater. There were two shotguns left, which were like new, and Leon took the more expensive one. Then Marion, a nephew that was closer to Coleman than was his brother, took the other gun. Leon looked over at the old '47 Chevy that was sitting in the yard and said that Eddis should have it for transportation. We answered that it was fine with us. Then he looked over to where the mobile home was parked, and the greed spilling out of his mouth could be seen. He said that he was going to take the mobile home and set it up to live in.

I looked at Shirley's husband, James, and asked him if he had a hitch on his truck and if he could haul the mobile home. He responded that he could handle it. I told James to remove the tires and wheels from the Chevy and put them on the mobile home and that the tires and wheels for the Chevy were on the back porch of the farmhouse. Coleman had switched them because the Chevy tires were worn-out.

Leon was beginning to object, and I pulled out my wallet and handed the title to the mobile home to sister Shirley. It was in the name of Bobby R. and Judith L. Dutton, signed and delivered to the one who had helped the most with Mom in her last few months. I had left it in our names because I expected this from some of Coleman's relatives. We said goodbye and headed north to home.

It was another long drive, and on the way home, Jim and I discussed all the crap that had happened and what could have happened if Leon had not done what I told him. I told Jim that this situation would never happen to my family because everything that needs to be done and the decisions that must be made regarding my death will have been made and put in legal documents long before I die. I told Judy what had happened when I got home and then began jotting down notes that I would later print out in the form of final instructions in a legal format, where no decisions would have to be made by my survivors when I die.

The plant was going well, and I wanted to reward Jim for his work. He was still being paid exactly the same salary that I made. I worked about sixty hours a week, and he worked about fifty.

I presented him with a stock certificate for 24 percent of the business. Unknown to me, the same thing that happened a few years before at

Mobilcraft when I gave him 24 percent of that company was brewing again. Our plant was outside the city, and we had no fire protection, except the county volunteers. Our woodworking company was always at risk of fire, and I had witnessed three of them in plants that someone else owned. The city was extending the water main up the street we were on, and when I inquired of them, they gave me a date that water would be available and what date the line would be installed in front of my property. Jim was the general manager and would be responsible to handle the situation. I gave him all the financial expenses with respect to our insurance premiums and the method we would use to depreciate the cost, which would be done on a leasehold improvement basis as Judy and I owned the real estate and rented the buildings to the company.

After a period of time, I asked Jim for a status report on the sprinkler project. He had done nothing with it. The date the city had given me was growing near, and if we could coordinate our installation with the city while their lines were being installed, we could save about five thousand dollars. I waited another week, during which Jim had become very sullen. I discussed the project with him, and again, he had done nothing. I proceeded to contract with a firm from Ohio who could meet the timetable required, and the system was installed and activated. Now we had fire protection.

Jim's sullenness continued, and it was beginning to affect production and employee attitude. Jim was upset that the company was paying for the sprinklers and that I owned the building. I explained and showed him the spreadsheet that Don, our accountant, had prepared. If I paid for it, the depreciation would be over the life of the building, and the rent would have to be increased. If the company paid for it on a leasehold basis, the depreciation would be much greater each year, which would reduce income tax. Once the final costs were calculated, the entire system would be paid for in twenty-two months using only the reduction in insurance premiums; plus we had fire protection twenty-four hours a day.

After the twenty-two months, profitability would increase by near thirteen hundred dollars per month. Jim either didn't understand or let something else get in the way of logic. Attitudes were turning sour, and I had to stop it. I met with Jim one morning, and he was in the worst mood I had seen him. I simply told him it was hurting the company, and if he couldn't get his act together by 4:00 p.m., he could hit the road. He told me I was shafting and cheating Randy and him by handling the sprinkler cost in this manner, and as stockholders, they should be entitled to a proportionate amount of money that was spent on the sprinklers.

At four o'clock, Jim left. It didn't take him long after I gave him the stock. Once again, I spent thousands of dollars buying back stock that I had given him within a few months of the date I had given it. He went on to set up his own little shop in his garage and started taking or attempting to take a few of our customers. I called the customers and told them that Jim had started his own place, and if they could give him some work, I would appreciate it. I have always believed that if you do a good quality job and honor your word, there will always be enough business out there waiting for you.

I had established a very good reputation of practicing a high level of honesty and integrity in every job I had ever done. It had always paid off. I expect the party on the other side that I'm dealing with to do the same; unfortunately, that has not been the case a lot of times. The world is filled with millions of greedy people; and when you deal with them, the possibility of getting cheated, lied to, and forced to contend with those circumstances until you can do better is a fact of life.

Randy and Jean had been married for one full year, and one day, they both approached me. Jean gave me a hug and stepped back, looking directly at me. She said, "Dad, you were right about me and Randy. We love each other, but just can't get along. We've tried everything, but we are totally incompatible as you had told us and have both tried. We really do love each other, but we can't be happy living together."

I suggested they give it some more time, get some professional help, pray, and really make a concentrated effort to work things out between them. They said they had been doing this with no success, but would continue trying.

Soon thereafter, they both came to me again and advised they were getting a divorce. I asked if they had talked with her parents, and they had. There were no children involved, so I advised them a course of action. They had already agreed to how they would share the material things they owned, and when they told me, I was truly impressed that these two youngsters could split their property in a way that I thought was absolutely fair to both.

Jean had come from a very fine family, and of course, we had raised Randy to always have a keen sense of fairness. I advised them to get one lawyer and draft the divorce papers, and under their circumstances, it would take a judge about three minutes to make the divorce declaration. They did this, and everything went very smoothly. Randy had bought Jean a new car, which she would keep. Randy would keep his car that he owned when they were married and would keep his house and the stock in the company.

Jean got what she wanted, and Randy got what he wanted. Randy helped Jean move into her own place and would check on her needs occasionally, and Jean would come to Randy's house and help with the housework and do his laundry. This continued for a long period of time, but eventually, they went their separate ways.

I promoted an employee to the plant manager position. His name was Stan Floerkey. Stan was one of the employees we inherited when we purchased the assets of Alpine Wood Products. I really needed Stan to take over the Dutton Industries operations because we had another project that would keep Randy and me very busy.

The owners of the Ryder Truck Company had gotten a divorce, with the wife getting ownership of Ryder. The husband started a new truck rental company called Jar-Tran and placed an order with a local company for 2,500 trucks in the twelve-to-fourteen-foot box size. Several companies were involved, and I was asked to paint all the unpainted parts that were to be used on these trucks. We had managed to get this job almost completed when Holiday Rambler began producing delivery trucks for companies like FedEx, UPS, and others under the name of Utilimaster. They needed someone to paint them for a year or so until they could build their own paint facility.

We were attempting to do this work at our cabinet paint facility, but there was a major conflict in types of paint materials used on these units and that which we used in the cabinet operation. The fire hazard was astronomical because the mixing of the dried dust of one type of paint with that of the other resulted in immediate spontaneous combustion. It didn't matter how well we kept them separated; we could not eliminate this fire hazard.

I began looking for a facility that we could rent with no success. The man that had purchased 49 percent of my old B&D Paint called me. Over the years, he had acquired full ownership from my ex-partner Don. The owner, Lionel Smead, said he would sell me all his equipment; and I could assume the lease on the building. This was the large paint facility where we had moved B&D into back in 1962.

I purchased the equipment, which included a roller coater, huge air compressors, and a multitude of miscellaneous paint equipment that had been accumulated over the past thirteen years.

We moved the Utilimaster paint operation to this location. Randy was still young, but I wanted him to get the experience; so I made a deal with him to take the operation over. I thought it would be a great opportunity and decided to do it in light of the fact that Dutton Industries really needed him, and if he wasn't there, it would pose a very hard but temporary hardship on the cabinet company.

I sent the best painter we had with Randy. His name was Merle Carr. Merle and I had been working together for the better part of twenty years, and he was good. Merle was to help Randy acclimate himself to all the new types of paint materials that had just come on the market, train the workers, and then return to work his old job at Dutton Industries. My plan was to give the new operation, Elkhart Industrial Painters, to Randy and help him plan for new customers after Utilimaster got their paint facilities under way, which would be about a year.

After a very short period of time, Randy advised me he would like to come back to the cabinet operation. The pressure of full control of this type of business was too much for the youngster. He wasn't ready yet, so he came back to the cabinet plant, and we left Merle to finish the Utilimaster contract.

The week before we moved the Utilimaster away from the cabinet operation, I received a call from the fire department in the middle of the night. Dutton Industries was on fire. By the time I reached the plant, there were three fire trucks getting set up for the fight. Stan came wheeling in and beat me to the side door of the plant and was about to open the door. The noise was deafening inside the plant, and a fireman grabbed Stan and pulled him back, telling him there was a great possibility that when he opened the steel door, a major explosion could occur.

Black smoke was billowing high in the rear corner of the building. Stan and I told the firemen there should be no problem. There were no flames, just smoke, and the noise we heard was not fire, but the huge industrial sprinkler system doing its job. Stan popped open the door and made a mad dash for the huge main electrical panel and cut off all the power. We told the firemen they needed not start pumping water. The system had contained the fire and put it out. The damage was limited to a couple of thousand dollars to repair the ceiling, roof, and water damages caused by the sprinklers. The firemen left while Stan and I began sweeping some of the water out of the building in the dark. We dared not turn the electric back on until we could see if any of the electric panels contained water.

The following morning, about fifty feet of the rear of the shop was a mess caused by the water. The crew cleaned it up; we put a tarp over the hole in the roof, turned the electric on, and went to work. The sprinkler system had saved the business and the building. Putting it in was the best investment I ever made, and it was unfortunate that brother Jim had not understood this.

The evidence of what caused the fire was on top of the trash in the trash trailer. It was spontaneous combustion caused by an accidental mixing of the paint dust from the fan filters of the two different types of paint. The cleanup man normally set the paint dust containers outside by themselves, away from the building, and topped the cans off with water. Someone had thrown about two gallons of this dust on the wood scrap trailer that was inside the building. The fire was contained within the perimeter of the trailer at floor level, but blew through the metal roof above it like a blowtorch until the sprinklers came on.

Two friends of mine, Don Matz and Hal Bechtel, were paint salesmen; and I had been purchasing paint from them for a long time. Because most of the paints used in the area were shipped in, it required purchasing large quantities to maintain a good cost level; plus if you had an emergency need, you had to wait on delivery from out of town. I convinced them to open a distribution point in Elkhart. I rented them the back part of the building on the street and furnished secretarial services through our secretary, Teri. They opened Paints and Solvents Company and were able to build a good-size business. I began thinking about greener pastures for my future and decided to sell the building to them.

Stan and Randy were running the production operations. I worked in the plant many hours a week but reported to Stan if I worked in the mill room and reported to Randy when I worked anywhere else. I decided I was going to leave the company, and I discussed it with both Randy and Stan to see if they wanted to work together and own the company. It wasn't going to require either of them to come up with any cash. We would design a takeover plan suitable to them. They discussed it and made the decision that they did not want the company. The company was profitable, but the work was hard, and the hours were long, but I never understood why they did not want to run it by themselves. Randy already owned 25 percent, and I wasn't asking for anything other than the company pay, the monthly rent, and to let Judy and I keep our health insurance.

I put the word out that the company was for sale. It had served its purpose. Each of the three kids had worked there at some point in time. I taught them how to do many things and tried to impress upon them the importance of always honoring your commitments because you are truly known by what you say and that it takes a long time to build a good reputation but only a moment to lose it. I felt they were ready to face the world on their own. I would almost have traded my soul to have had a close complete family and to have had an opportunity for a childhood and someone to give me on-the-job training as I was growing up. Well, it didn't happen. I had no security. My kids did.

Teri was about to get married. I took her aside and told her to take time off work and go off by herself without the influence of others and make her decision and, further, that the guy was not for her. I knew his father and knew of his ways and actions. This man was going to follow in his father's footsteps. Having said that, I told her it was her choice and that no one else can make it for her. I further stated, "If it is your decision to marry him, you will have to give 95 percent while he gives 5 to the marriage. If you're willing to do that, go ahead. If not, don't. Mom and I will support your decision." Teri married James Schenk in 1980.

Michael was still away at Indiana Central where he had gone to pitch baseball. Soon after he finished school, he married Michelle Iemma.

In October 1982, we sold Dutton Industries to George McMeekan and George Nielson. McMeekan was a very successful and well-liked businessman in Elkhart. Nielson had not been in town very long and was not well known. When we made the deal to sell, the books were audited by their accountants, and they confirmed the value of the business to be greater than what we were asking as I had told the buyers it would be. The books were audited September 30, and they did not want to take over until November 1.

We discussed how to handle this, and I told them I would run the operation until the end of the month, and I would personally pay for any losses during the month. They agreed to pay a separate check for the net profits. At the end of the month, they wrote me a check for the profits in the amount of slightly over twenty-seven thousand dollars. I deposited the check in my personal account and disbursed every penny to my employees based upon their positions and seniority.

I had a big bass boat that Stan loved, which was worth about ten to eleven thousand dollars. Stan had told me he wanted the boat if I sold it. I went to him and gave him his choice of his percentage of the twenty-seven thousand, which was under five thousand, or he could have the boat. He asked if I was crazy and took the boat.

Nielson came in to manage the business, and I was to remain for thirty days to teach him the ropes. Nielson had been a suit-and-tie executive salesman for either GE or Westinghouse since he graduated from Harvard and had always associated with executives of companies he dealt with. Now he found himself in the midst of all blue-collar fine-working people, and he did not quite know how to handle it. He got off the wrong foot with Stan.

The morning Nielson started, I walked into the plant with him, and Stan approached me with a question. Nielson put his hand on Stan's shoulder and said, "Stan, all you have working here are niggers and hillbillies, and you will be my shield from them."

This definitely did not sit well with Stan and me. Stan would leave the company within two weeks. One of the black men that worked there was one of my best friends. I had hired him twenty years ago when he was seventeen, and he had followed me wherever I started a company for all those years. He was married to a lady who also worked for us, and including me, we had several hillbillies there who made up a real good workforce.

Stan left the company, and Nielson hired a new production manager. My thirty-day workout ended, and in December, Judy and I went to Florida for a vacation. We came home at Christmastime, and between Christmas and New Year's, Nielson calls me. He said they were having some problems with the computer milling equipment and could not get production out and asked if I would come in and help. I went in to see him, and the production was in shambles. The production flow and procedures had been changed, and the workers had to handle goods through their workstations several times, and processes were out of order. To correct the mess would require direct personal supervision and work re-allocation at every line station for several days.

I told Nielson I would help under the condition that he give me 100 percent control from the office door on. He was not to order any employee to do anything, including sweeping the floor. They still had a good nucleus of my old employees, but the workstations had to be moved and the newer employees trained. I soon learned that what had created the problem was that Nielson did all the thinking from the office and would go to the plant and order line employees to do it his way; and in doing so, several processes were skipped, and it was very costly and time-consuming to make them up.

It was triple work to route glass openings after the cabinet doors had been sanded, ready for paint. They would have to be sanded the second time. Crazy stuff. I got the crew together without Nielson's presence and told them we, as a group, were going to make their jobs easier, get the job done, and have fun doing it. I asked everyone to think real hard as to how to make their operation easier, faster, more efficient, and less work for them. "Let's all work smarter, not harder" was the concept.

I got a few suggestions from the employees and approved them to try what they had suggested. I moved the employees to workstations that they were the best at that particular job because they liked it. I told them that if there was a job that was too hard, dirty, or dangerous, they should come get me; and I would do it until I was satisfied that the job parameter was fine for them.

I spent 99 percent of my time on the floor and put the plant on a ten-hour day. The employees were great and were a lot happier. The month ended on Thursday, and all our orders were caught up. I had accounting run a quick profit and loss statement for the month, and we had made close to twenty thousand dollars. They had lost near ten thousand in December. I had a quick meeting with all the employees and thanked them for their input, help, and total participation. I was proud of them, and they were proud of themselves. They thanked me, and I went to the office to speak with George Nielson.

When I entered the office, I ask Mr. Nielson for a private meeting because what I had to say should not be made known to anyone else. He closed the sliding window to the secretary's office, and I closed the door. I started by telling him that the company was profitable in January even though we had worked a lot of overtime and that every order scheduled to ship had been shipped. He thanked me for my work and offered payment. I refused the pay. "Give it to the people that made you the money."

Then I proceeded to tell him the real reason I wished to talk. I told him that it was obvious from his demeanor that he was a Harvard graduate, and I further understood that he had worked with and hobnobbed with people of high social standing, but if he were going to be successful running Dutton Industries, he would have to set the work parameters and allow the people to make decisions within the boundaries that he set and that there were no so-called niggers and hillbillies here. They were simply honest, hardworking people that wanted to earn a living and be prideful of the products they produced.

If you want that to happen, you will have to treat them with respect and utilize their individual talents and input. I stood up and told him I would not come back again. He was on his own. He shook my hand and thanked me, and I left, never to set foot on the premises again.

The company continued for a short period, and the other partner paid off all the bills and closed down the operations. I met with McMeekan much later to help him identify several drums of paint where the labels had been removed, which had been moved to another business he owned. I asked what he was going to do with the Dutton Industries corporate name, and he responded that he would not renew it, making it available to me in the future if I so desired.

Chapter Fifteen

For a period of time after Judy and I were married, I still had a longing to be in Alabama. We discussed the possibility of opening some type of business there. Both of us were partial to root beer barrels, and there was the new four-lane U.S. 78 Highway skirting my hometown, and several businesses were springing up. My dad knew the realtor who had the strip listed, so I asked my dad if he would make an appointment for me with the realtor. We drove to Alabama and looked at the parcel and told the realtor what we intended to do was to get a franchise for an A&W Root Beer barrel. The land was too expensive, so we declined.

By the following year, we had been interested in building a bowling alley, so we go back to the same realtor to look at some other property. We passed by the property that we had declined to purchase for the root beer barrel the year before, and there on the property was a big drive-in named Scherer's. What a coincidence. We also declined to purchase the land for a bowling alley because it was double the price it should have been. We let it go for two years, and still thinking we could possibly get some type of business there and because all my life I wanted to build a golf course, we learned that there was 150 acres for sale that was close to town. This would be a perfect size for a course.

We drove to Jasper, and as we went by the strip where the land was that we had hoped to put the bowling alley, there sat one. This was strange. We walked the property to see if it would be suitable for a course, and it was. For the third time, we could not negotiate a price that we could meet the debt service, so I made a firm decision. We had B&D Paint in operations by then, and I would forget having a business there and concentrate on doing my thing in Elkhart. From this point, strange got even stranger. When Mom died in 1964 while driving down U.S. 78 past the property that we were proposing to build a course, someone had. There on the entry way was a sign: Welcome to Skyline Golf and Country Club.

I thought about this for many years and sort of kept track of these three businesses that started an identical operation that Judy and I had wanted. Scherer's Drive-In went on to be a chain operation with several locations within Alabama. The bowling alley closed after about three or four years, and the golf course began growing up in field pine trees within five years.

I still wanted to build a golf course. When we moved into our house on Crawford Street in 1961, I designed a nine-hole course on a small sheet of plywood using modeling clay. I discarded it in 1973 when we moved to the lake. Discarding the clay model in no way dissuaded me from the desire to build one.

When I finished helping Nielson out at my old Dutton plant, I was now free to do whatever I wanted to. It was time to research building the course I'd wanted since I was eleven years old. If I could pull this off, my business life would be complete, and I would be satisfied with whatever I had accomplished in the business world. I had been involved on a working committee level at a golf club and worked with a major golf course architect, Mr. Gary Kerns. I had enough experience in general management to organize and develop a course, and I had a good engineer that could assist in obtaining all the various permits and help with streets, drainage, and utility design. I could design and build a golf course

By early 1983, all three of the kids were married, leaving Judy and I rambling around in a house that Judy would have to become a slave to. I hated to give up living on the lake, and I dreaded more to lose my big garden, but the fact was that the house was too large for us. We sold the house in midyear 1983 and rented the purchaser's house until we knew exactly what we were going to do. I had been searching for land and had looked at several parcels, but none of them were suitable.

In October 1983, I found 202 acres, part of which was inside the city limits of Elkhart. There were three parcels that the realtor had put together, making up the 202 acres. Forty-five acres was in the city, and the balance was in the county. This meant that we could build a clubhouse within the city limits and have city facilities and services, yet build the golf course in the county, which would be a tremendous savings in property taxes. Judy and I discussed the project at length. I was forty-five years old and did not need to be taking such a financial risk as this business would require substantial capital outlay before we put the key in the door and started getting cash flow.

I developed my plan. I only wanted to build it and did not want to operate it. I wanted to retire pretty soon. My initial plan developed at age seventeen had me retiring at age forty-seven. If I could build a course and get it profitable in two years, I could meet my initial plan. I decided to take investors, which would minimize my risk. I brought in a golf professional, Gary Keaffaber, and Gary concurred with me that the property was very good for our purpose.

We then added two more men, and collectively, we added ten more for a total of fourteen. This number was our maximum investors that we would take because of privacy. If you had fifteen investors in a company in Indiana, there would be a required public reporting of financial affairs. We named the new business Bent Oak Corporation. We wanted the name of a tree, but most of them had already been taken. The road to our east is Benham, and the road to our west is Oakland, and Ben-Oak didn't get the job done. If we added a *T* to Ben, we could then have BentOak, which sounds like a crooked tree. That would work.

I committed to writing my personal objectives and commitments and set the parameters for the same, using dates, finances, and conditions as the bases of all my commitments. I was to build the course and stay with the operations until it was profitable. We would begin as a public facility, and before I left, we would take it private. Now all I had to do was perform.

We set a date for the opening for June 19, 1985. No one had any idea why I chose that date, and twenty-four years later, only two or three people know. That date represented my thirty-year anniversary in Elkhart. No one builds a complex like ours in less than two to three years. We would have fifteen months to build a championship eighteen-hole course, a driving range and a practice putting green, maintenance facilities, two wells several miles of underground sprinkler lines and heads, over a mile of asphalt cart paths, and at least one and a half mile of concrete streets.

We purchased some equipment and began grubbing and clearing the land as soon as the frost left the ground in April 1984. We ran into one snag after another. The soil was clay and tough to work with, but we quickly learned. There were hundreds of yards of barbed-wire fencing, part of which had fallen to the ground and were buried over the years. About sixty-five acres were grown up, so thick that it was impassable, yet we managed to go forward. We removed hundreds of trees, dug up the roots, and filled the holes. We dug three ponds in the beginning and would dig three or four more before we were completely done.

Over the period of construction, we had hired a total of twenty-seven contractors for specific jobs. Some worked cutting in the streets while another hauled the borrowed material to sites on the course. We installed numerous storm drains and underground pipes to transfer excess water to the ponds. Everything was designed to accommodate a three-inch rainfall in twenty-four hours. We had an old barn that we used to work the crew out of and store our equipment there. It was a hectic pace, but by late June, all the acreage had been tilled. We used eighteen-inch-deep chisel knives pulled behind a dual-wheel, and four-wheel drive tractor. We plowed all the land, disced it, and began leveling and contouring areas as soon as the traffic had moved out. Kevin Fuller and a crew installed the sprinkler system. Sam Shrock directed the Bent Oak crew, and I handled the outside contractors.

Due to bad weather, we had fallen a little behind schedule and needed more equipment to catch up. Bent Oak did not have enough funds to purchase some of the equipment; so I bought my own personal dozer, backhoe tractor, and a drag line to work the ponds. I rented a rock picker and picked hundreds of tons of rocks off the surface as we began leveling. I was spending one hundred to 120 hours a week on the premises, but it had to be done.

We started the clubhouse. We drilled the two wells and got our pump installed. We had scheduled to sow seeds beginning on August 27, and just as we began, it started raining. Between then and November 10, it had rained twenty-one and a half inches, an all-time record. We were installing city water and utilities to service over two hundred residents and had the sanitary sewer being installed.

By early winter, the clubhouse was about finished, we had mowed all the grass at least one time, and now we have to wait for spring to do any more outside work. During the winter, we ordered forty-five golf carts and purchased all our course maintenance machinery and had everything ready to drive onto the course for maintenance as soon as weather permitted. We cut a swath through the grass area and asphalted about five miles of cart paths and dug fifty-five sand bunkers throughout the course. We were hurrying to get the Main Street paved before winter, but the in-climate weather held us to just one lane. I had four houses under construction, one of which would be my temporary home until after we opened the course.

In late February 1985, Judy and I moved into our house on the course, and I sold one of my houses across the street from me to a couple I'd known for a long time. They moved in soon after we did.

We were on time, and by opening day, the course was ready. On Friday, before opening day, we held a small party for our fourteen directors and played the first round of golf that had been played on the course. The directors presented me a gift of my own personal golf cart, and the pro and I were first off the tee.

Saturday morning came, and it was raining. We opened the course at 6:00 a.m. and had a steady stream on the course until dark, even in a light rain that lasted most of the day. Things went well, and in about a month, we leased our restaurant facilities to two chefs. Gary ran the pro shop and golf operations. I oversaw the whole operation. We set up an annual-fee structure and also had daily-greens fee. I was glad to see this day come. We had met our schedule, and now I would start drawing a salary. To this point in time, I had not received one penny from the corporation. Everyone else was paid from the first hour they worked.

We finished the streets throughout the complex. We had five different villages that had different restrictions regarding sizes of homes. This would allow couples, small families, and large families an opportunity of choice.

Our first half year was very good and had a positive cash flow. We sold a number of annual memberships and were considered semiprivate. We continued dolling up the course with trees and flower areas and installed advertising on the stone tee signs. Play continued to be good.

In the summer of 1986, we hosted the county Parade of Homes and had built eleven homes to show; and by the end of 1987, I personally had sold ninety-seven residential lots. We built a six-unit condo across the street from the clubhouse, which would provide from temporary to permanent housing. The units were from 1,550 to 2,250 square feet.

This project was difficult because we had to adhere to codes, rules, and regulations from several government agencies, ranging from local to federal and every agency in between. The DOT was a major problem. They had planned to construct the U.S. 20 bypass somewhere south of town and did not want permits issued even though they could not make up their minds where the road was going to be built. I visited with them before we finished the complex, and we agreed to the boundaries where our complex would end. They were so pleased that they sent me a certificate of commendation.

Two years after, we were open. They came in and took enough land from the golf course that we had to rebuild our thirteenth hole and lost three residential lots. They paid us for it, but after my going to the effort of confirmation of their location, they decided to change it.

I owned two acres in the middle of the golf course and intended to build my permanent home there. I sold one acre and built my home in 1987 on the golf course between holes number 16 and 17. Randy had married his childhood sweetheart, Alice Bowers; and they had a son, Christopher, and soon were to have another. They were planning to add on to their existing home. When Judy and I moved to our new house, we gave the kids a great deal on the one we were leaving. They live there today. We owned another new house a couple of blocks away and made our son Mike and his wife a great deal on that house.

Just before we were ready to move in, Judy's mother died ten years after her dad had passed away. We loved the house, but when I had it built with a one-acre yard, I had intended to retire soon and have our maintenance department maintain the yard because I was not going to become a slave to it as I had at the lake.

By the year-end 1989, I had honored all the commitments that I had originally made. I built the course, operated it until it was stable and profitable, and had prepared all the legal documents, and sold memberships in a private club. The restaurant was going strong, and the bar and pro shop were busy serving our members. Now it was time for me to leave. I had intended to keep my ownership, but due to circumstances, I decided it was in the best interest of everyone connected to the course that I sell. I sold my ownership and left the club on January 2, 1990.

For the new owners to reach debt service required a large payment to the bank to reduce the overall debt of the corporation. The only debt that the corporation had until the new owners financed the purchase was the real estate. I wrote the bank a check for $440,000 and purchased all the remaining residential real estate from the corporation and began selling the lots.

The rains of 1984 came at a time that the paving contractors were doing the streets. One strip of the streets began to fail, and since the corporation did not have adequate cash nor resources to help the city, I gave the city $100,000's worth of residential lots; and they, in turn, sold them. Now they were responsible for the streets forever.

I completely severed my ties with Bent Oak Corporation from an ownership standpoint. I purchased a lifelong membership and still continued living out my dream of building a course and playing golf there.

I began spending my time maintaining the residential lots that I had purchased from Bent Oak. I purchased a large mower the same as is used on the golf course. I enjoyed keeping the lots looking nice and even started mowing some of the lots that had not yet been built on for their owners. This provided enough money for the fuel and maintenance of my machine. Periodically, I would hire a contractor and build a spec house on one of my lots, simply to keep building activity going on within the complex.

Over five or six years, I had five houses built. I would sell a lot every now and then; and by 2000, I only had two left, which I would eventually give to my son Mike.

In the late spring of 1990, Randy came to me and wanted to start a cabinet shop. I told him I was tired of the race and was going to retire and take life a little easier. After a few days of on-and-off conversation, I agreed that I would help him start a company, but I set a very unchangeable schedule. I would provide the start-up capital, we'd find a building and develop a product, sell it, and produce it. That I would stay with the operation for exactly three years and regardless of circumstances, I was gone.

We found a cabinet company that had gone out of business. We purchased their equipment and leased the same building that they were in. By this time, the Dutton Industries name had been vacated; so the state gave us the corporate name of Dutton Industries Incorporated, the same name, we used in the seventies. We began soliciting the various recreational vehicle manufacturers and in particular the van industry, which was going nuts they were growing so fast.

Very soon after we started, the building was too small, so I purchased a building on south CR 3 toward Jimtown, which is just south of Elkhart, and moved the operation to that location. Most of our products were for the van industry and were made from solid oak or walnut. We hired a man who had been working in the company, whose machinery we had purchased. His name was Dave Murray. Dave was charged with production in the mill and assembly room; Randy was in charge of the entire plant and concentrated his efforts in the paint and shipping area. I was in charge of the office and worked in the plant with the crew in whatever capacity I was needed. We had about twenty-five employees and gradually added new or different products to service the custom needs of our customers.

My sister Ella Mae had died recently. She had developed cancer; however, regardless of any medical report—and I don't even know what the medical report said—Ella Mae died from Huntington's disease. She was fifty years old.

One day, Dennis, her son, stopped by the plant. The symptoms that I had detected when he was a young teenager had worsened over the years, and now they were getting to the critical point. Dennis and his wife had two sons but were recently divorced. In our conversation, I asked Dennis to please see a doctor. He went to a local doctor who suspected, as I had, that his illness could be Huntington's. Blood samples were sent to a special institute out east, and weeks later, the results came back positive. By now, his sister Kathy was quickly developing physical signs that she too had the disease. A short period after Ella Mae died, Jack died, and I had always been very fond of their kids and wanted to help them get through this disease the best they could.

The fact that Dennis had the disease prompted me to update what I called my "death book." That's what I called it from the day I started keeping it. When I opened the binder of the book, a couple of scrap pieces of paper fell out that were dated many years apart. It was a note to myself, saying, "This is a good idea . . . should refine and publish."

I continued updating information in my book, and as I turned the pages, another note saying the same thing popped up. I had made the decision to make my book when Jim and I were returning from Coleman's funeral after experiencing turmoil and disorder with family members after his death. My book was designed to completely eliminate any survivor from having to make any decisions upon my death and include my will, a living will with durable power of attorney in the event I became incapacitated, and numerous documents with directions and information, which would guide my family in the resolution of my affairs. It listed all my assets and the location, names, and phone numbers of the contact or representative who could provide details on investments, insurance, and the like. It included listings of personal things and who I wanted to have them if they were not designated in my will and included very simple things such as where the extra keys to autos, boats and other locks were located.

I believed all this information was necessary and would help anyone's survivors get back to a normal life after the death of a loved one. I decided to publish it.

I was extremely busy working the business with Randy, so I hired an agency to put the book together and had my best friend and lawyer, Dick, do the legal work. It would take some time to get all the legal work done since we had to have certain items in the book legally assessed in all fifty states.

Late spring of 1991 came, and my son Mike was getting married again. He and his first wife had a son that died after thirty-three days, and soon after, they just couldn't handle the aftermath and had gotten a divorce.

Dick came to the wedding, and during the reception, he and I stepped outside where he told me he did not have much longer to live. His heart was failing fast, and he asked me to do something for him. He said that whatever happens to him to make sure that his family did not keep him hooked up to any life-prolonging equipment. He also told me that the legal work on the book was done and on his desk, ready for his final OK.

The following weekend, Dick was taken to the hospital, and I was called immediately. Judy and I went to the hospital waiting room with the family, hoping to see Dick. We weren't allowed to at that moment. Soon after arriving, the doctor came into the room and told the wife that they had him hooked up to life support, that his heart would no longer function on its own, and that without the support he would die within forty-five minutes.

Bootie, the wife, and their five children—all practicing lawyers—discussed the matter. Two of the children wanted to pull the plug, and three wanted to leave him on support. Bootie pondered the situation and turned to me. She said, "Bobby, you're his best friend. What do you think?"

I responded by telling Bootie that I did not have to think because Dick had told me last week at Mike's wedding what he wanted done, and I relayed the message to her. She called the doctor back in and told him that her brother Joe, who was a doctor in Indianapolis, was en route to the hospital; and when he arrived, if he concurred with him, then remove the life support.

Joe arrived shortly thereafter and told Bootie he had seen the doctor already and that her decision was the right one. They pulled the plug, and less than an hour later, Dick had died. After the funeral, the eldest son advised me that he would assume my legal work and that he was driving his mother to their Florida home and returning via plane. He would take the information on the book with him and review it while flying home. His name was Rick and had been in the firm for a few years.

A few nights later, I received a call from Rick who was between flights from Chicago to South Bend. He apologized for such a late call, but told me the importance of it. He said that he would have given anything if his father would have had my book. He thought the book was a wonderful idea, which provided for the decision of whether to remove the life support or not. Since the family was split on that critical decision, it already was tearing the family apart. Dick had a will before his death, but even though there were eleven lawyers in his family (himself, five kids, and their spouses), no one had the forethought to include a living will with the durable power of attorney, which left the decision of the life support to someone else.

I took the final legal documents to the agency, and they completed the book. They had the books printed and set up several chain bookstores to sell it. Many of them were in Canada. After a few years, one of the distributors in Texas had their lawyer call me. They wanted to purchase the copyright and all the inventory in stock. They were setting up an Internet site to sell the books. My book was in the marketplace, and the best thing a person could do for their loved ones was to fill it out. The agency refused to use the name *My Death Book*, which was what I had called mine; instead, they named it *Personal and Comprehensive Testimony, PACT*, for the label. I proceeded to hold a book-signing session at the bookstore to promote the new book.

Book-signing session

Judy and I had started taking an annual trip to Florida in the wintertime. This began in 1977 where we would go for a week. Over the years, we continued to lengthen the time we stayed there to a couple of weeks before the holidays and then another couple of weeks after the holidays. We would come home for Christmas and stay until all the year-end books at work were closed out. By this time, we wanted to spend the entire winter there, or at least three months each year. I loved to fish and spent most of my time on the water. We rented a place on Lake Panasoffkee between Ocala and Tampa, which included a slip where I docked my bass boat. I would go out early in the morning and some days stayed on the lake all day. I fished for largemouth bass and caught my own bait, which was golden shiners that were up to ten inches long.

Over the years, I became a good bass fisherman and got the reputation of being the best on the lake at finding and catching shiners. I had caught my first ten-pound bass in 1980 and had it mounted for the wall. I began chasing the fish all over this seven-thousand-acre lake with hopes to one day catch one that would go fourteen pounds. Early on, Judy would fish with me; but by this time, she preferred to play golf or shop with her girlfriends. She told me the reason she stopped fishing was the pesky little gnats that would swarm on a hot day to the extent they would cast a shadow on the water. At times, they would completely cover the top of the engine and loved to hover around your head, eyes, and ears. They would get so bad that many times the fishermen would wear a net over their head to keep these pesky devils away.

The woodworking operation was going good, and the time for me to leave was coming soon. We had rented storage space to our hardwood supplier, Paul Minne, because it made it much more convenient for our operation and reduced our inventory. Paul had brought a lady, Jeannie, with him; and we shared offices in a residential building adjacent to the plant. Jeannie ran the office for our company as well as Paul's.

Judy and I had spent a couple of weeks in Florida in the fall of 1993 and had returned to Elkhart before Christmas. When I arrived back to work, I began talking to Randy and Dave about my leaving soon. Randy had hired a friend of his, John DeJohn, to handle the office routine; and they had installed a computer system in the offices, which included a direct hookup to an engineering facility in Texas where we could download direct to our computer milling machine the programs required rather than calculate all the measurements and enter them by hand. They had the operation under control, so I concentrated on working myself out of a job. Each time I would remind them I would be leaving soon, they would laugh and say, "You'll never retire."

In those days, I hated computers. It was the days of "garbage in, garbage out," and some bad experiences with computer results while I was still with Sheller Globe. Everyone knew this and would not even let me touch a computer. One day, as we were talking about computers, I made the statement that I would never own one for myself.

I continued to impress upon Randy, Dave, and John that soon, I'll be gone; and they had to set their course for the future to include that fact. I explained to Randy that my three years would end in March and that I was going back to Florida and would not return until early March, which would give me about two weeks to work when I returned. Time went on. Judy and I went to Florida and returned in early March.

The day my three-year commitment to Randy would be fulfilled was on a Thursday and *would* be my last day there. When that day came, I cleared out my desk and put my personal things in my car around lunchtime. When the crew finished at three thirty, I packed up my personal tools and belongings and told the three men I would see them around. They were all surprised that I was really retiring. Now they all got down to brass tacks and started planning the course the company would take. Within a month or so, the decision was made to sell the company to John DeJohn.

Chapter Sixteen

Soon after the sale was final, Randy began working in the van-painting business, Dave got employment elsewhere, and John changed his product line to coating steering wheels, and changed the name of the company to Forrest Products. I busied myself helping the owner of the golf course construct new ponds and sand traps and worked keeping my residential lots clean and mowed.

When we started building Bent Oak, Indiana changed their property tax system; and our new complex was hard hit. We were already paying the largest amount of any other similar complex in the state. Ours had increased 192 percent. Even though I no longer had ownership in the club and golf course, this was a serious problem that would thwart the selling of my residential lots. I took up the fight, and the politicians and tax officials were inept and did not have the ability to understand the new property tax manual. Their error rate in the assessment of the sixty-two homes we had at that time was 100 percent because they did not understand how to interpret the new assessing rules.

I had been working on the problem from early 1990. I obtained a state assessing manual from the state congress, and after proving hundreds of errors, the local assessor was too stubborn to correct them. I met with Judge Fisher, who was the judge of the state tax court, and advised that I had prepared a class action suit, and we're going to take the personal and political issues of the politicians to task. The new tax rules were unconstitutional, and any high school student that could read would clearly see that it was, yet the assessors who were elected officials thought it was all right and didn't care.

Judge Fisher asked me to withhold filing the suit because another one duplicating it had been filed a few days before, and the results of the outcome of this suit would extend and cover our problem. We elected a new assessor, and as the suit was in court and become known to everyone, local assessors begin making corrections. The final determination that the tax laws were unconstitutional was handed down by the courts around the end of 1996.

The tax system changed very slowly as the politicians had gotten used to having this extraordinary windfall income that had raped the property owners in the state and were reluctant to give up the hundreds of millions of extra dollars they had been squandering on their pet projects through the state. I developed an overall tax plan for the state congress to review.

My plan would abolish property taxes and replace the revenue in a manner that everyone paid their share based upon their income and the amount of goods they consumed. I had always believed that everyone should pay their fair share based upon what they could afford and what they spent and not this most regressive of systems known to man. All taxes should be progressive, and my new plan was and had been certified as to its accuracy by certified accountants before I submitted it. The committee liked my plan and took it to the legislature, where it died. I would take this issue up again in the future.

Some people say they will never retire. Retirement doesn't mean you're quitting and are going to spend the rest of your life sitting on the sofa watching the boob tube. Retirement means going to bed and getting up when you want to and doing those things that interest you. One of my favorite things that I love to do is to do something for someone else who will show their appreciation with a simple thank-you and mean it. I've always made the statement about retirement that after ninety days of retirement, if you're not thirty days behind, you're doing something wrong.

In 1998, Judy and I had become slaves to our home that was within the confines of the golf course and decided that all we needed were two bedrooms, living space, and a full drive under basement where I could have a garage for my boat and bait tanks, a place to park my golf cart, and a lot of room for a work shop, computers, and music equipment. I designed the house and contracted for it to be built on a lot we owned across the Main Street coming to the golf club, and we moved into the new house in March 1998, where we now live. I haven't stopped to count in detail how many places that I have lived during my life but a quick count from memory, it's twenty-one or twenty-two, and I hoped that this one was the last.

I continued with my interest on Huntington's disease, and soon after Dennis was diagnosed with it his sister Kathy begin showing signs that she had it also. Soon thereafter, the other sister Patsy began showing signs of the disease. The younger brother, Blair, was still in his twenties and had no signs that were detectable. I insisted that Kathy get immediate help, so she consulted a doctor.

During her several examinations, she had given the doctor my name, and I received a letter from a Dr. P. Michael Conneally, PhD, who was a distinguished professor at the School of Medicine at Indiana University. Dr. Conneally headed the National Huntington's Research Team and wanted as much information about our family and Huntington's that we could provide.

I was very glad to help. I went to Alabama and retrieved medical records on as many of my relatives as I could who appeared to have the disease, including the ones who had died before the name of the disease was known and their cause of death was listed as something else, usually a stroke. After several months of research, I began to better understand the disease and began distributing my newfound information through my widespread family, most of whom still lived in Alabama. I learned that Elkhart was one of the hot beds in the nation for Huntington's, but except for my sister and her children, none of the others were related to our family. Many new questions arose, and I wanted to learn more. I didn't have any signs of the disease, but I needed to know the probability of any of my offspring getting it.

I continued my research and was in contact with Dr. Roger V. Lebo, PhD, at Boston University School of Medicine. Their Center for Human Genetics was a front runner in this field and were the people who did the final testing on my niece Kathy.

From 1998 until about 2006, I spent numerous days working in this research, communicating with, particularly, Dr. Conneally, and his staff. I reached a point where I was convinced I could no longer be of any assistance, so I passed all the information I could garner on to my relatives. Today I am still on their mailing list and receive periodic information about the current status of the disease and what advancements medical researchers have made, but I cannot contribute any further because my sources of contribution have been exhausted over the years, and I personally do not qualify nor fit the criteria one must meet for personal testing for genetics. Kathy and Dennis did, and Kathy was a subject in the genetic testing program.

My research began with my maternal grandfather, and I followed it initially to their nine children and chose only two of them to continue the lineage to the next two generations. I chose only two because of a better personal knowledge of these two and could follow from Grandpa to them to their children and grandchildren, covering four generation that I had witnessed. Limited to this specific lineage I found a total of thirty-seven people, of which nineteen had died of Huntington's by December 1998.

After that date, there would be several of the living who would eventually prove to have the disease. My niece Patsy would be one of those.

Huntington's disease is a genetic disorder caused by a CAG repeater gene found in the fourth chromosome, which has a normal repeat of near twenty-five times. Anyone who has this abnormal repeating gene will develop Huntington's disease of a degree based upon the number of repeats. When the repeats exceed about thirty-six, that person will have a full-blown case of the disease.

The results of my family research found that the average age where the symptoms first become very noticeable is thirty to thirty-five years and will bring about death in about fifteen years. One of the nineteen people in my research died at age sixty, who was the oldest; and one died at age sixteen, who was the youngest. I did not include them in the average. All the others died between forty-eight and fifty-one years of age, with the average being fifty.

Dennis knew he was going to die about the time I started my research. During one of our conversations, he mentioned it and asked me if I would do something for him. I agreed. He told me that he had learned what transpired between brother Jim and me when Jim left Dutton Industries and thought that we were having a problem with each other. I told Dennis we never discussed what happened and had seen each other several times since. I had told no one about the incident but my immediate family, so either one of them had told Dennis, or Jim had told him.

In any event, I promised him that I would make a deliberate effort to assure that there was no problem. I immediately began going to Jim's home in Alabama twice a year and would spend one to three nights with him and his wife, Brenda. We got along really well. This continued through the year 2007.

In the spring of 2008, we made our last visit and couldn't go in the fall of 2008 and the spring of 2009. There were no known problems between Jim and me, but we could not stop to see them on two trips to and from Florida due to medical problems and appointments for medical help. I felt I had honored my commitment to Dennis because Jim and I had gotten along very well, and there was never a word mentioned about our conflict that caused Jim to leave the company.

I had done some wood carvings of musical instruments that took forty-three hours. I gave them to Jim, and he was pleased. Long before that, I had given him a beautiful new electric guitar that I could not play, and he could. He was pleased with that. In the spring of 2009, I sent a few of the biblical prophecy books that I had written and thought he would once again be pleased.

I received a handwritten letter from him that began by telling me how pleased he was to have received the books and that he really enjoyed them. The next paragraph was the nastiest things anyone could possibly say to me. He told me I cheated and stole from him and that I was greedy, and it went on to say I should practice what I had written in the books I had sent him. I was really hurt, so I laid the letter aside.

The following morning, I read it again. I was first inclined to not answer it, but after careful consideration, there was no way I could *not* answer it. I wrote him back and gave him the facts of his history from the time he was living at home with Mom, Coleman, and me and our business relationship from Mobilcraft, where I was forced to buy stocks back that I had just given him. I continued my description through Continental and to the final business relationship at Dutton Industries. I mailed the letter and concluded I had turned my cheek for the last time.

Since my retirement in 1994, I have fished and played golf a lot, but my old work habits never left. I still had an insatiable craving for knowledge. In 1985, I was introduced to karaoke and met a great musician, Wayne VanCuren, who had previously owned a restaurant and club on Lake Wawasee in Syracuse, Indiana. He had played and performed there for years and had tired of that lifestyle and sold the club. He started doing karaoke gigs, and I attended one. I loved it, and Wayne and I became friends. I went to karaoke and sang old country songs many times and had a real good time. I'd made the statement many times that I would never own a computer, but that was before I learned what could be done on one. I purchased my first one the week after I retired and wanted to produce karaoke songs on the computer. It wouldn't do it. I took the computer to Florida for the winter and continued trying.

Wayne and Patty, his wife, spent a few weeks in the winter about twenty-five miles from my home; and he did karaoke gigs while he was there. I went to most of them. Wayne needed new songbooks, so I began working them out on the computer. When I was ready to print them, the computer was so slow, I gave it the print command and went to bed. They were done when I got up the next morning. I began trying to get the computer to do things it wouldn't do and continued for a year without any success.

In the winter of 1995, I learned that a good friend had a son who was a computer geek and built custom computers. I discussed with him what I wanted, and he felt he could get it done. I told him that after speaking to all the big people in the computer and software world, they had told me it could not be done on a desktop computer. Those people included

Microsoft, Hewlett-Packard, Gateway, Adaptec, and a dozen more with the same answer. Curtis, the son, built me a computer. I picked it up one afternoon and paid him the $5,500 that all the equipment cost. (A regular computer cost about $2,700 then.)

When I tried to do what I wanted to do, it did not work. After several hours of trying, I put a sheet on the living room floor and disassembled every nut, screw, wire, and parts of the machine. I was determined to make it work. While I had it torn down, Curtis's dad came and saw what I was doing and called Curtis. I told him I'd have it fixed by morning, and he told me to bring it back to him.

By morning, I had it working good but would only do parts of what I wanted done. I took it back to Curtis, and he wrote a few DOS commands, and it worked good. This was the beginning of my interest in home computers.

Back home in Elkhart I continued my quest learning about karaoke. I had a good machine and could sing over two hundred songs, but I still wanted to write some karaoke songs and put them on a disc that could be used in anybody's karaoke machine. The word was out, and I got a call from a man named Andy. He told me he wrote computer programs and was working on the same project. We talked on and off for almost a year about the technical aspects of doing the job, color, timing, etc.

One day, Andy sent me a disc that had a program on it representing what we had been discussing for a year. I installed it in my computer, and after learning how to maneuver through the program, I could do what I wanted to do. I began writing songs or taking existing old songs that were not on karaoke discs and made karaoke out of them. My karaoke library now has over five hundred discs, containing fifteen to nineteen songs each.

Chapter Seventeen

Having come from a broken family, I vowed to everything that was holy that my marriage would be for a lifetime. I came from a broken home, and the memories remain. I dedicated myself to having a family and taking care of that family so they could have a better and easier life than I had.

When my children were considering marriage, I spoke with each of them suggesting that they carefully review all the conditions and circumstances before making a final decision, but the decision would be theirs; and whatever their decision, I would support it. Randy got married to a wonderful girl, but I knew and told both of them of their incompatibilities and how hard each would have to work to make the marriage successful. After a year, they got a divorce.

In 1981, he married the girl who was my choice by a mile. Her name was Alice Bowers, and the two of them had been good friends and dated long before Randy had married the first time. Judy and I got to know Alice very well and really liked her and were very happy when they decided to get married. Alice has been as close to us as if Judy had given birth to her. They have been married twenty-eight years on Valentine's Day and have given us two great boys, Chris and Matt, and we are proud to call them grandsons. They are smart and industrious, and both are out of college and have very good jobs. Chris is married to Kristin Groh; and they have a son, Cole, who is the apple of the eye for Grandma and Grandpa. Matt is engaged to marry LeAnne Matthews in 2010.

Teri got married in 1980, and I objected to her marrying this man and discussed my reasons. Once they were married, I did everything in my power to accept him and got along well with him. After about eight years, he left her with two children, and she was pregnant with the third. The three kids are great, but the girl was spoiled rotten as she grew up because she is the only girl of the seven grandchildren we have. Their names are Jammie, Justin, and Brandon. Jammie is married to Tony Butler, and they recently had a baby boy, Charlie. Justin is married to Mandie and has a little boy, Garret, and recently had a baby girl, Carley. Brandon is in his last year of college and stays on the dean's List. He will continue to graduate school. We are proud of all of them.

Michael followed the same path as Randy and Teri. He married in 1980; and after a few years, he and his wife had a baby boy, Robert Michael, who only lived for thirty three days. The trauma tore them apart, and they got a divorce. Mike married Michaele King in 1991; and they have a son, Hunter Michael, who is approaching the age of six and doing second-grade schoolwork.

Our family is a close-knit group; but in today's economy, most of them work, leaving social time to be short but frequent sessions. Once any of our family marries, we consider the spouse as another one of our kids. When the whole group is together, we have a house full. There are twenty of us at this date.

The twenty people in these two photos make up our entire family.

Space in this book has not allowed me to write much about my half brother and sister nor a few really good friends. They, along with many others, have greatly contributed to my happiness and well-being and to my success in business. As a simple token of my appreciation of their contribution, I have herewith submitted some photographs. For the many others who have faithfully supported me who are not mentioned or shown within, you have my heartfelt thanks for your loyalty and contribution; for without your support, success would not have been possible.

My brother and sisters (Ella Mae insert, deceased.)

1981

Judy, Bob, and good friends Keith and Marilyn Bates, 1981

**Wayne Barrentine, 1956
Birthday party for both of us**

Ginny and Dwayne Curtis, 1959

David Kidder

Chapter Eighteen

Since retirement I have not changed my routine very much. I'm still an early riser and must have a project to keep occupied.

It's almost like I go on a binge with work. When I get something started, I'll work on it until something I like better comes along. I love doing things for people. After my first major surgery, I had to do something I could do while seated for an extended period. I started carving small musical instruments and making framed wall displays and did so over about three years in spare time. I sold enough of them to pay for my materials and then gave them to friends.

Thirteen musical instruments displayed

Two years ago, I spent almost the full spring and summer months working on our poor Indiana property tax system with some positive results—not nearly what the people deserve. Most of last year, I spent my time writing about Biblical prophecy. I have always been intrigued by prophecy and am a member of the generation who has seen more prophecy come true during this generation's lifetime than all the other generations before collectively have seen. To date, I have written thirteen books.

Biblical Prophesy Books Written

I play golf as often as I can, and I love to build golf clubs. The last few years, I have built several hundred clubs and love to help the players on the high school teams. I have custom-fitted several of the team players who could not afford clubs, and I was very glad to do it. I still remember what it was like for me at that age.

One of my more favorite activities is to fish. I have been a bass fisherman for many years and go whenever I get the chance. One of my good catches is pictured below.

A Good Catch Of Bass

Summary

As a child, without the comforts of life that is normal today, on occasion, I would get a fleeting glimpse of things that filled me with desire. Once, I went to a buddy's to play basketball, and the mother invited me into the house. She was having hamburgers for dinner and invited me to stay. I had never had one before. While I was in the house, I noticed there were electric lights, carpet on the floor, and an oil-fired heater. My house had no electricity, so we used coal oil to burn in the lamps for light. Our floors were wood with a lot of cracks between the planks, and we had a wood-fired stove and used either wood or coal in the heater. Our coal oil cost a nickel a gallon, we cut the wood for the cookstove, and we'd find coal alongside the railroad tracks on the curves where it had fallen off the coal cars.

Getting out of bed in the morning and walking barefoot on a very cold floor with air coming in between the cracks was miserable, and chopping wood was a cold job in the winter. When I saw this difference in the way it was and the way it could be, I craved something more and attempted to better myself; but due to family illness and conditions, maintaining the status quo was difficult, and bettering myself was almost impossible in the poverty-ridden hills of Alabama.

With few choices, I chose to give up my childhood and gamble that with an early start, I could make things better and that where I went would become better than before I came. To do this would require strength and diligence in the pursuit of my rainbow. God provided the strength and has continued doing so every day of my life, and I will be eternally grateful. Because he has led me on the path to success, I was able to help my old family and make a better and easier life for my new family.

I had never possessed any material things, so when I first began earning a decent wage that was slightly more than daily needs, I made a choice. Rather than spend the money, I would use it as a down payment on my family's future. That decision and a willingness to walk into a world of unknowns, unafraid to tackle a new project with the confidence that through honest and hard work and a diligent pursuit, I could conquer the roadblocks and reach the objective. It's a hard road, but a very rewarding one if you're willing to make the sacrifices to do it. You can't do it alone. There's only one word you have to know that can calm and lead you. That word is "Jesus," who will give you wisdom and strength if you only ask for it.

The true reward isn't money—it's self-satisfaction and in knowing you have done your job in securing a decent life for your family and preparing for your future.

My life experiences has proven to me that it doesn't take expensive cars, big houses, and a lot of jewelry to be rich. My car is eleven years old, Judy's car is five years old, and we live in a very comfortable, modest home. My watch is a Timex. I am rich in experience that I wouldn't trade for a truckload of money.

You can't purchase it; you have to live it. Opportunity is there for anyone who has the desire to grasp it and diligently pursue it with high morals and integrity.

In all you're endeavors, may God bless and keep you!

Bob Dutton, 2009

Photos of Bobby

Aged seven

Aged fifteen

Aged twenty-five

Aged thirty-two

Aged fifty

Bobby and Judy
Aged seventy-one

Edwards Brothers, Inc.
Thorofare, NJ USA
October 5, 2011